T0305598

FOOD JUSTICE IN AMERICAN CITIES

This book documents food insecurity in urban communities across the United States and asks whether emerging urban food and agriculture initiatives can address the food security needs of American city dwellers.

While America has sufficient food to feed its entire population, 38 million people are food insecure, with urban communities and communities of color having long borne the brunt of food inequalities. This book traces the evolving story of food by describing the people behind food system statistics, focusing on cities and suburban communities across America. In doing so, it raises questions not only about food security but about a food economy that can foster justice and sustainability and combat hunger and waste. By linking human faces to the data, the book reveals the many connections between food insecurity and unsustainable practices. The book concludes by discussing some of the pathways toward a more sustainable and just food system by linking the food system to the larger economy and the many sectors that are connected to food. Because of these multifaceted connections, food can be a unique catalyst for creating pathways toward a more just and sustainable economy that is more aligned with nature.

This book will be of great interest to students and scholars of food justice, food security, urban food and agriculture, urban sustainability, and sustainable food systems more broadly.

Sabine O'Hara is a distinguished professor and Ph.D. Program Director in the College of Agriculture, Urban Sustainability and Environmental Sciences (CAUSES) at the University of the District of Columbia, USA. Prior to her current appointment, she served as the founding Dean of CAUSES and led the university's efforts to build a cutting-edge model for urban agriculture that integrates urban sustainability.

ROUTLEDGE STUDIES IN FOOD, SOCIETY AND THE ENVIRONMENT

Critical Mapping for Sustainable Food Design
Food Security, Equity, and Justice
Audrey G. Bennett and Jennifer A. Vokoun

Community Food Initiatives
A Critical Reparative Approach
Edited by Oona Morrow, Esther Veen, and Stefan Wahlen

Food Futures in Education and Society
Edited by Gurpinder Singh Lalli, Angela Turner, and Marion Rutland

The Soybean Through World History
Lessons for Sustainable Agrofood Systems
Matilda Baraibar Norberg and Lisa Deutsch

Urban Expansion and Food Security in New Zealand
The Collapse of Local Horticulture
Benjamin Felix Richardson

Evaluating Sustainable Food System Innovations
A Global Toolkit for Cities
Edited by Élodie Valette, Alison Blay-Palmer, Beatrice Intoppa, Amanda Di Battista, Ophélie Roudelle, and Géraldine Chaboud

How to Create a Sustainable Food Industry
A Practical Guide to Perfect Food
Melissa Barrett, Massimo Marino, Francesca Brkic, and Carlo Alberto Pratesi

Food Justice in American Cities
Stories of Health and Resilience
Sabine O'Hara

For more information about this series, please visit: www.routledge.com/ Routledge-Studies-in-Food-Society-and-the-Environment/book-series/RSFSE

FOOD JUSTICE IN AMERICAN CITIES

Stories of Health and Resilience

Sabine O'Hara

Routledge
Taylor & Francis Group

LONDON AND NEW YORK

Designed cover image: © Getty

First published 2024
by Routledge
4 Park Square, Milton Park, Abingdon, Oxon OX14 4RN

and by Routledge
605 Third Avenue, New York, NY 10158

Routledge is an imprint of the Taylor & Francis Group, an informa business

© 2024 Sabine O'Hara

British Library Cataloguing-in-Publication Data
A catalogue record for this book is available from the British Library

ISBN: 978-1-032-34494-2 (hbk)
ISBN: 978-1-032-34490-4 (pbk)
ISBN: 978-1-003-32239-9 (ebk)

DOI: 10.4324/9781003322399

Typeset in Times New Roman
by Taylor & Francis Books

CONTENTS

Acknowledgements   vi

1   Introduction   1

2   Why are people in the richest country on earth food
    insecure?   25

3   Who is food insecure and who is not? The story of too
    much and not enough food in US cities   67

4   Food is more than food: Connecting the dots between food
    and green cities   87

5   Finding the friends of food security: The diverse faces of
    new urban and regional food system innovators in US cities   116

6   How do we get there from here? Pathways toward the food
    system we want   137

7   Conclusions   172

Index   *185*

ACKNOWLEDGEMENTS

Why are 38 million people in the country with the world's largest economy food insecure? And why is the world's most productive food system so vulnerable against external shocks like the recent COVID pandemic? And are there pathways to a more sustainable and just food system in a country where 80 percent of the population live in cities and metropolitan areas? This book suggests that the answer is an emphatic "yes." In fact, the pathways to a more sustainable and just food system are already emerging in the work, experiences, and stories of everyday Americans in cities across the United States. This book seeks to capture these stories.

In writing this book as well as numerous research projects before it, I have learned more than I had hoped for from the generous people who shared their stories with me. They are the people living with food insecurity in American cities, those who work with them, and the food innovators who want to change the way we grow, distribute, process, and eat food across this country. My sincere thanks and gratitude go to those who shared their stories with me for this book and to the many others whose stories have deeply influenced my thinking.

Yet, since I am an agricultural economist and ecological economist by formal training and profession, this book also includes a good bit of data, historical information, and analysis. This work too has relied on the counsel and collaboration of many who have shared their time and expertise with me. First and foremost, I thank Leslie Glover, Program Manager of Urban Agriculture & Innovation Production of the Natural Resources Conservation Service at the US Department of Agriculture, who offered many useful comments and suggestions on earlier drafts of this book and especially on the policy chapter (Chapter 6). I also thank Dr. Alisha Coleman-Jensen from the Economic Research Service at the US Department of Agriculture, who has not only influenced my thinking about food access and food security for many years but also connected me with those working in food pantries and food banks across the country.

This book also relied on the capable research assistance of Margaret Fornes from Butler University in Indianapolis, who worked with me on a semester-long research internship, Campbell Jackson, a Ph.D. student in the University of the District of Columbia's Urban Leadership and Entrepreneurship Program, and Dr. Golnar Ahmadi, also from the University of the District of Columbia. All three contributed to collecting data, tracking data sources, and assisting with numerous other research-related tasks. I sincerely thank them for their commitment and diligent work. Dr. Ahmadi, who collaborated with me on previous research projects, also provided especially helpful contributions to Chapter 2 of this book.

There are many other colleagues and students from the College of Agriculture, Urban Sustainability and Environmental Sciences (CAUSES) at the University of the District of Columbia, from the Resource Economics Group at Humboldt-Universität, Berlin, from Wageningen University & Research in the Netherlands and its Green Cities and Regions Program, and from the Economic Research Service at the US Department of Agriculture who have contributed to my work over the years in countless ways. I thank them for their collegiality, friendship, and generosity in sharing their insights with me.

My hope is that this book will get us one step closer to a sustainable and just food system in the United States and around the world.

1

INTRODUCTION

In 2022 the world population reached 8 billion people. This is a vast increase from the 3 billion who lived on Planet Earth only 60 years earlier. Global agricultural production stands at 13 billion tons per year today, compared to just 3.4 billion tons in 1960. Most of this growth in agricultural production was realized by conventional and cultural agricultural practices. Annual crop production (i.e., the production of agricultural plants but not meat production) grew to 9.8 billion in 2020, up from 2.7 billion tons per year in 1960. This suggests good news overall. While the world's population grew by a factor of 2.7, crop production grew by a factor of 3.6, and overall agricultural production by a factor of 3.8. This implies that the so-called "Malthusian trap," which predicted that population growth would outpace humanity's ability to grow sufficient food, has not materialized (Hollander, 1997; Welling, 1888). Instead, the so-called "Green Revolution," which began in the 1960s, made it possible to accelerate food production largely through the use of fertilizers, pesticides, and new crop varieties (Trewavas, 2002; Evenson and Gollin, 2003; Pingali, 2012).

These achievements are impressive. On a per capita basis, agricultural production increased from 1.13 tons per person per year to 1.67 tons per person—an almost 50 percent increase for every man, woman, and child on Planet Earth. Table 1.1 summarizes this substantial increase in agricultural production between 1960 and 2020 by world region.

Crop production grew at similar rates (see Table 1.2). As a result, extreme poverty, defined as living on less than $1.9 per day (adjusted for inflation), declined from roughly 1.6 billion people in 1960 to 800 million in 2020, even though the world's population grew from 3 billion to almost 8 billion in the same time frame. In 1960 more than half of the world's population (53 percent) lived in extreme poverty, compared to less than 10 percent today.

DOI: 10.4324/9781003322399-1

TABLE 1.1 Agricultural production in million tons by world region between 1960 and 2020

	1960	1970	1980	1990	2000	2010	2020
World	3,435	4,468	5,445	6,905	9,127	11,483	12,932
Africa	228	306	356	472	664	925	1,139
Asia	1,104	1,517	1,947	2,814	4,459	5,786	6,839
Europe	1,174	1,461	1,638	1,787	1,570	1,585	1,575
Latin America & Caribbean	428	583	743	955	1,272	1,947	2,119
North America	449	522	671	771	999	1,082	1,128
Oceania	54	78	90	106	160	156	131

Source: FAO (2022)

TABLE 1.2 Crop production in million tons between 1960 and 2020

	1960	1970	1980	1990	2000	2010	2020
World	2,680	3,563	4,287	5,512	6,533	8,224	9,820
Africa	192	266	307	411	544	759	984
Asia	1,117	1,391	1,763	2,496	3,320	4,217	5,094
Europe	780	971	1,089	1,143	919	904	1,062
Latin America & Caribbean	361	493	621	813	968	1,518	1,669
North America	303	369	501	580	681	734	765
Oceania	28	44	56	69	101	93	86

Source: FAO (2022)

This is tremendous progress overall as a large proportion of the world's population have escaped extreme poverty and more people are being fed today than at any time since global food production records started to be kept. Indeed, one might almost have the impression that we are about to solve the problem of food insecurity. Yet, unfortunately, the reality is rather different than the average calculations would suggest. Regional differences in food security are substantial, and recent estimates by the Food and Agriculture Organization (FAO—an agency of the United Nations) project that by 2050 the world will have to produce 60 percent more food to feed a world population of an estimated 9.3 billion people (FAO, 2020). Goal number 2 of the United Nations' 17 Sustainable Development Goals (SDGs)—"Eliminate Hunger"—continues to be elusive. Yet, the fact that hunger has not been eliminated may not be so much a failure to produce enough food for everyone as a failure to address disparities in food distribution.

Regional progress in food production and food security

A closer look at six world regions—Africa, Asia, Europe, Latin America and the Caribbean, North America, and Oceania—shows tremendous progress in both overall agricultural and specifically crop production in every part of the world (see Tables 1.1 and 1.2). Yet, the picture is by no means uniform. As Table 1.3 indicates, the largest population growth rates occurred in Africa, which saw an almost fivefold increase in its population between 1960 and 2020. Meanwhile, the populations of Asia and Latin America and the Caribbean almost tripled in the same time frame. In contrast, Europe's population has remained essentially flat over the past 30 years, and some European countries have even seen their populations shrink. The percentage of Europeans over 65 years of age grew from 8 percent in 1960 to 19 percent in 2020, making Europe the world's oldest continent. North America is the second-oldest region, with 17 percent of the population 65 years old or older. In contrast, Africa is the youngest continent, with a steady 3 percent of the population at 65 years of age or older—a percentage that has remained virtually unchanged since 1960. The 65-and-older populations of Asia and Latin America and the Caribbean increased from 3.6 to 9 percent between 1960 and 2020 as their population growth slowed. In terms of individual countries, Japan has the world's oldest population, while China marked a turnaround in 2022 when its birth rate fell below its rate of population losses (Peng, 2022). While China remains the most populous country in the world for now, its population growth has slowed considerably.

Asia achieved the steepest growth in agricultural production, increasing its agricultural output more than sixfold. Meanwhile, both Africa and Latin America and the Caribbean saw fivefold increases in their agricultural production. These significant gains in some of the world's poorest regions contributed to the overall decline in extreme poverty. However, Africa saw the lowest gains in per capita agricultural production, which increased from 0.8 to just 0.85 tons per person per year. In contrast, Asia saw an increase in its per capita agricultural

TABLE 1.3 Population in millions of people by world region between 1960 and 2020

	1960	1970	1980	1990	2000	2010	2020
World	3,030	3,680	4,430	5,280	6,110	6,920	7,860
Africa	283	363	476	630	811	1,039	1,341
Asia	1,705	2,142	2,650	3,226	3,741	4,210	4,641
Europe	605	657	693	721	726	736	747
Latin America & Caribbean	220	287	361	443	522	591	654
North America	205	231	254	280	312	343	369
Oceania	16	20	23	27	31	37	43

Source: World Bank (2022a)

production from 0.6 to 1.1 tons per person per year—a tremendous feat, especially in light of the region's steep population growth. The world's two most populous countries, India and China, experienced the steepest declines in extreme poverty. North America consistently saw the highest levels of per capita agricultural production, which increased from 2.2 to 3.1 tons per person per year. Yet, Latin America and the Caribbean has almost caught up—the region now stands at 3.0 tons of agricultural products per person per year, up from just 1.8 tons per person per year in 1960. This would seem to imply good news for the people of the Latin America and Caribbean region. Yet, the picture is rather more complex.

The Gini coefficient (or index)—named after the Italian statistician Corrado Gini (Gini, 1997)—is a measure of a population's income distribution. In a population in which income is perfectly equally distributed, 10 percent of the population would earn 10 percent of the income generated. This would give a Gini coefficient of 0. In contrast, a Gini coefficient of 1 would indicate that a single person earns 100 percent of the income while everyone else receives nothing at all. Measuring income inequality across countries and world regions is challenging. Data availability varies considerably, so comparing cost of living, income, and consumption levels is difficult, to say the least. There are also big differences in subsistence levels, meaning that in some countries most people grow at least some of their own food, while in other countries almost no one does, so they are dependent on the money economy to feed themselves and their families.

Despite these limitations, it is informative to consider measures like the Gini index alongside figures for per capita production as they give a sense of the distribution of incomes. Figures 1.1 and 1.2 show the Gini index by world region for 2000 and 2020, respectively. These figures indicate that the southern part of Africa and Latin America still have very high levels of inequality, with Gini indexes of 0.6 or higher. Meanwhile, central Asia and northern Europe have the lowest levels of inequality, with Gini indexes of less than 0.3. Changes between 2000 and 2020 were modest, with only slight declines in inequality levels in the regions with the largest inequalities. This raises important questions about the gains in per capita agricultural production in Latin America and the Caribbean.

Four countries have emerged as the world's top agricultural producers: China, India, the United States, and Brazil (Ross et al., 2022). These four countries are also among the world's top ten countries by land area. China is the world's largest grain producer: although it has only 10 percent of the world's arable land, it produces 25 percent of the world's grain. It is also the world's leading producer of cotton, fruits and vegetables, poultry, and eggs. In 2020 China's total food production was valued at $1,500 billion, slightly lower than its overall agricultural production, which was valued at $1,560 billion (FAO, 2022). It also continues to have a very large agricultural workforce. Nevertheless, despite some impressive gains in agricultural production, it remains dependent on food imports, in large part due to the necessity to feed a population of over 1.4 billion people.

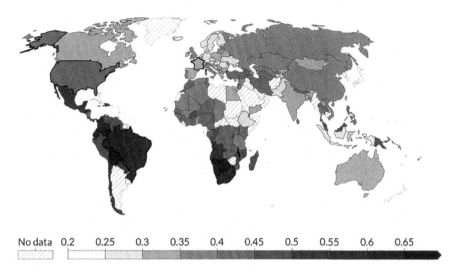

No data 0.2   0.25   0.3   0.35   0.4   0.45   0.5   0.55   0.6   0.65

FIGURE 1.1 Global measure of income inequality in 2000
Source: Hasell et al. (2023)

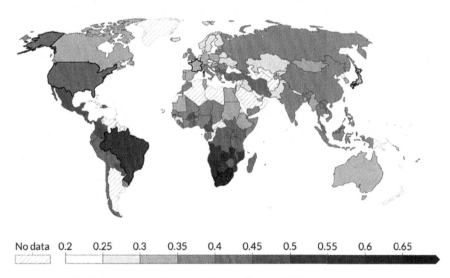

No data 0.2   0.25   0.3   0.35   0.4   0.45   0.5   0.55   0.6   0.65

FIGURE 1.2 Global measure of income inequality in 2020
Source: Hasell et al. (2023)

India is the world's second-largest agricultural producer. In 2020 its agricultural output was valued at $404 billion, $383 of which was food production. Both its agricultural production and its consumption are focused on local markets, and it has achieved self-sufficiency in grain production. It did this through a large network of small farms that produce at or just above subsistence levels due to their reliance on cultural and conventional practices.

India's large population of over 1.4 billion people means that its per capita agricultural output remains relatively low. The country also lacks a robust agricultural infrastructure, which limits its ability to use resources, such as energy and water, efficiently. As a result, India's agricultural production experiences significant seasonal fluctuations resulting in below-average crop yields and growing climate risks. Despite these challenges, however, it is the world's largest producer of milk, jute, and legumes, and the second-largest producer of rice, wheat, sugarcane, fruits, vegetables, and cotton (FAO, 2022).

Brazil is the world's fourth-largest agricultural producer and the world's largest beef exporter. In 2020 its total agricultural output was valued at $136 billion, $125 billion of which was food production. That same year, Brazil's agricultural exports were valued at $85 billion, making it the world's third-largest food exporter after the United States and the Netherlands. (The latter's high position on this list is almost entirely due to the fact that it is the world's largest exporter of flowering plants and plant seedlings (see Jukema et al., 2022.) Brazil's top export products were soybeans, sugar, poultry, and beef. Its largest trading partner by far was China, which purchased more than $30 billion worth of Brazil's agricultural exports. The tremendous expansion of Brazil's agricultural sector came at a cost, however: namely, the loss of vast swathes of rainforest. Large-scale deforestation began in the 1960s, when Brazil's government implemented financial incentives to encourage the transformation of native forest into farmland. Between 1980 and 2004 an estimated 20,000 square kilometers of forest were destroyed every year. By 2010, deforestation had declined to under 5,000 square kilometers per year, but thereafter it started to increase again, pushing up the country's agricultural output per capita as well as its food exports (Roy, 2022; Estoque et al., 2022).

The United States is the world's third-largest agricultural producer and its largest food exporter by far. In 2020 it produced almost 100 million tons of agricultural products, with a total value of $307 billion. Food crops accounted for $306 billion of this figure, although some of them, especially corn and soybeans, were used primarily as animal feed. Given its smaller population of 332 million people, US agricultural production per capita is considerably higher than the figures for the world's other top agricultural producers. The US agricultural sector is almost the opposite of India's. US agriculture is characterized by large conventional farms that produce high crop yields and rely on a robust, highly centralized infrastructure. These farms have been subsidized and supported in many ways to reach their current levels of productivity. The United States heavily subsidized its agricultural sector during the New Deal era, when support for the country's farmers became a cornerstone of President Roosevelt's efforts to turn the tide on the Great Depression (Rasmussen et al., 1976). Yet, even before the inauguration of the US Department of Agriculture and the farm subsidies introduced in the 1930s, government programs encouraged and actively supported farming. The Homestead Act of 1862, for example, reappropriated so-called "unappropriated public land" occupied by native peoples (Lincicome,

2020). After the passage of the country's first Farm Bills, subsidies were also integral to the development of high yield crop varieties (HYVs). One of the leaders in developing these revolutionary varieties was the agricultural scientist and 1970 Nobel laureate Norman Borlaug, who is known as the "Father of the Green Revolution." His initial research focused on developing wheat varieties that produced higher yields and were less susceptible to pests, but his work was then adapted to produce other HYVs, including corn, soybeans, and rice, with the latter particularly influential in achieving breakthroughs in agricultural yields in Asia (Farmer, 1986; Hazell, 2009).

By 2020, US agricultural exports were valued at $148 billion. China imports the most US agricultural products each year ($33 billion worth), followed by Canada, Mexico, and Japan. The state of California is the largest agricultural producer in the United States, producing almost twice as much as any other state. However, the states of Iowa, Nebraska, Texas, Kansas, Minnesota, and Illinois are also major producers.

Despite its sophisticated infrastructure, the United States leads the world in food waste (RTS, 2023). An estimated 23 million tons of food (or one-quarter of the country's total agricultural production) is wasted every year, much of it in the form of on-farm losses that occur when products do not meet the expectations of food buyers and processors (Dou et al., 2016).

The new HYVs typically came as a package deal, since they required higher applications of fertilizers, pesticides, controlled irrigation, and new cultivation methods. This also meant that farmers had to make upfront investments that were generally funded through loan programs. In the international arena these loan programs often came with strings attached. For example, private sector seed banks were established, petrochemical industries began to supply fertilizers and pesticides, and farmers no longer owned their seeds. While many scientists point to the tremendous successes of HYVs, some have argued that yields of traditional crop varieties could have increased to comparable levels with better irrigation and cultivation methods. This illustrates that the efficiency gains in conventional agricultural production did not come without costs. In Brazil, for example, the expansion of food production meant that the country's forest coverage declined by 81.7 million hectares between 1960 and 2020 (Estoque et al., 2022). Other environmental impacts increased as well. For example, the effects of increased fertilization on ground and surface water quality were documented as early as the 1960s (O'Hara, 1984; Bijay-Singh and Craswell, 2021). When high rates of nitrogen fertilizer are applied and the plants cannot take up all of the nutrients, soluble nitrates leach into the ground water or are carried into surface water. This may seem counterintuitive as one would assume that any farmer will want to avoid the loss of valuable nutrients. Yet, every application of fertilizer is time consuming and generates costs in the form of labor, fuel, machine hours, and other inputs. At the same time, the leachate of fertilizers (e.g., in the form of water-soluble nitrates) is dependent on precipitation patterns that are difficult to predict. Navigating heavy machinery through fields of growing plants also becomes more difficult as the plants grow. This means that higher doses of nutrients are applied earlier in the growing cycle. It is therefore near impossible to apply fertilizers in very small doses at precisely the right time—that is, when the plants are ready to absorb all the available nutrients and when there is no prospect of heavy rainfall that will result in leaching nutrients into the ground water or losing them in surface-water run-off. The latter may result in eutrophication—that is, the contamination of streams, lakes, and eventually coastal areas with nitrogen and phosphorous—which in turn leads to excessive algal blooms and oxygen depletion to the point where fish and other aquatic organisms can no longer survive. Similarly, contamination of ground water may impact private water wells and municipal sources of drinking water and make it impossible to stay within safe nitrate contamination limits recommended by the World Health Organization. Urea, the largest component of nitrogen fertilizers, contributes more than half of all nitrous-oxide (N_2O) emissions and releases carbon dioxide (CO_2) that was embedded within the fertilizers during the manufacturing process. An estimated 9 percent of all CO_2 emissions are attributable to this decomposition process (Neelis et al., 2005; Reay et al., 2012). Emissions of N_2O from synthetic fertilizers are estimated at 2.3 million tons per year. This is the equivalent of about 40 percent of the direct CO_2 emissions of the chemical sector. On the other hand, the increased crop yields of the Green Revolution may have prevented an estimated 25 million hectares of land from going into agricultural production, since higher yields mean less land is needed (Stevenson et al., 2013).

The negative effects of pesticides—which, like fertilizers and HYVs, were important tools in the Green Revolution—were also documented as early as the 1960s. For example, in her book *Silent Spring*, Rachel Carson reported the bioaccumulation of pesticides in food chains—from insects to birds, fish, mammals, and ultimately humans (Carson, 1962). Observed results include biodiversity loss, reduced pollinator populations, increased cancer rates in animals and humans, lower rates of reproduction, and even birth defects. Yet, more than 500 active pesticide ingredients have been approved since the 1970s, including 72 that have since been banned in the European Union (El Bilali et al., 2019; Donley, 2019). The United States lags far behind in its regulation of pesticides, still allowing the use of 85 that have been outlawed in other countries. Regulations also tend to be more lax in low-income countries, which means that millions of farmers and farm workers are still routinely exposed to harmful pesticides even though the negative health effects of these substances are well documented (Boedeker et al., 2020; Farmworker Justice, 2016).

Economists call the environmental and social side-effects of agriculture's productivity gains "negative externalities." These occur when the production or consumption of a product results in costs to a third party. When negative externalities are present, markets tend to overestimate a product's benefits. The benefits of agricultural products may be overestimated because the full costs of production are not entirely known or accounted for. There are also no incentives to reduce the negative externalities of production since their costs are borne by those most affected by them, not by those who create them (Gowdy and O'Hara, 1996). This often means that the costs of negative externalities are borne by those living at a considerable distance, those without the political capital to effect change, and future generations. Clearly, the gains in agricultural production make it possible to feed more people, and increased yields have also resulted in lower food and commodity crop prices. Yet, these lower prices may be more costly than meets the eye, as agricultural prices would be far higher if the external costs of production were included. However, since such costs are not borne by those who benefit from the higher yields but by third parties who suffer the negative consequences, adjustments in production levels and in the way we produce our agricultural yields fail to take place. Changes in production methods that would lower the negative externalities of agricultural production are slow to be adopted unless they also reduce production costs.

Of course, there can also be positive externalities. For example, sustainable agricultural practices (including some urban agriculture schemes) can facilitate the sequestration of carbon in the soil and counteract the negative impacts of deforestation and the loss of green space. Third parties will benefit from such practices even though the farmers who implement them bear their costs. Year-round green cover can reduce ground water contamination and surface water pollution, and more frequent fertilizer applications in small doses may reduce nutrient run-off and leachate. In urban environments, where paved streets, sidewalks, and rooftops result in high rates of storm-water run-off that may contribute to flooding, plants can absorb storm water and may also mitigate urban heat islands. Improved access to healthy, nutritious food therefore does more than reduce hunger and the negative physical, cognitive, and emotional consequences of malnutrition. The direct benefits of having sufficient nutritional food and better physical, mental, and emotional health are increased capacity to learn and work, improved productivity and creativity, better quality of life, and higher levels of satisfaction (Leroy et al., 2015; Evans et al., 2015). The social tensions associated with food shortages and rising food prices are well documented, even though their severity may vary depending on other institutional factors (Bellemare, 2014; Weinberg and Bakker, 2015; Rudolfsen, 2021). Since improved access to healthy food also lowers the incidence of food-related illnesses, it also reduces third-party costs associated with food-related health problems. Women and children are disproportionately impacted by these problems, and the benefits of improved food security are further multiplied as negative impacts on future generations are reduced. Therefore, as countries around the world contemplate the next frontier of agricultural innovation, they must decide which types of food production and agricultural practices will lead to reductions in negative externalities and increases in positive externalities.

The gains in global agricultural production also ushered in a dramatic shift in where people live. As the productivity of the agricultural sector continued to grow, fewer farm workers were needed. Global data prior to 1990 is sparce, but according to the World Bank (2022a), the percentage of the global workforce employed in agriculture declined from 44 to 25 percent between 1990 and 2020. This led to a major demographic shift from rural to urban communities in virtually every region of the world. In 1960 just 36 percent of the global population lived in cities; by 2020, this figure had increased to 56 percent. North America led the world in urbanization, so that today 82 percent of the region's population live in cities and metropolitan areas. Latin America and the Caribbean is a close second, with 81 percent of its population living in urban areas, followed by 74 percent in Europe, 68 percent in Oceania, 51 percent in Asia, and 44 percent in Africa (FAO, 2022).

This shift to the cities was accompanied by a shift in people's relationship with their food. In 1960 the majority of people around the world grew at least some of their own food. By 2020, the majority of the world's population were food consumers who relied on an ever-smaller percentage of their fellow citizens to grow that food. The workforce that moved from the countryside to urban communities produced new consumer goods and provided ever more services. In the process, the world's gross domestic product (GDP)—that is, the monetary value of all final goods and services—rose dramatically from $1.3 trillion in 1960 to $85 trillion in 2020. Yet, at the same time, the value of so-called primary-sector products, such as those produced by agriculture, forestry, and fishing, dropped from 10 percent to only 4 percent of global GDP. Table 1.4 shows the percentage contributions of agriculture, industry, and the service sector to the GDPs of the world's four largest agricultural producers. With a GDP of $21 trillion in 2020, the United States has the largest economy in the world; China is second largest, with a GDP of almost $15 trillion; India's GDP is $2.7 trillion; and Brazil's is $1.5 trillion. However, there a far greater differences in these countries' GDP per capita—from $61,800 per person per year in the United States to just $1,940 per person per year in India. Table 1.5 summarizes the changes in GDP per capita in all four countries between 1960 and 2020.

TABLE 1.4 Percentage contributions to GDP by sector for selected countries

	GDP 2020 ($ billion)	GDP from agriculture (%)	GDP from industry (%)	GDP from services (%)
World	85,000	4	–	–
USA	21,000	1.1	18.4	80.1
China	14,700	7.7	38	54.5
India	2,700	18.2	25	49.4
Brazil	1,500	7	18	63.8

Source: World Bank (2022a)

TABLE 1.5 Changes in GDP per capita between 1960 and 2020 (in constant US dollars)

	1960 GDP per capita ($)	2020 GDP per capita ($)
World	3,500	11,000
USA	19,100	61,800
China	238	10,360
India	306	1,940
Brazil	2,500	8,200

Source: World Bank (2022b)

As urbanization gathered pace around the world, the distance between food consumers and food producers also increased, meaning that food had to travel ever further distances. This brought a new set of challenges. Food that travels longer distances has to be stored and processed, both of which require energy, leading to an increase in negative externalities. Twnety-five percent of global CO_2 emissions are attributed to food transportation. Agriculture also uses an estimated 75 percent of the world's fresh water (Pimentel et al., 2004) and appropriates a sizeable proportion of the world's petrochemicals in the form of fertilizers and pesticides (International Energy Agency, 2018). Food that travels has to be harvested earlier, which can have negative effects on its nutritional value. However, the implications of food transportation and storage vary tremendously across the world. North America and Europe both have robust infrastructures consisting of efficient road, water, and rail systems, cold-storage facilities for perishable food products, and sophisticated distribution centers. Losses of unprocessed agricultural products therefore occur primarily pre-harvest, when agricultural products are deemed unsuitable for sale as they do not meet narrowly defined quality criteria relating to color, shape, and size. In contrast, in other world regions, especially Africa and parts of Asia, pests, mold, and related problems cause far more post-harvest losses due to a lack of proper storage and processing facilities (Malhotra, 2019; Mandyck and Schultz, 2015).

The vulnerabilities of a food system that stretches across the globe came into sharp focus during the recent COVID-19 pandemic (O'Hara and Toussaint, 2021). In an effort to curb the number of infections and deaths, curfews, quarantines, and other restrictions described as "social distancing," "lockdown," and "stay at home orders" were implemented around the world. By April 2020, almost 4 billion people (more than half of the global population) had been placed under some kind of mobility restriction by their governments. Additional measures to constrain the spread of the virus included frequent handwashing, wearing face coverings, contact tracing, and isolating infected persons. Research indicates that these measures were effective in reducing the spread of COVID-19, but the economic impact was significant. Global GDP declined by 5 percent in 2020, which resulted in a sharp increase in global poverty. An estimated 97 million people slid back into extreme poverty, while the global poverty rate increased from 7.8 to 9.1 percent, setting the world back an estimated three to four years in the struggle to eradicate extreme poverty.

Disparity increased during the pandemic, too. A World Bank study (Sanchez-Paramo et al., 2021) reported that people in the world's two lowest-income quintiles lost 6.6 percent of their income in 2020 and 6.7 percent in 2021. In contrast, those in the highest-income quintile lost 5.1 percent in 2020 and only 2.6 percent in 2021 (see Figure 1.3).

Globally, food insecurity grew by almost 10 percent during the same two years. Women and children in low- to middle-income countries (who had already been vulnerable before the pandemic) were especially hard hit and suffered a particularly high decline in food security. By 2022, an estimated 144 million children under five were exhibiting stunted growth, and 47 million children were suffering life-threatening levels of malnutrition. A study of households in Africa and Asia revealed that disruptions in food supply chains and rising food prices were among the main causes of the dramatic increases in poverty. As a result, millions of families were forced to go hungry for longer periods of time or adopt poorer diets (Fernandez, 2022).

Further pressures on the global food system were triggered by the war in Ukraine. According to the United States Department of Agriculture Foreign Agricultural Service (2022), Ukraine is the world's seventh-largest wheat producer and the sixth-largest producer of corn. Egypt, China, Turkey, and

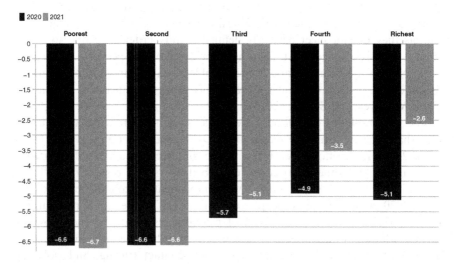

FIGURE 1.3 Percent of income loss by income quintile due to COVID-19 in 2020 and 2021

Source: Sanchez-Paramo et al. (2021)

Nigeria are the biggest buyers of Ukrainian wheat, while Mexico, Japan, South Korea, and Vietnam are the biggest importers of Ukrainian corn. Grain deliveries were initially suspended as a result of Russia's blockade of Ukrainian ports, export prices for wheat and corn skyrocketed, and there were severe disruptions in the supply chain for food-importing countries. As a result, the FAO (2022) estimated that an additional 8 to 13 million people would be unable to meet their daily minimum food-intake requirements and so could become undernourished in 2023. Women, children and the elderly have been particularly hard hit by these food shortages and high food prices. These are some of the same people who were disproportionally affected by the COVID-19 pandemic (Osendarp et al., 2023).

One might imagine that the world's largest economy, and its largest food exporter, with one of the world's highest household incomes, would have mastered the supply chain disruptions triggered by an external shock event like COVID-19. Yet, COVID-19 brought the vulnerabilities of the US food system into focus as well. Over 6 million people had lost their lives to the pandemic by the time vaccines became widely available, with over 1 million of them in the United States. This means it is the country with the greatest number of COVID-19 fatalities, followed by Brazil (690,000), India (530,000), Russia (390,000), and Mexico (320,000). Of these five countries, the United States had the highest rate of COVID-19 fatalities per 100,000 of the population. While the global COVID-19 mortality rate was 0.8 percent, the US rate was almost 3 percent. At the same time, US households with children that reported low to very low food security increased from 14.7 percent to 17.5 percent (Coleman-Jensen et al., 2021; Parekh et al., 2021). Not surprisingly, those with low household incomes, high unemployment, and low education levels were especially vulnerable to becoming food insecure. An estimated 25 million Americans—8 percent of the population—sought food assistance during the pandemic. Low-wage earners in the hospitality sector were especially hard hit as restaurants and hotels shut down and households shifted to home cooking and take-out meals. These figures are alarming, especially since those in food-insecure households were also more likely to suffer other health issues that would have made them more susceptible to the effects of COVID-19 (O'Hara and Ivanic, 2022; World Health Organization, 2008; Popkin et al., 2020).

These figures show how precarious the livelihoods of vulnerable people, including those who live in the world's largest economy (and the world's largest food exporter), can be. They also illustrate the multi-layered disparities that are an integral part of food insecurity and its corollary, hunger. As countries around the world aspire to a higher level of affluence for their citizens, and ever more exports to fuel their economic aspirations, it may be instructive to ask what can be learned from the US experience. This warrants a closer look, especially at US cities, where over 80 percent of US citizens live.

Lack in the midst of plenty

Although agriculture is no longer one of the United States' major employers, food exports still exceed imports, making a positive contribution to the US trade balance. Moreover, while agriculture officially constitutes only 1.1 percent of the United States' GDP, as mentioned earlier, GDP measures *final* goods and services. A significant portion of agricultural products are considered *intermediate*, since they are used in processed foods and as ingredients for meals in hotels and restaurants. Hence, such products are counted in the "retail" and "services" categories, rather than listed under "agriculture." More importantly, food is a necessity that no one can do without. Ensuring food security is therefore essential, and low food security can trigger a chain of deficiencies. A certain number of calories and critical nutrients are necessary to maintain an active, productive life, fight disease, and ultimately increase life expectancy. Yet, too many calories—as well as too few nutrients—can create health problems such as obesity, diabetes, and heart disease, reduce energy levels, hinder productivity, compromise the body's immune system, and lead to sluggishness or even depression. This is why the USDA defines "food security" as: "access by all people at all times to enough nutritious food for an active, healthy life" (United States Department of Agriculture, 2014). Therefore, "low food security" implies that not enough food is available at least some of the time, or that the available food is of low quality and cannot support an active and healthy life at least some of the time. As COVID-19 made clear, ready access to healthy food is critically important to reducing the negative health effects of an external shock event. Identifying ways to improve access to food took on a new sense of urgency during the pandemic. Reliable access to an adequate supply of healthy, nutrient-rich food can be considered an important determinant of health, and an indicator of vulnerable communities.

As entire industries shut down, agricultural products like grain, meat, and perishable fruits and vegetables, consumer goods like refrigerators and cars, and manufacturing components like steel plates and computer chips were left stranded in ports, at airports, and in rail yards all over the world. A new term—the "essential workforce"—emerged to describe those workers who ensure the supply and delivery of essential goods and services such as food, water, cleaning products, and medical supplies (Geary et al., 2022). Employees in meat-processing plants and distribution centers suffered exceptionally high rates of COVID-19 due to working conditions that made social distancing nearly impossible (Whitehead and Brad Kim, 2022). Crops withered in the fields as farm workers sat at home under lockdown, unable to reach the farms where they were scheduled to harvest strawberries, tomatoes, artichokes, and lettuces (Lusk and Chandra, 2021). Meat ran low as slaughter houses were unable to maintain normal processing rates. Animals that could not be slaughtered in time outgrew the allowable processing weights and had to be destroyed (Cima, 2020). These examples illustrate how vulnerable highly industrialized food supply chains can be. Any highly industrialized process has little flexibility to deviate from the norm. Animals must have just the right slaughter weight for the conveyor belt of processing machines to remain functional. Cold chains are carefully calibrated, and either too much or too little of a perishable product can cause serious problems. As food travels long distances, there is little capacity to accommodate variations in the slaughter weight of animals or the storage conditions of fruits and vegetables. Anything that is too ripe, too big, or too heavy cannot be processed. The economies of scale that drive the unprecedented efficiency levels of a highly industrialized, highly centralized food system also make it vulnerable. This is a perfect description of the US agricultural sector. The United States leads the world not only in food exports but also in market concentration, with a food economy shaped by enormous agribusinesses and highly processed foods.

Like almost everything else, the disruptions of the COVID pandemic were not evenly distributed. Poor communities and communities with high percentages of non-white populations were hardest hit. An examination of the statistical relationship between food-related health conditions such as obesity, diabetes, and heart disease and COVID-19-related deaths is instructive. A study of more than 3,000 US counties found that the presence of several pre-existing health conditions had a statistically significant impact on COVID-19 fatality rates (O'Hara and Ivanic, 2022; Ariya et al., 2021). In the United States, food-related illnesses are higher among African Americans, other non-white populations, and the elderly (Harrison et al., 2021; Chatters et al., 2021), and COVID-19-related fatalities were higher among these same groups. Food access is often limited in urban areas with predominantly non-white populations, and full-service grocery stores are often conspicuously absent from low-income neighborhoods where black and/or brown populations constitute the majority. For example, Washington, DC, the nation's capital, is organized into eight administrative wards, each with a population of approximately 80,000 people. Income levels vary significantly between the wards, with the households in Ward 3 earning almost five times as much as those in Ward 8. Ward 3's residents are predominantly white and live, on average, 15 years longer than the predominantly non-Hispanic, black residents of Ward 8. There are nine full-service grocery stores (0.12 per 1,000 residents) in Ward 3, compared to just two (0.026 per 1,000 residents) in Ward 8. Therefore, it is hardly surprising that food-related illnesses also vary significantly between these two wards.

The lower food security rates that many low-income, black and brown neighborhoods experience are not a recent development stemming from the COVID-19 crisis. They are an injustice that stems from a long history of disinvestment, neglect, and negative or erroneous belief systems about food. For example, in such areas, Small Business Administration (SBA) loans favor fast-food chains instead of small independent food vendors. Sugar subsidies have translated into high-sugar snacks and beverages that have cemented the lack of access to unprocessed, nutrient-rich snacks and sugar-free alternatives in low-income neighborhoods. As a result, food access remains uneven across socio-economic and racial lines. Disparities in food access are therefore not simply a reflection of differences in supply chain disruptions. They are also an expression of discriminatory practices that enable some to afford freshly made smoothies that are low in sugar and high in nutrients while others cannot; some to dine in high-end restaurants that offer seasonal menus of locally sourced produce while others eat exclusively in fast-food restaurants; and some to work from home while others must take crowded public transport to reach their places of (often "essential") work.

As concerns about the fragility of long food supply chains and worries about pre-existing health conditions have increased, calls for more local food alternatives have also grown. There is evidence that some progress has been made in this area. For instance, local farmers' markets have almost doubled over recent years, with Washington, DC, now boasting more than 50 (the highest number per 100,000 residents in the country). Unfortunately, though, the high prices often make these markets prohibitively expensive for low-income residents, undermining their transformative potential (Martinez et al., 2010; Hu et al., 2021).

In 2020, the USDA launched a pilot project under the direction of Congress to form 17 Farm Service Agency (FSA) Urban Agriculture Committees across the United States. The purpose of the scheme was to create committees in locations with relatively high concentrations of urban and suburban farms. County Committees have been vehicles for farmers to provide input into FSA programs since the 1930s. They represent the nation's farmers and set priorities at the local level. The new Urban Agriculture Committees similarly work to encourage and promote urban, indoor, and other emerging agricultural practices, and address local issues of interest to consumers, such as food access, community engagement, and food waste reduction. They also make recommendations, listen to appeals, and conduct outreach programs to urban and suburban farms and farmers for both the FSA and the Natural Resources Conservation Service (NRCS). These and other developments suggest that the USDA is trying to establish a framework for shoring up the food supply chains and making the country's food system more resilient. For instance, it has already invested in climate-smart practices, organic transition initiatives, and programs to relocalize meat and poultry processing, as well as urban agriculture initiatives.

Some agencies within the USDA have also made programmatic changes to include urban producers in their clienteles. For example, the Risk Management Agency has changed both its Whole-Farm Revenue Protection Program and its Micro Farm Program to include urban and innovative producers, reduce the revenue threshold for approvals, and minimize underwriting and record-keeping requirements that are especially onerous for small farmers. Similarly, USDA Rural Development has launched a Business and Industry Food Supply Chain Guaranteed Loan Program and a Meat and Poultry Processing Expansion Program to accommodate projects in urban areas.

Meanwhile, the Natural Resources Conservation Service has formulated new conservation practices and payment schedules for small-scale and urban producers. Nevertheless, much more work still needs to be done to address the gaps in the food system.

Since these are new developments, we must ask how we got here. A review of the US Farm Bills reveals that US agriculture has historically been defined almost exclusively as commodity crops and large-scale operations with the goal of realizing economies of scale and keeping food prices low. The majority of US commodity crops are grown in rural Midwestern and southern states, and the nation's food and agriculture are commonly associated with rural communities and large farms that grow commodity crops such as corn, soybeans, cotton, and dairy products (United States Department of Agriculture Economic Research Service, 2022). The association of agriculture with rural America is also evidenced by the latter's strong representation within the leadership of the USDA: throughout the department's history, 23 of the 32 secretaries (72 percent) have been from rural Midwest communities (United States Department of Agriculture, 2023). Therefore, agricultural producers and the lived experiences of rural communities have been well represented in the leadership and policy priorities of the US Department of Agriculture.

In the most recent Farm Bill (2018), the combined producer and consumer programs received $428 billion in funding for FY19–FY23 (Johnson and Monke, 2019). Producer-focused programs and subsidies help with loans, crop insurance, and conservation efforts. Consumer-focused programs include the Supplemental Nutrition Assistance Program (SNAP), the Women, Infant, and Children (WIC) Program, and the Senior Farmers Market Program. Over their 50-year history, these programs have grown to account for 65 percent of the total USDA nutrition-assistance funding (Jones et al., 2021). Consumer-focused programs constitute 76 percent of the 2018 Farm Bill budget, compared to 24 percent for producer-focused programs (Johnson and Monke, 2019). This illustrates a shift in funding priorities from agricultural production to programs supporting consumers, which has resulted in a dramatic change in the end-users utilizing USDA programs. While, historically, producers in rural Midwest communities were the main stakeholders of food- and agriculture-focused programs, the new constituents are food users who live in diverse urban communities. For example, in 2020, 82 percent of SNAP users lived in cities and metropolitan areas. These users reflect the diversity of urban communities across the country, with 37 percent of SNAP users white, 26 percent black, 16 percent Hispanic, 3 percent Asian, 1.5 percent Native American, 16 percent identified as "race unknown," and 1 percent reported as "multiple races" (Cronquist, 2021). These urban constituents experience significant disparities compared to Americans who are not in need of food and nutrition support. These disparities are commonly referred to as differences in the social determinant of food security and health. In 2021, six times as many households in urban and metropolitan areas experienced food insecurity compared with those in rural areas (Coleman-Jensen et al., 2021).

Given the high level of participation in the USDA's consumer programs and the need for food and nutrition access for urban constituencies, one might expect the USDA to shift toward more programs that increase food production in urban areas. However, such a shift in producer-focused programs toward small-scale, urban, and suburban agriculture has been largely absent to date. There are a couple of exceptions—two financial assistance programs initiated by the Office of Urban Agriculture and Innovative Production, and the launch of the aforementioned 17 FSA Urban Agriculture Committees—but subsidies are still focused on large producers in rural America. Nevertheless, there is growing awareness of the diversity of stakeholders—and diversity within the individual stakeholder groups—in the US food system. This warrants a closer look at the country's food consumers and the newly emerging food producers in urban and metropolitan areas. Since the latter group are new arrivals in the food and agriculture space, it is worth exploring whether they will make a difference in addressing the needs of urban food consumers.

This is the focus of this book. It examines six cities and metropolitan areas in the United States and identifies those who are struggling with food security and those who are seeking to reform the food system. Chapter 2 takes a closer look at the history of food insecurity in the United States and how it came to be known by that term, rather than "hunger" or "nutritional deficit." It then examines the complexities of food insecurity in six cities: namely, Albuquerque, NM, Atlanta, GA, Chicago, IL, New York City, NY, Oakland, CA, and Washington, DC. All but one of these cities (the sole exception is Washington, DC) are participants in the FSA's new Urban Agriculture Committees project. The selected cities span different geographic locations and all three of the United States' time zones, and they demonstrate some of the common characteristics of food insecurity across vastly different growing conditions.

Chapter 3 introduces the people and stories behind the food insecurity data in the same six US cities by sharing the stories of food-insecure individuals and those who run food banks and food pantries to address their needs. These stories illustrate how prevalent characteristics captured in data on food insecurity actually play out in the lives of real people and organizations.

Chapter 4 takes a closer look at the other side of the urban food system by tracing the history of urban food innovations in cities across the United States. Such innovations have the potential to reduce the food miles traveled from the farm to the forks of US consumers, and to address the supply chain vulnerabilities associated with a highly centralized, large-scale food system. The chapter provides a brief overview of the data on food sector innovations in the six US cities discussed in Chapter 2. It also introduces linkages between urban food sector innovations and other sectors of the economy both upstream and downstream from the food and agriculture sector.

Chapter 5 introduces the people behind some of the emerging food system innovations in the same six US cities. These innovators come from all walks of life, yet they share a commitment to implementing a more decentralized, sustainable food system. Their stories reveal that food system innovations can generate win–win outcomes of improved food security *and* improved sustainability, even in cities that may have less than optimal growing conditions.

Chapter 6 outlines the pathways between food security and the new urban food initiatives that can create a sustainable and just food system in cities across the United States. Despite the vastly different locations of the six cities discussed in this book, a number of commonalities emerge from the stories of those who experience food insecurity and those who are seeking to address it by building alternatives to the existing food system. These pathways point to new policies that can smooth the transition to a more sustainable and just food system rather than place boulders in the path. The chapter thus highlights promising solutions as well as critical barriers, including existing food and agriculture policies.

Finally, Chapter 7 summarizes the key issues discussed in this book along with insights gained from the data presented in Chapters 2 and 4 and the personal stories introduced in Chapters 3 and 5. In so doing, it offers a concluding review of various pathways toward a more sustainable and just food system and the changes in policy and mindset we need to get there from here.

Throughout, this book cautions against the risks associated with maintaining the status quo and argues that solutions-oriented pathways to a new food system that is sustainable and just for people and the planet are already emerging and must be actively supported through policy. Trade-offs between more food and less sustainability and equity are no longer an option. The second of the United Nations' 17 Sustainable Development Goals—"Eliminate Hunger"—can be achieved only in concert with commitments to achieve the other SDGs—end poverty, improve health and wellbeing, reduce inequality, provide high-quality education, make cities and communities sustainable, build resilient infrastructure, promote inclusive and sustainable industrialization, foster innovation, make production and consumption more responsible, provide affordable and clean energy, promote decent work, take action on climate change, sustain life on land and under water, and ensure peace, justice, and strong institutions for all.

References

Ariya, M., Karimi, J., Abolghasemi, S., Hematdar, Z., Naghizadeh, M., Moradi, M. and Barati-Boldaji, M. (2021). Food insecurity arises the likelihood of hospitalization in patients with COVID-19. *Scientific Reports*, 11: 20072. https://doi.org/10.1038/s41598-021-99610-4.

Bellemare, M. (2014). Rising food prices: food price volatility, and social unrest. *American Journal of Agricultural Economics*, 97(1): 1–21. https://doi.org/10.1093/ajae/aau038.

Bijay-Singh and Craswell, E. (2021). Fertilizers and nitrate pollution of surface and ground water: an increasingly pervasive global problem. *Applied Science*, 3: 518. https://doi.org/10.1007/s42452-021-04521-8.

Boedeker, W., Watts, M., Clausing, P. *et al.* (2020). The global distribution of acute unintentional pesticide poisoning: estimations based on a systematic review. *BMC Public Health*, 20: 1875. https://doi.org/10.1186/s12889-020-09939-0.

Braveman, P. and Gottlieb, L. (2014). The social determinants of health: it's time to consider the causes of the causes. *Public Health Reports*, 129(2): 19–31. https://www.ncbi.nlm.nih.gov/pmc/articles/PMC3863696/.

Carson, R. (1962). *Silent Spring*. New York: Houghton Mifflin.

CDC. (2022). Adult obesity facts. https://www.cdc.gov/obesity/data/adult.html.

Chatters L.M., Taylor H.O. and Taylor R.J. (2020). Older black Americans during COVID-19: race and age double jeopardy. *Health Education & Behavior*, 47(6): 855–860. https://doi.org/10.1177/1090198120965513.

Cima, G. (2020). Slaughter delays lead to depopulation: farms short of room as processors halt or slow meat production because of COVID-19. *Journal of the American Veterinary Medical Association*, 28 May.https://www.avma.org/javma-news/2020-06-15/slaughter-delays-lead-depopulation.

Coleman-Jensen, A., Rabbitt, M., Gregory, C. and Singh, A. (2021). *Household Food Security in the United States in 2020*. Washington, DC: Economic Research Service of the USDA.

Cronquist, K. (2021). *Characteristics of Supplemental Nutrition Assistance Program Households: Fiscal Year 2019 (SNAP-20-CHAR)*. Washington, DC: USDA. https://fns-prod.azureedge.us/sites/default/files/resource-files/Characteristics2019.pdf.

Donley, N. (2019). The USA lags behind other agricultural nations in banning harmful pesticides. *Environmental Health*, 18(44). doi:10.1186/s12940-019-0488-0.

Dou, Z., Ferguson, J., Galligan, D., Kelly, A., Finn, S. and Giegengack, R. (2016). Assessing US food wastage and opportunities for reduction. *Global Food Security*, 8: 19–26.

El Bilali, H., Callenius, C., Strassner, C. and Probst, L. (2019). Food and nutrition security and sustainability transitions in food systems. *Food and Energy Security*, 8: e00154. doi:10.1002/fes3.154.

Estoque, R., Dasgupta, R., Winkler, K., Avitabile, V., Johnson, B., Myint, S.W., Gao, Y., Ooba, M., Murayama, Y. and Lasco, R. (2022). Spatiotemporal pattern of global forest change over the past 60 years and the forest transition theory. *Environmental Research Letters*, 17(8). https://iopscience.iop.org/article/10.1088/1748-9326/ac7df5.

Evans, A., Banks, K., Jennings, R., Nehme, E., Nemec, C., Sharma, S., Hussaini, A. and Yaroch, A. (2015). Increasing access to healthful foods: a qualitative study with residents of low-income communities. *International Journal of Behavioural Nutrition and Physical Activity*, 12(1). https://doi.org/10.1186/1479-5868-12-S1-S5.

Evenson, R.E. and Gollin, D. (2003). Assessing the impact of the Green Revolution, 1960 to 2000. *Science*, 300(5620): 758–762. doi:10.1126/science.1078710.

FAO. (2020). Value of agricultural production. https://data.apps.fao.org/catalog/dataset/value-of-agricultural-production-global-national-annual-faostat.

FAO. (2022). Crops and livestock products. https://www.fao.org/faostat/en/#data/QCL.

Farmer, B. (1986). Perspectives on the "Green Revolution" in South Asia. *Modern Asian Studies*, 20(1): 175–199. doi:10.1017/s0026749x00013627. S2CID 145626108.

Farmworker Justice. (2016). *Exposed and Ignored: How Pesticides Endanger Our Nation's Farm Workers*. Washington, DC: Farmworker Justice.

Fernandez, G. (2022). Food insecurity in the time of COVID. https://publichealth.jhu.edu/2022/food-insecurity-in-the-time-of-covid.

Forum on Child and Family Statistics. (2022). POP1 child population: number of children (in millions) ages 0–17 in the United States by age, 1950–2021 and projected 2022–2050. https://www.childstats.gov/americaschildren/tables/pop1.asp.

Geary, C., Palacios, V. and Tatum, L. (2022). Who are essential workers? The US economy depends on women, people of color, & immigrant workers. https://www.law.georgetown.edu/workers-rights-institute/publications/brief/.

Gini, C. (1997). Concentration and dependency ratios. *Rivista di Politica Economica*, 87: 769–789. [First published in Italian, 1909.]

Gollin, D., Hansen, C. and Wingender, A. (2021). Two blades of grass: the impact of the Green Revolution. *Journal of Political Economy*, 129(8): 2344–2384. doi:10.1086/714444.

Gowdy, J. and O'Hara, S. (1996). *Economic Theory for Environmentalists*. Florida: St. Lucie Press.

Harrison, E., Monroe-Lord, L., Carson, A., Jean-Baptiste, A.-M., Phoenix, J., Jackson, P., Harris, B., Asongwed, E. and Richardson, M. (2021). COVID-19 pandemic related changes in wellness behavior among older Americans. *BMC Public Health*, 21: 755. https://doi.org/10.1186/s12889-021-10825-6.

Hasell, J., Arriagada, P., Ortiz-Ospina, E. and Roser, M. (2023). Economic inequality. https://ourworldindata.org/economic-inequality.

Hazell, Peter B.R. (2009). *The Asian Green Revolution*. IFPRI Discussion Paper 00911. https://core.ac.uk/download/pdf/6257689.pdf.

Hollander, S. (1997). *The Economics of Thomas Robert Malthus*. Toronto: University of Toronto Press.

International Energy Agency. (2018). *The Future of Petrochemicals: Towards More Sustainable Plastics and Fertilizers*. Paris: OECD.

Hu, X., Clarke, L. and Zendegdel, K. (2021). Farmers' market usage, fruit and vegetable consumption, meals at home and health: evidence from Washington, DC. Sustainability, 13(13): 7437. https://doi.org/10.3390/su13137437.

Johnson, R. and Monke, J. (2019). What is the Farm Bill? (RS22131). Congressional Research Service. https://sgp.fas.org/crs/misc/RS22131.pdf.

Jones, J.W., Toossi, S. and Hodges, L. (2021). *The Food and Nutrition Assistance Landscape: Fiscal Year 2020. Annual Report*. https://www.ers.usda.gov/publications/pub-details/?pubid=104145.

Jukema, G., Ramaekers, P. and Berkhout, P. (eds.). (2022). *De Nederlandse agrarische sector in internationaal verband*. Wageningen: Wageningen University and Research.

Leroy, J.L., Ruel, M., Frongillo, E.A., Harris, J. and Ballard, T.J. (2015). Measuring the food access dimension of food security: a critical review and mapping of indicators. *Food and Nutrition Bulletin*, 36(2): 167–195.

Library of Congress. (n.d.). History of the United States Farm Bill. https://www.loc.gov/ghe/cascade/index.html?appid=1821e70c01de48ae899a7ff708d6ad8b&bookmark=What%20is%20the%20Farm%20Bil.

Lincicome, S. (2020). Examining America's farm subsidy problem. *The Dispatch*, 15 December. https://www.cato.org/commentary/examining-americas-farm-subsidy-problem#:~:text=The%20United%20States%20has%20subsidized,parts%3A%20(1)%20various%20types.

Lusk, J. and Chandra, R. (2021). Farmer and farm worker illnesses and deaths from COVID-19 and impacts on agricultural output. *PLOS ONE*, 16(4): e0250621. https://doi.org/10.1371/journal.pone.0250621.

Mahler, D., Yonzan, N. and Lakner, C. (2022). *The impact of COVID-19 on Global Inequality and Poverty*. Policy Research Working Paper No. 10198. Washington, DC: World Bank. https://openknowledge.worldbank.org/handle/10986/38114.

Malhotra, S. (2019). Measuring and reducing food loss in developing countries. IFPRI Blog: Research Post. https://www.ifpri.org/blog/measuring-and-reducing-food-loss-de veloping-countries.

Mandyck, J. and Schultz, E. (2015). *Food Foolish: The Hidden Connection Between Food Waste, Hunger and Climate Change.* Palm Beach Gardens, FL: Carrier Corporation.

Martinez, S., Hand, M., Da Pra, M., Pollack, S., Ralston, S., Smith, T., Vogel, S., Clark, S., Lohr, L., Low, S. and Newman, C. (2010). *Local Food Systems: Concepts, Impacts, and Issues.* Economic Research Report No. 97. Washington, DC: United States Department of Agriculture Economic Research Service.

Narayan, A., Cojocaru, A., Agrawal, S., Bundervoet, T., Davalos, M., Garcia, N., Lakner, C., Mahler, D., Montalva Talledo, V., Ten, A. and Yonzan, N. (2022). *COVID-19 and Economic Inequality: Short-Term Impacts with Long-Term Consequences.* Policy Research Working Paper No. 9902. Washington, DC: World Bank.

Neelis, M.L., Patel, M., Gielen, D.J. and Blok, K. (2005). Modelling CO_2 emissions from non-energy use with the non-energy use emission accounting tables (NEAT) model. *Resources, Conservation and Recycling*, 45(3): 226–250.

O'Hara, S. (1984). *External Effects of Nitrate Fertilization: Assessment Problems and Valuation of Reduction Measures under Economic and Ecological Considerations* (in German; translated by the author). Kiel: Verlag Vauk.

O'Hara, S. (2018). *Five Pillars of Economic Development.* Washington, DC: College of Agriculture, Urban Sustainability and Environmental Sciences, University of the District of Columbia. https://docs.udc.edu/causes/Five-Pillars-DC-Final-05-2018.pdf.

O'Hara, S. and Ivanic, M. (2022). Food security and lifestyle vulnerabilities as systemic influencers of COVID-19 survivability. https://esmed.org/MRA/mra/article/view/2989.

O'Hara, S. and Toussaint, E. (2021). Food access in crisis: food security and COVID-19. *Ecological Economics*, 180: 106859.

Osendarp, S., Verburg, G., Bhutta, Z., Black, R.E., de Pee, S., Fabrizio, C., Headey, D., Heidkamp, R., Laborde, D. and Ruel, M.T. (2023). Act now before Ukraine war plunges millions into malnutrition. *Nature*, 604: 620–624. https://publichealth. jhu.edu/2022/food-insecurity-in-the-time-of-covid.

Parekh, N., Ali, S.H. and O'Connor, J. (2021). Food insecurity among households with children during the COVID-19 pandemic: results from a study among social media users across the United States. *Nutrition Journal*, 20: 73. https://doi.org/10.1186/s12937-021-00732-2.

Peng, X. (2022). China's population is about to shrink for the first time since the great famine struck 60 years ago: here's what that means for the world. *The Conversation*, 29 May. https://theconversation.com/chinas-population-is-about-to-shrink-for-the-first-tim e-since-the-great-famine-struck-60-years-ago-heres-what-it-means-for-the-world-176377.

Pimentel, D., Berger, D., Filiberto, D., Newton, M., Wolfe, B., Karabinakis, E., Clark, S., Poon, E., Abbett, E. and Nandagopal, S. (2004). Water resources: agricultural and environmental issues. *BioScience*, 54(10): 909–918. https://doi.org/10.1641/ 0006-3568 (2004)054[0909:WRAAEI]2.0.CO;2.

Pingali, P.L. (2012). Green Revolution: impacts, limits, and the path ahead. *PNAS*, 109(31): 12302–12308. https://doi.org/10.1073/pnas.0912953109.

Popkin, B., Du, S., Green, W., Beck, M., Algaith, T., Herbst, C., Alsukait, R., Alluhidan, M., Alazemi, N. and Shekar, M. (2020). Individuals with obesity and COVID-19: a global perspective on the epidemiology and biological relationships. *Obesity Reviews*, 21(11): e13128.

Rasmussen, W., Baker, G. and Ward, J. (1976). A short history of agricultural adjustment, 1933–1975. United States Department of Agriculture Economic Research Service, Agriculture Information Bulletin No. 391.

Reay, D., Davidson, E. and Smith, K. (2012). Global agriculture and nitrous oxide emissions. *Nature Climate Change*, 2: 410–416. https://doi.org/10.1038/nclimate1458.

Ross, S., Boyle, M. and Eichler, R. (2022). 4 countries that produce the most food. *Investopedia*, 22 August. https://www.investopedia.com/articles/investing/100615/4-countries-produce-most-food.asp.

Roy, D. (2022). Deforestation of Brazil's Amazon has reached a record high: what's being done? Council on Foreign Relations. https://www.cfr.org/in-brief/deforestation-brazils-amazon-has-reached-record-high-whats-being-done.

RTS. (2023). Food waste in America in 2023: statistics and facts. https://www.rts.com/resources/guides/food-waste-america/.

Rudolfsen, I. (2021). Food price increase and urban unrest: the role of societal organizations. *Journal of Peace Research*, 58(2): 215–230. https://doi.org/10.1177/0022343319899705.

Sanchez-Paramo, C., Hill, R., Mahler, D., Narayan, A. and Yonzan, N. (2021). COVID-19 leaves a legacy of rising poverty and widening inequality. https://blogs.worldbank.org/developmenttalk/covid-19-leaves-legacy-rising-poverty-and-widening-inequality.

Stevenson, J., Villoria, N., Byerlee, D., Kelley, T. and Maredia, M. (2013). Green Revolution research saved an estimated 18 to 27 million hectares from being brought into agricultural production. *Proceedings of the National Academy of Sciences*, 110(21): 8363–8368. doi:10.1073/pnas.1208065110.

Trewavas, A. (2002). Malthus foiled again and again. *Nature*, 418: 668–670. https://doi.org/10.1038/nature01013.

United States Department of Agriculture. (2014). Food security. http://www.ers.usda.gov/topics/food-nutrition-assistance/food-security-in-the-us.aspx#.U77pLpRdXQg.

United States Department of Agriculture. (2022). US regions. https://www.fns.usda.gov/fns-regional-offices.

United States Department of Agriculture. (2023). Former secretaries. https://www.usda.gov/our-agency/about-usda/history/former-secretaries.

United States Department of Agriculture Economic Research Service. (2022). *FAQs*. https://www.ers.usda.gov/faqs.

United States Department of Agriculture Foreign Agricultural Service. (2022). Ukraine agricultural production and trade. https://www.fas.usda.gov/sites/default/files/2022-04/Ukraine-Factsheet-April2022.pdf.

United States Department of Agriculture National Agricultural Statistics Service. (2022). Quick stats. https://quickstats.nass.usda.gov/.

UT Health. (2022). A resource for improving measurable impacts of COVID-19 on food insecurity. https://sph.uth.edu/research/centers/dell/legislative-initiatives/Impact-of-COVID-19-on-Food%20Insecurity-6.28.2022.pdf.

Weinberg, J. and Bakker, R. (2015). Let them eat cake: food prices, domestic policy and social unrest. *Conflict Management and Peace Science*, 32(3): 309–326. https://www.jstor.org/stable/26271391.

Welling, J.C. (1888). The law of Malthus. *American Anthropologist*, 1(1): 1–24. http://www.jstor.org/stable/658457.

Whitehead, D. and Brad Kim, Y.H. (2022). The impact of COVID-19 on the meat supply chain in the USA: a review. *Food Science of Animal Resources*, 42(5): 762–774. doi:10.5851/kosfa.2022.e39.

World Bank. (2022a). Population, total. https://data.worldbank.org/indicator/SP.POP. TOTL.

World Bank. (2022b). Rural population. https://data.worldbank.org/indicator/SP.RUR. TOTL.

World Health Organization. (2008). *Closing the Gap in a Generation: Health Equity through Action on the Social Determinants of Health*. Geneva: World Health Organization.

2
WHY ARE PEOPLE IN THE RICHEST COUNTRY ON EARTH FOOD INSECURE?

US cities are relatively young. Most were established by European settlers who arrived in North America in the early sixteenth century. St. Augustine, in Florida, which is considered the oldest US city, was founded in 1565 by the Spanish explorer Pedro Menéndez de Avilés. Jamestown, founded in 1607, is the second-oldest city and the first permanent English settlement in North America. Santa Fe, established in 1610, holds the distinction of being the oldest state capital. Albany, the capital of New York State, was settled by Dutch traders in 1614 before England took control of the city in 1664. The immigrant populations of the New World grew quickly and reflected the diversity of their countries of origin. Some came from privilege in pursuit of new opportunities; some fled religious persecution and economic hardship; others were brought forcibly against their will. In 1800 the United States had a population of 5.31 million; by 1900 this had grown to 76 million; in 1970 there were 203 million US citizens; and in 2020 the US population was 332 million strong. There are slightly more female (50.2 percent) than male (49.8 percent) US residents. Almost 17 percent are older than 65, while 22 percent are younger than 18. Based on the racial and ethnic designations in the 2020 US Census, 204 million (61 percent) identify as "Non-Hispanic White," 47 million (14 percent) as "Non-Hispanic Black," 24 million (7 percent) as "Asian," 10 million (3 percent) as "American Indian" or "Alaskan Native," and 1.6 million (less than half a percent) as "Native Hawaiian" or "Other Pacific Islander." Almost 19 percent (62 million) identify as "Hispanic," which represents a more than tenfold increase since 1970. The percentage of white US citizens declined from 88 percent in 1970 to 61 percent in 2020. This is reflected in the fact that Generation Z, which is defined as those born between 1997 and 2012, is the first majority non-white generation in US history (United States Census Bureau, 2020).

DOI: 10.4324/9781003322399-2

At $71,000 per year, the median income of US households is one of the highest in the world. A review of the historical data, however, indicates that the era of increased prosperity for all came to an end in the 1970s. Between 1940 and 1970, incomes across the whole range of low-, middle-, and high-income groups grew at nearly the same rate. Consequently, income inequality declined considerably following the Great Depression of the 1930s. There were two main reasons for this shift to greater equality: first, government programs initiated during President Roosevelt's New Deal sought to ease the stifling poverty of the Great Depression, which was exacerbated by a collapse in agricultural yields during the Dust Bowl years of 1931 to 1938; second, as the US entered World War II, the country's economy shifted from agricultural to industrial production. These two developments lifted millions of Americans out of poverty. The first Farm Bill, which was drafted in 1933, was a cornerstone of the New Deal. A second transformative piece of legislation was the Social Security Act, which was passed in 1935. This provided unemployment benefits, disability payments, and pensions for older Americans for the first time in the nation's history. However, the newly enacted law excluded farm and domestic workers from receiving benefits. At the time, almost 85 percent of black and brown workers were in one of these two categories. Scholars differ in their assessments of the motivation for these exclusions, but there is broad agreement on their consequences: a generational gap in income security between those who were covered by the Social Security Act and those who were not (DeWitt, 2010).

Also in 1935, the Works Progress Administration (WPA) created millions of permanent jobs in support of various infrastructure projects. In total, the WPA employed 8.5 million people between 1935 and 1943. One regional project orchestrated by the WPA was the Tennessee Valley Authority, which put thousands of impoverished residents to work on new hydro-electric ventures. Also in 1935, Congress established the Soil Erosion Service, now known as the Natural Resources Conservation Service (NRCS), an agency of the United States Department of Agriculture (USDA). It launched the Prairies States Forestry Project, which encouraged local farmers to plant trees as windbreaks on farmland across the Great Plains. The aim was to reduce the enormous losses of topsoil that the Dust Bowl states of Colorado, Kansas, Nebraska, New Mexico, Oklahoma, and Texas had experienced as a result of extended droughts and unsustainable agricultural practices. In the wake of this and other NRCS measures to combat soil erosion, over the next 50 years a series of Farm Bills introduced subsidies, price controls, risk management, and other initiatives to help producers adopt more sustainable agricultural practices. This was essential as the soil erosion of the Dust Bowl years was so severe that entire neighborhoods were coated in dust carried more than 1,000 miles from the American heartland to the East Coast on prevailing westerly winds (Lee and Gill, 2015; National Weather Service, 2023). Sadly, though, US agriculture may be on its way to creating another Dust Bowl, due, in part, to changing climate patterns (Union of Concerned Scientists USA, 2020).

The first food assistance program—the Food Stamp Program (FSP)—was launched in 1939. It provided people who qualified for food assistance with orange stamps that could be used to buy any kind of food, as well as blue stamps that could only be spent on items the USDA designated as food surplus. Retailers redeemed the orange stamps while various government-supported organizations redeemed the blue ones. During its first four years of operation, the FSP reached an estimated 20 million Americans in nearly half of the country's 3,000 counties. Milo Perkins, the scheme's first administrator under Secretary of Agriculture Henry Wallace, is quoted as saying: "We got a picture of a gorge, with farm surpluses on one cliff and under-nourished city folks with outstretched hands on the other. We set out to find a practical way to build a bridge across that chasm" (USDA FNS, 2010).

The new food stamps were clearly identified as a means to address the hardships of the Great Depression. As a result, no real stigma was attached to the program and it was widely used. However, it promptly ended in 1943, due to the fact that the widespread unemployment of the 1930s had started to give way to unprecedented industrialization and accompanying rising wages. Despite the efforts of President Roosevelt to put Americans back to work and provide those unable to work with a minimal social safety net, there is widespread agreement that it was the war and then the post-war recovery that turned the tide of the US economy and ushered in the boom years of the late 1940s and 1950s (Goodwin, 2001; Field, 2008). As unemployment rates dropped and social programs took effect, wages shifted from the wealthiest households to middle- and lower-income households. The Gini coefficient, which measures the equality of household incomes, remained essentially flat between 1940 and 1970. However, income disparities started to increase in the 1970s as upper incomes grew faster than middle and especially lower incomes. As a result, the Gini coefficient rose from 0.38 in 1970 to 0.49 in 2020 (Ruffing, 2013; Horowitz et al., 2020). The latter figure represents the highest level of income disparity in the United States since the 1920s. Table 2.1 shows the changes in median household incomes between 1970 and 2020 (adjusted for inflation, in 2020 US dollars).

In 1961 President John F. Kennedy announced the launch of a new Food Stamp Program. This retained the orange stamps of the original FSP, which once again could be redeemed by any food retailer. However, on this

TABLE 2.1 Changes in low, middle, and upper US household incomes from 1970 to 2020

	1970 median household income ($)	2020 median household income ($)	Percentage change
Low incomes	20,600	29,900	45
Middle incomes	59,900	90,100	50
Upper incomes	130,000	220,000	69

Source: United States Census Bureau (2022).

occasion, there were no blue stamps for surplus food. The pilot program fulfilled a campaign promise Kennedy had made after viewing the plight of the nation's poor. It had the specific goal of "promoting the general welfare"—a well-known principle established in the Preamble of the Declaration of Independence (Kennedy, 1961). Launched in West Virginia's southern coalfields, with the first official sale taking place in McDowell County, the program was soon extended to locations in the states of Illinois, Kentucky, Michigan, Minnesota, Montana, New Mexico, and Pennsylvania. Isabelle Kelley was the first director of the new scheme, and thus became the first woman to lead a USDA action program.

In 1964, after President Kennedy's assassination, President Lyndon B. Johnson asked Congress to pass legislation to make the pilot program permanent. The stated objectives of the resulting Foodstamp Act were to strengthen the agricultural economy and improve access to better nutrition for low-income households (United States Government, 1964). Once again, West Virginia was the first state to implement the new FSP. Each state could set its own eligibility criteria for participants, although the legislation stipulated that recipients should receive an amount of food stamps commensurate with their normal expenditure on food. One of the stated objectives was to provide low-income households with nutritionally adequate diets, so, unsurprisingly, alcoholic beverages were excluded from the program. A budget of $75 million was allocated to the FSP during the first year of funding, which increased to $100 million in the second year, and $200 million in the third year. The number of participants reached 10 million by the end of 1970, and 15 million four years later (Caswell and Yaktine, 2013).

Not everyone welcomed this rapid expansion of the FSP. In particular, a group of southern senators voiced concerns about the cost of the program and disputed that poverty and hunger were serious issues in the United States (United States Government, 1968). However, there were also some notable supporters of the program, including some who were associated with the US military. In 1955, the Interdepartmental Committee on Nutrition for National Defense (ICNND) had been established to explore health concerns relating to hunger and malnutrition (Combs, 2005; Sandstead, 2005). The ICNND's *Manual for Nutrition Surveys* became the go-to resource for nutrition surveys in countries around the world that the US considered of strategic importance (Interdepartmental Committee on Nutrition for National Defense, 1957). However, in 1967, the ICNND was disbanded and its nutrition research was placed under the auspices of the US Center for Disease Control (CDC), which was charged with undertaking "a comprehensive survey of the incidence and location of serious hunger and malnutrition, and health problems incident thereto, in the United States and to report these conditions to the Congress" (quoted in Sandstead, 2005: 1262). The resulting survey was conducted across ten states and pointed to serious nutritional deficiencies, particularly in the southern states (Center for Disease Control, 1971). Most disconcerting were the report's findings about malnutrition among children and its long-term effects. These painted a picture of children going to school hungry, which left them unable to concentrate and learn, and thus robbed them of any chance to escape intergenerational poverty. In response, the Women, Infants, and Children (WIC) supplemental nutrition program was launched in 1972. Nutrition programs for the elderly followed in 1974, and Congress authorized the USDA's school breakfast program in 1975.

Although driven primarily by military concerns, ICNND scientists also conducted groundbreaking research into the effects of caloric deficits and deficiencies in specific nutrients. For instance, they examined the impact of vitamin A, vitamin C, carbohydrates, and iron (Anderson et al., 1980; Hodges, 1978). Their findings resulted in guidelines for a balanced diet as well as recommended daily allowances of vitamins, minerals, water, and various other dietary components (Kuemmerlin, 1974). However, in 1980, the ICNNC's successor, the Letterman Army Institute of Research (LAIR), was suspended and the US Army's nutritional research was transferred to the USDA's Western Human Nutrition Research Center in Davis, California (United States Department of Agriculture Agricultural Research Service, 2020).

A 1970 amendment to the Foodstamp Act tried to ease the ongoing tension between program access and program accountability. Access to food stamps was deemed necessary to ensure the health and productivity of the nation's population, including the ability to meet the physical demands of military service. However, free riding was (and still is) frowned upon in a country that prides itself on its rugged individualism, where everyone is expected to pull themselves up by their own bootstraps. The amendment attempted to address long-standing regional differences by regularizing access to food assistance and establishing more uniform eligibility criteria. It also sought to tighten accountability by adding the requirement that all recipients of food stamps must register for work. Households with monthly gross incomes (i.e., before taxes and other deductions) at or below 130 percent of the poverty line would be eligible to receive assistance. The amended law further established that the food and nutrition support must be equivalent to the cost of a nutritionally adequate diet. An additional amendment was passed in 1973, courtesy of the Agriculture and Consumer Protection Act, which required states to expand the program to every jurisdiction, and to include people with drug and alcohol addictions, provided they were in treatment. This piece of legislation also added a new category of eligible purchases—namely, seeds and seedlings—to encourage recipients to grow their own fresh food and thereby reduce their nutritional deficit.

The two principal objectives of the original FSP had been to strengthen the agricultural economy and to reduce hunger and malnutrition. However, later amendments reduced the focus on agriculture and increased the focus on hunger and malnutrition. At the same time, a subtle shift in terminology took place as references to "hunger and malnutrition" were gradually dropped in favor of references to "food security." In marked contrast to the developing world, where a chronic lack of food often impacted an entire population, in the United States food shortages tended to occur in the midst of food abundance. Consequently, even though hunger was still a very public issue in the 1960s, some politicians from the most poverty-stricken parts of the country objected to suggestions that their constituents were going hungry. Moreover, while everyone understood that both "hunger" and "malnutrition" related to a lack of food, there was little agreement on how to define or measure either term. Government agencies, academic researchers, nonprofit organizations, and advocacy groups therefore undertook numerous studies to try to reach a consensus (Radimer et al., 1990). Some of these studies used the two terms interchangeably and based their recommendations on medical data. Others advocated the use of economic data relating to poverty as proxies for hunger (Eisinger, 1998).

In the midst of these discussions, the country suffered a succession of crop failures. To make matters worse, an oil embargo in the Middle East led to hikes in energy prices, spiraling inflation, and a stagnating economy. Given these economic pressures, the general perception was that hunger was on the rise. In response, in the early 1980s, President Ronald Reagan established a task force to examine the nation's food assistance programs. After much investigative work, despite conceding that the issue of hunger was complex and still lacked a clear definition, the task force concluded that there was no evidence of widespread hunger and malnutrition in the United States, with the possible exception of the nation's homeless population (US President's Task Force on Food Assistance, 1984).

This somewhat unsatisfying conclusion led to more studies: the Food Research and Action Center sponsored a series of surveys as part of the Community Childhood Hunger Identification Project (Kleinman et al., 1998); researchers at Cornell University's Division of Nutritional Sciences suggested indicators to measure hunger (Radimer et al., 1990; 1992); the USDA began to analyze information from its Nationwide Food Consumption Survey; and the National Center for Health Statistics (NCHS) added questions about hunger to its National Health and Nutrition Examination Survey (Centers for Disease Control and Prevention, 1995). Most significantly, in 1990, the Life Sciences Research Office (LSRO) of the Federation of American Societies for Experimental Biology convened an expert panel and published its findings in the *Journal of Nutrition* (Anderson, 1990). This report contained what became the consensus definitions for "food security," "food insecurity," and "hunger." Specifically, the panel defined "food security" as: "access by all people at all times to enough food for an active, healthy life, and includes, at a minimum: (a) the ready availability of nutritionally adequate and safe foods and (b) an assured ability to acquire acceptable foods in socially acceptable ways." Similarly, its definition of "food insecurity" was: "limited or uncertain availability of nutritionally adequate and safe foods or limited or uncertain ability to acquire acceptable foods in socially acceptable ways." Finally, hunger was defined as "the uneasy or painful sensation caused by lack of food." However, the USDA has not had a measure of "hunger" since 2006; instead, it now uses the term "very low food security." While there is a recognition that the two terms are related, the former implies a physiological condition, while the latter implies economic and social conditions (United States Department of Agriculture Economic Research Service, 2022).

Throughout this period, there was a parallel debate in the international arena regarding how to define and tackle hunger. Two seasons of crop failures in North America and Asia in the early 1970s, coupled with the aforementioned oil embargo, had a devastating impact on global food supplies. As a result, food prices doubled. Yet, rather than acknowledging that rising energy and food prices were undermining poor countries' efforts to achieve food self-sufficiency, the international community laid the blame squarely on the developing nations themselves by highlighting their high population growth rates and slow technological progress. The United Nations' Food and Agriculture Organization (FAO), which had been established in the late 1940s specifically to improve agricultural efficiency and reduce world hunger, recommended abandoning national self-sufficiency as a goal and instead started to encourage farmers in poor countries to develop cash crops for export (Mitchell, 2003). This highlights the tension between the FAO's goal of agricultural efficiency and self-sufficiency as the driver for reducing world hunger (Jarosz, 2014). At the 1974 World Food Conference the term "food security" was defined, with a firm emphasis on supply, as the "availability at all times of adequate, nourishing, diverse, balanced and moderate world food supplies of basic foodstuffs to sustain a steady expansion of food consumption and to offset fluctuations in production and prices" (Food and Agriculture Organization, 2010). Demand and access issues were subsequently added, so by 1996, when the first World Food Summit was held, the official FAO definition read as follows: "when all people, at all times, have physical and economic access to sufficient, safe and nutritious food to meet their dietary needs and food preferences for an active and healthy life" (Food and Agriculture Organization, 1996).

From the Dust Bowl to the city

In the 1930s, the United States faced not only an unprecedented economic crisis that had catapulted 30 percent of the country into unemployment and poverty but also an unprecedented environmental crisis. The Dust Bowl can be considered an exemplar of a human-made environmental disaster. The Homestead Act of 1862 had provided every settler, including women and immigrants, with the opportunity to become landowners of 160 acres of so-called "public land," provided they agreed to farm it (National Archives, 2001). A special provision, Field Order No. 15—commonly known as "40 Acres and a mule"—allowed formerly enslaved people to produce food, feed, and fiber on 40-acre plots. In addition to farming these plots, the new landowners were required to reside on them for a minimum of five years, build a home, and improve the land. By 1934, over 1.6 million homestead applications had been processed, and more than 270 million acres (10 percent of all the land in the United States) had been transferred to individual landowners. Of course, much of this land had been seized from indigenous communities who were forcibly displaced and relocated to reservations.

In January 1865, the US government rescinded Field Order No. 15, and formerly enslaved people were subsequently excluded from any reasonable chance to become landowners. In addition, administrative barriers were created by the Southern Homestead Act, which made it almost impossible for formerly enslaved people to gain access to farmland. By contrast, white citizens and new immigrants gained a stable economic foundation at minimal cost through landownership. Expansions of the Homestead Act were passed in 1904 and 1909, resulting in a massive influx of new (and often inexperienced) farmers into the Great Plains and the Western states. These new settlers started to farm grasslands across the Midwest and West without adopting any conservation measures to keep organic material in the topsoil of their plots. To make matters worse, several dry years started to turn the depleted topsoil to dust and massive erosion ensued. Crops failed on an immense scale, forcing many settlers to leave their land and migrate to the cities in search of work. By 1938, an estimated 700,000 farms had been abandoned, and by 1940 an estimated 33 percent of heads of households had moved to a different state (Long and Siu, 2016). Moreover, inward migration to rural counties in the Dust Bowl states slowed over subsequent decades (Gregory, 1989). As a result, the proportion of US residents in urban areas grew from 55 percent in 1930 to 70 percent in 1970, and 83 percent in 2020 (O'Neill, 2022).

The Homestead Act remained in effect for 114 years: it was repealed only in 1976, with the passage of the Federal Land Policy and Management Act. The latter piece of legislation was implemented in the 48 contiguous states, but not in Alaska, which was granted a ten-year extension on land claims. Farmers who remained in the Midwest, Mountain, and West regions during and after the Dust Bowl received millions of dollars in conservation and risk-mitigation funding that enabled them to keep their land and stay in business even when crops failed due to droughts or other natural disasters. By contrast, historically under-served groups received no or only minimal assistance. This resulted in numerous lawsuits that highlighted longstanding discrimination and the provision of targeted assistance to some privileged groups while others were excluded. The USDA lost most of these cases and settled others out of court.

The demographic shift from rural to urban areas was not uniform. Rather, it reflected the growing income disparities captured in the Gini coefficient. Those who could afford the American dream of a single-family house, a car, and 2.4 children moved to the suburbs. Those in lower income brackets moved to the urban core and joined other inner-city dwellers in low-paid jobs.

While cities in Europe and Asia often have high-income earners living in affluent, historic, central neighborhoods, few US urban areas mirror this pattern. Instead, most of the latter were redesigned to accommodate highways that allowed middle- and upper-income workers to drive from their homes in the suburbs to their downtown workplaces and back again. Four-lane roads dissected countless historic neighborhoods, destroying their social fabric. Between 1945 and 2010, the proportion of Americans living in suburbs increased from 13 percent to more than 50 percent (Nikolaides and Wise, 2017). This massive growth in suburban living shaped the nation's dependency on motor vehicles, commuting patterns, and spending habits, and reinforced segregation based on race, ethnicity, and social class (Norton, 2016). Suburban single-family homes with front and back yards generated higher property tax revenues than the run-down rental properties in the urban core, and since property taxes are the primary source of funding for US public education, suburban schools were well funded while urban schools were not. Not surprisingly, retail parks, office complexes, and new high-tech industries all preferred the suburbs, while neighborhoods in the urban core became retail and food deserts. A "food desert" is defined as an area that has minimal access to healthy, nutritious food (Dutko et al., 2012). In spatial terms, it is considered to be an urban area that is more than one mile from a full-service grocery store, or a rural area that is more than ten miles from such a store. Commonly, food deserts are populated by low-income residents from ethnic and racial minority groups. More recently, the term "retail and food apartheid neighborhoods" has started to be used in place of "retail and food deserts." The word "apartheid" reflects the fact that there is nothing organic about the exodus of department and grocery stores from US city centers. Deserts are ecosystems shaped by water deprivation. By contrast, the deprivation of urban neighborhoods can be attributed to political decisions that favor the majority of voters who live in suburban neighborhoods.

Prior to the exodus of mostly white, higher-income citizens to the suburbs, US inner cities had vibrant food cultures. In downtown Washington, DC, for example, food access was provided by a network of small mom-and-pop grocery stores and food carts called hucksters, supported by the DC Grocery Store Cooperative (DGS). The DGS consolidated these small businesses' purchasing power and community capital, facilitating a degree of economic autonomy, self-determination, and collective upward mobility for its members (Bockman, 2016). Launched in 1921, at its peak it consisted of over 300 grocery-store members. Many of these small outlets, as well as the hucksters that sold fresh produce, meat, and other food products door to door, were shaped by the ethnicity and food culture of the neighborhoods where they conducted their business. There were Italian, German, Puerto Rican, Colombian, Chinese, Vietnamese, and African American neighborhoods, all with their own distinct food cultures and food retailers. However, in the wake of the 1968 race riots, even more white residents migrated to the suburbs. The DGS soon folded, and most of its former members ceased trading, unable to compete with the suburban supermarkets and their wide range of products. The end result was a rapid loss of purchasing power and jobs, followed by a steady divestment of food businesses in lower-income urban neighborhoods (Crowe et al., 2018; Jones, 1972).

Chicago has a similar history. Beginning as a frontier town on the edge of white settlements, it quickly grew into a boomtown, attracting immigrants from overseas and elsewhere in the United States. It was also the place where the transcontinental railroads met. Many downtown restaurants catered specifically to passengers transferring between trains at one of the city's five major railroad stations. Both the city itself and the surrounding area were also shaped by small-scale farms that produced food for the urban area and shipment elsewhere. Before long, the inner city was home to a host of industrial food processors, including meat processors at the stockyards, candy makers such as Brach's, and food manufacturers like Kraft. In addition, it boasted every kind of ethnic restaurant as well as a plethora of independent mom-and-pop stores. There were Jewish, Polish, German, Scandinavian, and African American grocers, meat markets, vegetable stands, and bakeries. Households rarely owned any refrigeration equipment aside from an icebox, so it was common to shop for food almost daily. Hence, convenience was at a premium. The stores had to be within walking distance of home, and they had to supply everything from meat to fruits and vegetables, baked goods and more. Most proprietors could expect only a few hundred regular customers (although those with stores on the intersections of streetcar lines might attract rather more). To protect themselves from the fierce competition that characterized their industry, the retailers formed many associations. For example, there was an Early Closing Association, which was devoted to ensuring its members had at least some time off in the evening; the Chicago Grocer and Butcher Clerks Protective Association, which joined the Retail Grocers and Butchers Association in a crusade for Sunday closing; and the independent store owners' Associated Food Dealers of Greater Chicago. The city also had one of the first chain-store companies— A&P—which introduced the concept of "economy stores." These large, stores sold a full line of groceries at low prices on a cash-and-carry basis. The idea was to generate high-volume sales at prices that were barely above cost, while generating savings by circumventing wholesalers and instead buying in bulk directly from manufacturers. This new arrangement created what we know today as "store brands." The likes of A&P and Kroger acquired hundreds of small, independent stores and formed grocery chains that offered any food item conveniently on one large site. As a result, by the 1980s, the number of food stores in Chicago had declined from more than 17,000 to just 3,600, with further declines thereafter (Chicago Historical Society, 2005). The giant new chain stores utilized computer scanners to control inventories and keep track of costs. They also added school supplies, cosmetics, and other non-food items to their inventories to make it even more convenient for consumers to shop at one large store rather than go to multiple small food outlets, drug stores, and other retailers. As more and more independent food stores were eliminated and the new chains built ever larger stores in the suburbs, dozens of neighborhoods, especially in Chicago's south side, were left without a single grocery store, drug store, department store, or bank (other than a few ATMs). Today, approximately 500,000 Chicagoans live in food apartheid neighborhoods, primarily in the city's south and west, while another 400,000 live in areas with an abundance of fast-food restaurants but no full-service grocery stores (Varley, 2021).

As Washington, DC, and Chicago both illustrate, urban residents lose more than food access when their local food networks fold. They also lose diverse expressions of cultural value and the financial support of localized sharing economies that extend credit when needed and accept in-kind contributions along with monetary payments (Chicago Metropolitan Agency of Planning, 2014; Kolak et al., 2018; Varley, 2021).

On the other hand, over time, US suburbs started to become more diverse. Segregated neighborhoods characterized by middle-income white households began to reflect the cultures, values, and ways of life of more recent arrivals, including African Americans, immigrants, diverse ethnic groups, and various types of households. At the same time, those seeking more urban lifestyles started to move back to the city center. This migration back to the urban core brought new demographic shifts. Once predominantly African American, impoverished neighborhoods started to become whiter and more gentrified. During "gentrification" affluent residents and businesses buy up and renovate existing homes and commercial buildings, increasing property values in the process. This often precipitates what the National Community Reinvestment Coalition calls an "unnecessary cultural displacement of … existing residents, who are often black or Hispanic" (Richardson et al., 2019), which in turn prevents the latter groups from benefiting from the economic growth and greater availability of services that come with increased investment. Gentrification thus presents a challenge to communities that are trying to achieve economic revitalization without the disruption that comes with displacement. Cities that have seen especially high rates of white gains are Brooklyn, Washington, DC, Denver, Philadelphia, and Austin.

Throughout the ebbs and flows of urbanization and suburbanization, the disparities that have long characterized US cities and metropolitan areas have remained, notwithstanding countless attempts to alleviate them and promote more socially and environmentally sound development (O'Hara, 2001; 2018). A study of 87 big cities—those with populations of over a quarter of a million people—suggests that 55 of them are experiencing slower growth rates than in the past (Frey, 2018). More recently, during the COVID pandemic, many of those who could afford to do so relocated from city centers to larger homes in the suburbs. Furthermore, studies indicate that only 50 percent of office workers have since returned to their former places of work on a full-time basis (Brody et al., 2020; Chun et al., 2022). This implies that households, businesses, and government agencies will all have to negotiate ongoing urbanization trends. An important part of this negotiation process will be determining the right mix of amenities in America's cities as the decoupling of workspace and personal living space continues.

In 2020, households in urban and metropolitan areas were six times more likely to experience food insecurity than those in rural areas (Coleman-Jensen et al., 2021). In the same year, 82 percent of those enrolled in Supplemental Nutrition Assistance Program (SNAP—the current term for food stamps and related programs) lived in cities and metropolitan communities. The participants in these programs reflected the diversity of the country's urban communities: 37 percent were white; 26 percent non-Hispanic black; 16 percent Hispanic; 3 percent Asian; 1.5 percent Native American; and 16 percent identified as "race unknown" (Cronquist, 2021). These figures indicate that, on average, non-Hispanic white and Asian populations are underrepresented in SNAP, while non-Hispanic black populations are overrepresented, constituting 26 percent of recipients but only 14 percent of the total US population. In addition, it would be wrong to assume that the 38 million recipients of SNAP actually receive all of the money that the government has allocated for consumer-focused food programs. This is because the SNAP budget also includes training programs, assistance for food retailers to update their processing capacity, payments to agencies that distribute food to eligible Native American populations on reservations, and more. These auxiliary services under various SNAP allocations illustrate the two-pronged purpose of the SNAP program and its history of providing better nutrition to low-income households while also strengthening the agricultural economy of the nation. Both of these components are still evident in today's food assistance programs.

In 2020, the average food stamp allocation was approximately $110 per person, per month, while the poverty level was about $1,100 per month, which meant the income eligibility level was less than $1,470 per month. Given the cost of living in US cities, food assistance recipients are forced to purchase the cheapest food available to prevent their families from going hungry. Studies show that most of the beneficiaries of SNAP are children, many of whom are obese. This raises serious questions about whether the current programs can meet their objectives of not only reducing hunger but improving the nutritional health of low-income households in the United States.

In addition to living in neighborhoods with limited food access, urban populations experience what are known as social determinants of health and well-being. These include poor housing or outright homelessness, lack of health insurance and limited access to healthcare, poor education, high unemployment rates, and discrimination on the basis of race and gender. All of these factors may impact a person's health, quality of life, and life expectancy. Research conducted by the Center for Poverty Research suggests a strong connection between length of time spent in poverty and chance of escaping poverty. For example, on average, individuals who live in poverty for one year or less have a 56 percent chance of escaping poverty, whereas just 13 percent of individuals who have lived in poverty for more than seven years manage to escape (Huff Stevens, 2021). This has serious implications, especially as the recent COVID pandemic condemned many people to longer periods of poverty than might otherwise have been the case.

The second component of US food assistance, which is administered alongside SNAP, is The Emergency Food Assistance Program (TEFAP). In 2020, nearly 3 million food-insecure older adults who were excluded from SNAP because their incomes were slightly too high could apply for TEFAP. This number increased significantly at the height of the COVID pandemic. TEFAP is coordinated by approximately 370 regional food banks, with about 200 of them forming a network known as Feeding America (Feeding America, 2021; Foodbank News, 2023). The food banks supply approximately 60,000 food pantries in urban, suburban, and rural communities across the United States. These range from soup kitchens that provide warm meals, to churches that distribute boxes of food, to store-like establishments where clients can choose their own food items. Food kitchens across the country are heavily dependent on volunteers. Some are open daily, but others operate only once a week or even once a month. This means it is often challenging for those in need of food assistance to find up-to-date information on the location and/or operating hours of a pantry in their community. Moreover, given the pantries' heavy reliance on volunteer labor, they are not necessarily located close to those with the greatest food assistance needs.

For those who are not reliant on TEFAP, more grocery stores might give urban communities better access to food, yet it is often argued that increased food access does not necessarily lead to an increase in food security. Since a majority of US cities have had limited access to fresh, unprocessed food since the 1970s, some households have lost the ability to prepare their own food, while others may not even have a kitchen. Food security therefore requires more than improved access to food. It must also address other factors that stand in the way of healthier eating. Nonetheless, improved access to fresh, nutritious food would at least be a step in the right direction, and studies indicate that increased food access can improve healthy eating habits. For example, one study conducted in New Orleans found that local residents ate an additional 0.35 servings of vegetables per day for each additional meter of shelf space devoted to fresh vegetables (Bodor et al., 2008). Similarly, a study of over 900 urban households found that African American households ate an additional 0.7 servings of fruits and vegetables per day if they lived in neighborhoods with full-service grocery stores, while Hispanic households in such neighborhoods ate an additional 2.2 servings per day (Zenk et al., 2009). These findings bode well for identifying food security solutions in the six cities that are the focus of this book.

The food-insecurity landscape in six US cities

The United States stretches from the Atlantic to the Pacific, and from the temperate north to the sub-tropical south. The most densely populated areas extend along the East Coast, with a somewhat smaller number of population centers on the West Coast and a sprinkling of cities in the center. While these urban areas exhibit countless differences in terms of wealth and demographics, all of them have one thing in common: disparity.

Five of the six cities under discussion here have been selected from the seventeen in which the USDA has established its first Urban Agriculture Committees; the sixth is the nation's capital, Washington, DC. In the remainder of this chapter, the focus is on these cities' historic, socio-economic, and demographic characteristics.

Washington, DC

Washington, DC, is located on the East Coast, specifically in the so-called mid-Atlantic region. It is an unusual city, established as the nation's capital in 1790 to fulfill an article of the US Constitution. From the very beginning, it was embroiled in political maneuvering. Alexander Hamilton and the northern states wanted the newly established federal government to assume each individual state's Revolutionary War debts. Thomas Jefferson and his southern allies agreed to this proposal, but only on condition that the new capital would be located sufficiently close to their slave-holding states that their agricultural interests would not be ignored. As a result of this compromise, the city was founded at the intersection of Virginia, Maryland, and West Virginia. The first President of the United States, George Washington, chose the exact location, on the banks of the Anacostia and Potomac rivers, which meant that Maryland and Virginia had to cede some of their territory to the new "District of Columbia." (It was termed a district to distinguish it from the states.) The famous architect Pierre Charles L'Enfant, who was hired to design the new capital, envisioned a modern city based on a bold grid pattern, featuring grand boulevards and public ceremonial spaces reminiscent of his native Paris, with the US Capitol Building in the center and four quadrants of streets and avenues emanating from it.

The city grew slowly at first, but then began to expand dramatically toward the end of the Civil War. Its slaves were freed nine months before President Lincoln's Emancipation Declaration of 1863. As a result, it quickly became a hub for liberated slaves and home to a vibrant African American population. By 1950, it boasted over 800,000 permanent residents, plus a daytime population of a several hundred thousand more who commuted to jobs in the federal government. Nicknamed the "chocolate city" on account of its predominantly African American population, its wealthier white residents started to move increasingly to the suburbs from the 1950s onwards. Later, prompted by the race riots of the late 1960s, the African American middle class began their own exodus to the suburbs. This resulted in a steady decline of the city's African American population from a high of 538,000 in 1970 to just 309,000 in 2000. Meanwhile, the total population dropped to a low of 570,000 residents over the same 30-year period. However, thereafter, the number of permanent residents started to grow again, reaching 700,000 in 2020. Significantly, the proportions of non-Hispanic white, Asian, and Hispanic residents all increased during that time, while the proportion of non-Hispanic black residents stagnated (United States Census Bureau, 2023). This demographic shift coincided with some of the most rapid gentrification in the country.

Administratively, Washington, DC, is divided into eight wards with roughly equal populations (see Figure 2.1), ranging from 82,500 in Ward 3 to 89,000 in Ward 7 (which has seen the fastest growth in recent years). Socio-economic and demographic characteristics vary significantly, however. Ward 3 has one of the highest per capita incomes in the country, and its population is 76 percent white. By contrast, the per capita income of Ward 8 stands at just 27 percent of the Ward 3 figure, and its population is 87 percent non-Hispanic black. Unemployment rates also vary dramatically, from a low of 4 percent in Wards 2 and 3 to 17 percent in Ward 8. The latter also has the highest percentage of households with children under 18, while Ward 3 is the oldest ward. Table 2.2 highlights the demographic and socio-economic differences across all eight wards.

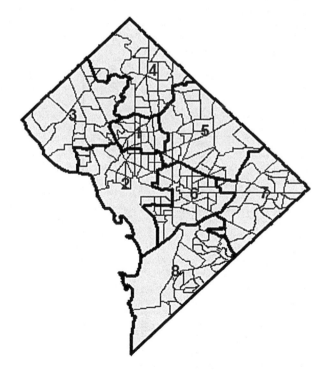

FIGURE 2.1 The eight wards of Washington, DC
Source: O'Hara (2018)

TABLE 2.2 Socio-economic and demographic characteristics of Washington, DC, by Ward

Demographic	Ward 1	Ward 2	Ward 3	Ward 4	Ward 5	Ward 6	Ward 7	Ward 8
Total population	83,397	85,916	82,518	86,075	88,839	83,050	88,915	84,275
Children under 18 (%)	15	6	16	23	19	14	24	30
People over 65 (%)	7	11	19	15	13	10	13	10
Non-Hispanic black (%)	26	11	9	49	61	24	87	87
Non-Hispanic white (%)	50	70	76	29	26	63	7	7
Hispanic (%)	13	10	10	22	9	8	4	4
Asian (%)	5	9	7	2	3	5	1	0.6
American Indian (%)	1	1	0	0	0	0	0	0
Household income ($)	117,814	122,151	130,056	116,325	92,083	126,765	65,237	49,382
Per capita income ($)	73,234	91,978	101,492	58,479	49,656	82,257	33,922	28,802
Unemployment (%)	5	4	4	6	8	5	16	17

Source: United States Census Bureau (2023)

Unsurprisingly, food-related illnesses also vary dramatically across the eight wards. Figure 2.2 shows the various percentages of the adult population with obesity and diabetes across the wards. The lowest rates are in the areas with the highest per capita incomes, and vice versa. Other commonly referenced health and food security indicators are summarized in Table 2.3. This shows that Ward 8 has the lowest life expectancy, at just 70 years, while residents of Ward 3 live 15 years longer, on average. Only 1 percent of households in the latter ward receive SNAP benefits, compared to 15 percent of households in Ward 8. The row that shows percentage of the population living more than a mile from a full-service grocery store highlights the problem of food access in the two most deprived wards. That said, it also serves as a reminder that food access is not the same as food security. The third-worst ward in terms of the food access metric is the

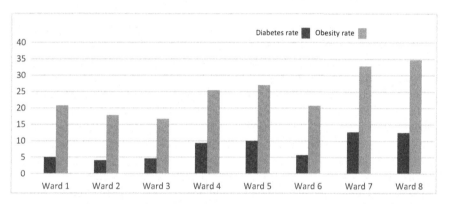

FIGURE 2.2 Percentage of the Washington, DC, adult population with obesity and diabetes by ward
Source: Centers for Disease Control and Prevention (2022)

TABLE 2.3 Health indicators across the eight wards of Washington, DC

Health indicators	Ward 1	Ward 2	Ward 3	Ward 4	Ward 5	Ward 6	Ward 7	Ward 8
Life expectancy (years)	78	80	85	79	75	77	72	70
Population more than one mile from a full-service grocery store (%)	0	0	5	3	0	0	16	8
Households receiving SNAP benefits (%)	4	2	1	3	6	3	10	15

Source: Centers for Disease Control and Prevention (2022)

affluent Ward 3. However, this is explained by the fact that a significant portion of the city's largest green space, Rock Creek Park, lies within the ward's boundaries. Consequently, rich households close to the park may be more than a mile from the nearest grocery store, yet almost all of them own a car, so the extra distance is not a problem. Therefore, while distance to the nearest full-service grocery store may be a useful indicator of food access, it may not tell the whole story with regard to food security. For instance, car ownership and sufficient discretionary income to afford food delivery may be equally or even more important factors in a household's ability to meet its basic needs (O'Hara and Toussaint, 2021).

Albuquerque, NM

Albuquerque is located in the state of New Mexico in the southwestern United States. It was founded in 1706 as La Villa de Albuquerque, named in honor of the 10th Duke of Albuquerque of New Spain. At the time, it was an outpost of the famous El Camino Real trade route, which linked Mexico City to the northernmost territories of New Spain. It is flanked by mountains to the east and west, while the Rio Grande flows from north to south right through the center. According to the 2020 US Census, Albuquerque has 565,000 residents, up from 450,000 in 2000 (United States Census Bureau, 2023). This makes it one of the fastest-growing urban areas in the country, and the fourth-largest city in the southwestern United States (after Phoenix, Las Vegas, and El Paso). In total, the metropolitan area of Albuquerque now has just under 1 million residents.

The city was built in the traditional Spanish pattern, with a plaza in the center surrounded by government buildings, stately homes, and a church (which dates from the mid-1780s). Today, this area is referred to as "Old Town." Long before European settlers arrived in Albuquerque, the Tanoan and Keresan people had lived on the banks of the Rio Grande for centuries. By the 1500s, more than 20 Tiwa pueblos stretched for more than 60 miles (100 km) along the course of the river. Two of these remain on the outskirts of the modern city: Sandia Pueblo, which was founded in the fourteenth century; and Pueblo Isleta, which dates back to the sixteenth century. There is also evidence of the Navajo, Apache, and Comanche peoples in the Albuquerque area, and along the trade routes of the Rio Grande.

In 1821, Mexico gained its independence from Spain following the Mexican War of Independence, and Albuquerque, along with the entire state of New Mexico, became part of the new country. By 1830, the city's population had grown to over 2,500, yet it quickly dwindled following the Mexican–American War of 1846–1848, which led to New Mexico joining the United States. Four years later, Albuquerque had 1,500 residents, one-third of whom were members of the city's army garrison.

Modern Albuquerque is a hub for technology, media companies, and the arts. It also has a thriving restaurant scene, with diverse New Mexican and global food options. Like most cities in the United States, the downtown area

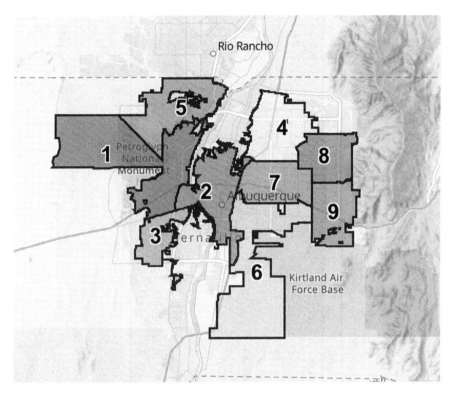

FIGURE 2.3 The nine districts of Albuquerque, NM
Source: City of Albuquerque (2022)

went through a period of urban decline in the 1960s and 1970s, when many historic buildings were razed to make way for shopping plazas, high-rises, and parking lots. More recently, the city has undergone significant urban renewal and gentrification. Thanks to a planned growth strategy, launched in 2002, it has slowly regained its historic urban character. Now the focus is on a more sustainable urban development strategy. Since urban sprawl is limited on three sides by the Rio Grande and the Sandia Mountains, most of the sub-urban growth is to the west and outside of the city limits (see Figure 2.3).

Administratively, Albuquerque is divided into nine districts, five of which have majority Hispanic populations. One of these majority Hispanic districts (District 5) has the highest median household income, although the only majority white district (District 8) has the highest per capita income and the second-highest median household income. The latter district also has the highest percentage of residents over the age of 65. Albuquerque has the lowest median household income of the six cities in this study. In addition, it has the largest American Indian population and the smallest non-Hispanic black population. Unemployment rates are uniformly low across the city's nine districts.

TABLE 2.4 Socio-economic and demographic characteristics of Albuquerque, NM, by district

Demographics	District 1	District 2	District 3	District 4	District 5	District 6	District 7	District 8	District 9
Total population	64,669	59,584	65,433	61,067	72,522	58,414	61,876	59,483	59,980
Children under 18 (%)	22	18	30	21	26	21	20	18	18
People over 65 (%)	15	18	7	19	12	14	18	23	20
Non-Hispanic black (%)	2	2	2	3	3	4	3	2	3
Non-Hispanic white (%)	27	36	9	46	38	34	44	58	47
Hispanic (%)	63	54	84	35	50	52	43	28	37
Asian (%)	1	2	1	8	2	2	2	4	4
American Indian (%)	4	4	2	5	3	5	4	3	6
Median household income ($)	64,850	52,057	50,084	70,007	84,809	43,687	56,196	83,890	65,678
Per capita income ($)	31,835	33,757	21,414	40,218	37,511	25,082	31,156	48,117	36,197
Unemployment (%)	6	6	5	7	5	6	6	5	6

Source: United States Census Bureau (2023)

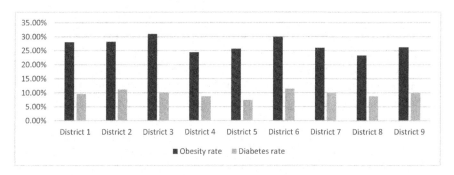

FIGURE 2.4 Percentage of the adult population of Albuquerque, NM, with obesity
and diabetes by district

Source: Centers for Disease Control and Prevention (2022)

TABLE 2.5 Health indicators across the nine districts of Albuquerque, NM

Health indicators	District 1	District 2	District 3	District 4	District 5	District 6	District 7	District 8	District 9
Life expectancy (years)	78	77	76	79	81	74	78	81	79
Population more than one mile from a full-service grocery store (%)	12	7	13	6	31	7	35	2	13
Households receiving SNAP benefits (%)	16	18	22	12	9	27	18	7	16

Source: Centers for Disease Control and Prevention (2022)

Life expectancy ranges from 74 to 81 years, with the highest figures in the two most affluent districts. Obesity and diabetes rates do not vary as much as in other US cities, ranging from 24 to 31 percent for obesity, and from 7 and 11 percent for diabetes. Given the wide variations in the percentage of the population that lives more than a mile from the nearest full-service grocery store, these relatively narrow ranges are somewhat surprising. Less surprisingly, the percentage of SNAP recipients ranges from lows of 7 and 9 percent in the two districts with the highest median household incomes to highs of 21 and 27 percent in the two districts with the lowest per capita and median household incomes. Albuquerque's high proportions of Hispanic and Native American populations distinguishes it from the other cities in this book. It is also known for its active urban food scene, which is influenced by the area's dual Hispanic and Native American heritage.

Atlanta, GA

Atlanta, the capital of Georgia as well as the state's largest city, is located in the southeastern United States. Founded in 1837 as a state-sponsored railroad hub, it soon became the convergence point of several railroads, the largest of which was the Western Atlantic Railroad, which gave the city its name. Today, it has a population of 500,000 within the city limits, or 6.1 million in the wider metropolitan area. This makes it the eighth-largest metropolitan area in the country. Located in the foothills of the Appalachian Mountains, it is characterized by a topography of rolling hills, a lush tree canopy, and a wealth of agricultural resources.

For thousands of years prior to the arrival of European settlers, the area was inhabited by indigenous Creek people. The village of Peachtree Creek, close to Atlanta, was one of the earliest settlements. After becoming a British colony, Georgia was one of the 13 colonies that signed the Declaration of Independence in 1776. Two years later, it ratified its articles of confederation, and ten years after that it became the fourth state to ratify the US Constitution. Throughout the early nineteenth century, European settlers systematically encroached on the territory of the Creek people, eventually forcing them to cede 22 million acres of land and driving them from the area following the Battle of Horseshoe Bend in 1814. Similarly, the second-largest indigenous group in Georgia, the Cherokee, were forcibly removed from their lands less than a decade after the Indian Removal Act was signed into law in 1830 (Saunt, 2020; Garrison, 2018). During the Civil War, Atlanta was a strategically important city of the Confederacy until it was captured in 1864 and almost burned to the ground. However, it rebounded in the post-war era, rapidly becoming an industrial center and the unofficial capital of the so-called "New South." Following World War II, it became a center of activism for returning veterans who sought full rights as US citizens. In 1948, the mayor ordered the hiring of the first eight African American police officers, and by the 1960s Atlanta had become a major organizing center of the Civil Rights Movement under the leadership of Dr. Martin Luther King, Ambassador Andrew Young, Ralph David Abernathy, and others. Nevertheless, full desegregation came slowly. Public transportation was desegregated in 1959, restaurants in 1961, movie theaters in 1963, and public schools only in 1973, nearly 20 years after the US Supreme Court had ruled that the segregation of public education was unconstitutional.

Atlanta lost more than 100,000 residents (more than 20% of the population) between 1970 and 1990. In response, it developed new office space and a modern transportation system in the hope of attracting major corporations. Hartfield-Jackson International Airport quickly became one of the busiest airports in the world in terms of passenger traffic. Spurred on by the 1996 Summer Olympics, Atlanta underwent a profound physical, cultural, and demographic transformation. Young, college-educated professionals were drawn to the city, which coincided with a decline in the percentage of African American residents from 67 percent in 1990 to just 54 percent in 2010. With a GDP of $406 billion, Atlanta's economy ranks tenth in the United States and twentieth of all cities in the world. It is a leading center of the transportation, aerospace, logistics, healthcare, news and media, film and television, information technology, finance, and biomedical industries. In 2005, the city approved the $2.8 billion BeltLine project, which planned to convert a 22-mile freight railroad loop around the central city into an art-filled, multi-use trail and light-rail transit line that would simultaneously increase the city's green space by 40 percent. Although the project has stimulated retail and residential development around the loop, it has been criticized for its adverse impact on some of Atlanta's historic, mostly black neighborhoods. Once completed, the interconnected BeltLine and Silver Comet Trail will be the longest paved trail surface in the United States, totaling some 300 miles (480 km).

Administratively, Atlanta is organized into 12 districts ranging in population from 34,000 to over 50,000. These districts reflect the city's history of segregation in that they tend to have large black or white majorities, with far smaller percentages of Hispanic and Asian residents. Both median household and per capita incomes vary widely, with per capita income in the poorest

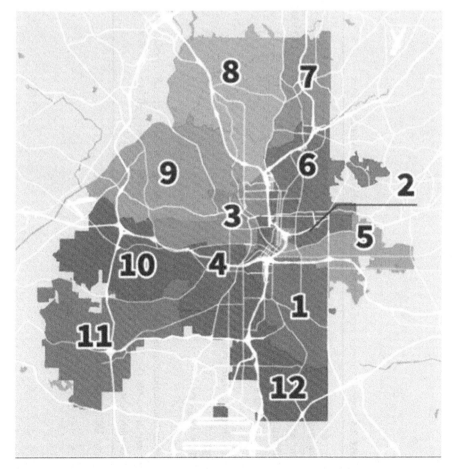

FIGURE 2.5 The 12 districts of Atlanta, GA
Source: Atlanta Civic Circle (2021)

TABLE 2.6 Socio-economic and demographic characteristics of Atlanta, GA

Demographics	District											
	1	2	3	4	5	6	7	8	9	10	11	12
Total population	36,681	50,695	41,564	38,753	42,942	46,712	46,430	39,371	40,039	34,294	41,628	31,885
Children under 18 (%)	24	9	11	15	14	13	15	18	23	23	26	23
People over 65 (%)	9	7	8	9	10	9	14	18	11	18	14	15
Non-Hispanic black (%)	59	19	54	73	36	15	13	12	59	93	95	80
Non-Hispanic white (%)	31	64	26	14	48	65	70	81	31	2	2	8
Hispanic (%)	6	5	6	4	6	8	5	3	5	3	1	6
Native Asian (%)	2	6	11	6	5	8	9	5	2	0	0.3	1
American (%)	0	0	0	0	0	1	0	0	0	0	0	1
Median household income ($)	72,328	101,903	49,609	45,320	86,108	99,485	103,222	89,092	86,596	46,794	48,063	42,137
Per capita income ($)	40,599	81,428	27,488	23,361	50,715	75,429	94,047	118,938	49,363	26,756	28,024	26,201
Unemployment (%)	13	10	11	11	7	4	4	3	3	10	10	11

Source: United States Census Bureau (2023)

district merely 25 percent of that in the wealthiest district. The districts with the largest non-Hispanic black majorities have the lowest incomes.

Food-related illnesses mirror income distribution in Atlanta. The three districts with the highest obesity and diabetes rates (more than 40 percent and more than 17 percent, respectively) have the largest non-Hispanic black populations and the lowest income levels. Not surprisingly, life expectancy also varies widely, from an average of 72 years in the majority black districts to 83 years in the majority white districts. The three districts with the highest proportions of non-Hispanic black residents also have the highest proportions of residents who have to travel more than a mile to the nearest full-service grocery store. SNAP recipient rates vary widely—from 2 percent and 33 percent—and follow the expected pattern of higher proportions of recipients in lower-income districts.

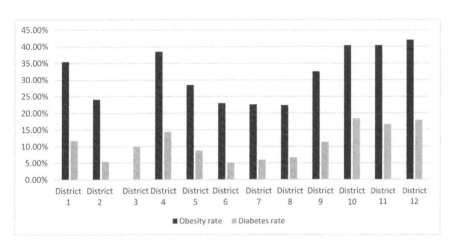

FIGURE 2.6 Percentage of the Atlanta, GA, adult population with obesity and diabetes by district

Source: Centers for Disease Control and Prevention (2022)

TABLE 2.7 Health indicators across the 12 districts of Atlanta, GA

Health Indicators	District											
	1	2	3	4	5	6	7	8	9	10	11	12
Life expectancy (years)	75	78	71	72	75	80	80	83	75	74	76	72
Population more than one mile from a full-service grocery store (%)	6	6	7	3	5	1	2	8	13	14	14	12
Households receiving SNAP benefits (%)	22	5	21	30	11	4	2	2	18	27	28	33

Source: Centers for Disease Control and Prevention (2022)

Chicago, IL

Chicago is located in the Midwest, on Lake Michigan, one of the great freshwater lakes that form the border between the United States and Canada. According to the 2020 Census, the Chicago metropolitan population is just under 10 million residents (United States Census Bureau, 2023). In part, the area's growth is due to a substantial increase in the already large Hispanic population of "Chicagoland," as the metropolitan area is sometimes known. However, this area also has large numbers of white, non-Hispanic black, Asian, and Arab American residents, making it a very diverse region.

In addition, Chicago has one of the largest and most diverse economies in the world, with more than 6 million full or part-time employees, over 400 major corporate headquarters, including 35 Fortune 500 companies such as McDonald's, United Airlines, and Blue Cross Blue Shield. Its annual GDP is $800 million (FRED, 2022). With so many big companies opting to base themselves in Chicagoland, the area ranked as the nation's top metropolitan area for corporate relocations and expansions for nine consecutive years (Ori, 2023). It is also home to a number of the nation's leading research universities, including the University of Chicago, Northwestern University, the University of Illinois at Chicago, Loyola University, and the Illinois Institute of Technology.

Before it was incorporated as a town in 1833, Chicago's primary industry was fur trading, particularly with the powerful Canadian Northwest and Hudson Bay companies. In addition, it was the traditional homeland of the Council of the Three Fires: the Odawa, Ojibwe, and Potawatomi nations. Many other tribes, including the Miami, Ho-Chunk, Menominee, Sac, and Fox, also called the area home. The first permanent non-indigenous resident was a fur trader named Jean Baptiste Point du Sable, a black freeman from Haiti who settled in the area with his Native American wife. More freemen and fugitive slaves had established the city's first black community by the 1840s, and the first black person was elected to public office at the end of that century. Between 1910 and 1960, the so-called "Great Migration" brought hundreds of thousands of African Americans from all over the southern United States to Chicago's south and west sides, which subsequently became major centers of the Civil Rights Movement.

During World War II, the city's steel mills accounted for 20 percent of US (and 10 percent of global) steel production. Over 200,000 people were employed in the industry at its peak in the 1950s and 1960s, but mass layoffs in the 1970s and 1980s devastated many working-class families on the south side of the city. Downsizing and plant closures continued into the 1990s and 2000s, and today fewer than 25,000 people are employed in Chicago's steel industry.

By contrast, Chicago remains a crucial trading hub, with 50 percent of US rail freight continuing to pass through the city. There are also extensive storage facilities for grain and other commodities, the Chicago Board of Trade and the Mercantile Exchange, two of the world's leading commodities-trading centers. Meanwhile, O'Hare and Midway international airports accommodate the most air traffic in the United States.

Administratively, Chicago is organized into no fewer than 50 wards. Twelve of these have been selected for this book, including those with the lowest and highest median household incomes, while those that mirrored the socio-economic and demographic profiles of their immediate neighbors were disregarded. The studied wards have populations that range from just above 46,000 residents to almost 61,000, and they display tremendous ethnic and racial diversity, reflecting Chicago's long history as a free city. There are majority white, majority black, and majority Hispanic wards, as well as several in which Asian residents account for more than 20 percent of the total. The wards' per capita income levels range from a low of $17,000 to more than $95,000, and unemployment rates vary from a low of 3 percent to a high of 21 percent. These figures make Chicago both the most diverse city in our sample and the one with the greatest disparities.

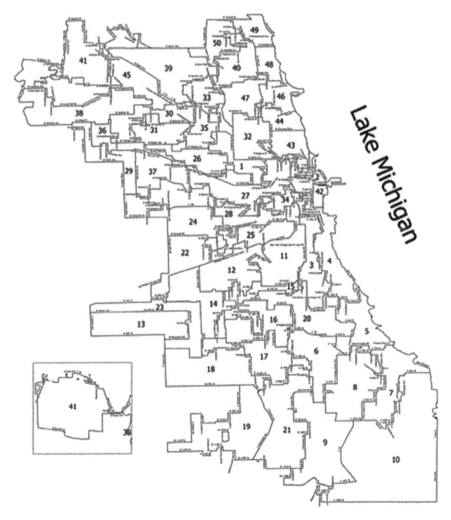

FIGURE 2.7 The 50 wards of Chicago, IL
Source: City of Chicago (2022)

TABLE 2.8 Socio-economic and demographic characteristics of Chicago, IL, by ward

Demographics	Ward											
	1	16	18	20	21	25	27	32	34	48	49	50
Total population	57,031	44,625	60,928	47,989	58,627	54,728	54,259	57,637	48,856	57,178	57,221	59,178
Children under 18 (%)	13	24	24	26	23	19	18	20	8	11	17	29
People over 65 (%)	6	17	14	12	18	10	9	6	4	16	10	14
Non-Hispanic black (%)	6	70	50	71	94	8	44	4	7	14	27	9
Non-Hispanic white (%)	63	1	7	7	2	19	33	75	57	53	43	45
Hispanic (%)	20	27	40	17	3	67	15	11	9	15	20	20
Asian (%)	6	0	1	2	0	4	5	7	23	13	5	22
Native American (%)	0	0	1	0	0	1	0	0	1	0	0	1
Median household income ($)	120,670	33,282	69,233	33,042	56,539	66,903	95,281	154,445	122,775	63,816	51,752	66,055
Per capita income ($)	72,677	17,310	26,396	20,142	24,634	28,297	56,294	95,340	89,211	46,920	32,825	29,373
Unemployment (%)	3	21	13	19	16	7	10	3	5	7	5	7

Source: United States Census Bureau (2023)

The two highest-income wards both have majority white populations. Meanwhile, the ward with the highest proportion of Asian residents (23 percent) not only has very few children under the age of 18 (8 percent) but an equally low percentage of residents over the age of 65 (4 percent), indicating a very high percentage of working-age single-person households. The two highest-income wards both have diabetes rates below 4 percent and obesity rates below 23 percent. By contrast, the two lowest-income wards, both of which have majority black populations, have diabetes rates of 17 percent and 15 percent, respectively, and obesity rates of well above 40 percent. Unsurprisingly, the wards with the lowest obesity and diabetes rates have the highest life expectancies (80 and 81 years), compared to just 71 years in the lowest-income wards. The percentage of SNAP recipients ranges from a low of 3 percent in the highest-income ward to a high of 42 percent in the lowest-income ward.

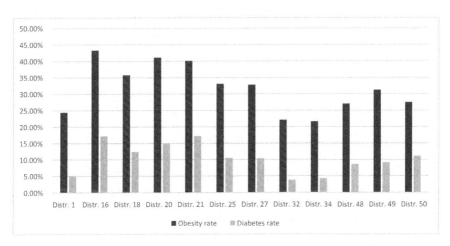

FIGURE 2.8 Percentage of Chicago's adult population with obesity and diabetes by ward

Source: Centers for Disease Control and Prevention (2022)

TABLE 2.9 Health indicators across the wards of Chicago, IL

Health Indicators	Ward											
	1	16	18	20	21	25	27	32	34	48	49	50
Life expectancy (years)	80	71	77	71	73	78	74	80	81	78	77	79
Population more than one mile from a full-service grocery store (%)	0	0	4	4	8	0	0	0	0	0	0	0
Households receiving SNAP benefits (%)	6	42	19	38	31	19	24	3	3	12	17	20

Source: Centers for Disease Control and Prevention (2022)

Brooklyn, New York

New York City is the largest city in the United Staes and a historic landing point for millions of Europeans who came to the New World in search of a better life. It is situated on one of the world's largest natural harbors, which extends into the Atlantic Ocean, making it a perfect port of entry. According to the 2020 US Census, New York City has a population of almost 8.9 million, which makes it the most densely populated city in the country (Roberts, 2020). In total, its metropolitan area has a population of more than 20.1 million people (the largest in the country) and a GDP of $2.4 trillion (the largest in the world). Indeed, if the New York metropolitan area were a country, it would have the world's eighth-largest economy. Over 58 million people live within 250 miles (400 km) of the city, which houses a host of world-renowned cultural, financial, media, and entertainment organizations, as well as the headquarters of the United Nations. Reflecting its history as the United States' foremost port of entry, an estimated 800 languages are spoken in New York, making it the most linguistically diverse city in the world. It also has the largest foreign-born population of any city on earth (Roberts, 2010).

The city comprises five boroughs—Brooklyn, Queens, Manhattan, The Bronx, and Staten Island—each of which overlaps with a county of the State of New York. (For instance, Brooklyn overlaps with Kings County.) The boroughs were created in 1898 when local governments were consolidated into a single municipal entity. The origins of the modern city can be traced back to a trading post founded on the southern tip of Manhattan Island by Dutch colonists in approximately 1624. Originally called New Amsterdam, it was renamed New York in 1664 after falling under British control. Today, New York City is a global node of creativity and entrepreneurship, as well as a symbol of cultural diversity. Many of its districts and monuments are considered major landmarks, and it boasts several of the most visited tourist attractions in the world, including Times Square, Broadway, and the Empire State Building.

FIGURE 2.9 The five boroughs of New York City
Source: Wikipedia (2023)

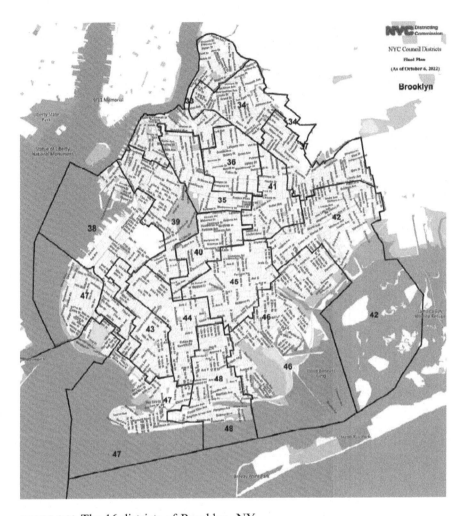

FIGURE 2.10 The 16 districts of Brooklyn, NY
Source: New York City Districting Commission (2023)

With over 2.7 million residents, Brooklyn is New York's most populous borough, as well as its second-most densely populated (after Manhattan). Several bridges and tunnels connect it to Manhattan and Staten Island. It has a distinct culture of ethnic neighborhoods, including a Jewish population that is larger than that of Jerusalem. Its official motto is *"Eendraght Maeckt Maght,"* which translates (from early modern Dutch) as "In Unity is Strength."

After a period of decline, Brooklyn is currently experiencing a renaissance, in part due to its high-tech startups, postmodern art, and creative food scene. Real estate prices have risen dramatically and gentrification has displaced many long-time residents. Some new housing developments are now required to include affordable housing units, but these are unlikely to compensate for

TABLE 2.10 Socio-economic and demographic characteristics of Brooklyn/Kings County

Demographics	District 35	District 36	District 38	District 39	District 40	District 42	District 44	District 46
Total population	179,159	173,765	59,033	163,368	152,935	167,396	161,482	178,240
Children under 18 (%)	18	19	13	23	19	25	36	22
People over 65 (%)	13	11	11	12	14	15	14	18
Non-Hispanic black (%)	38	53	5	4	51	70	1	55
Non-Hispanic white (%)	37	21	20	64	23	3	71	25
Hispanic (%)	14	19	37	14	15	22	9	9
Asian (%)	6	3	35	12	7	3	15	7
Native American (%)	0	0	1	0	1	0	1	0
Median household income ($)	100,555	77,182	65,264	133,757	72,704	44,008	60,464	85,155
Per capita income ($)	54,116	39,990	27,744	67,966	38,685	22,631	24,179	38,253
Unemployment (%)	8	9	9	6	6	12	7	5

Source: United States Census Bureau (2023)

TABLE 2.11 Health indicators across the eight districts of Brooklyn/Kings County

Health indicators	District 35	District 36	District 38	District 39	District 40	District 42	District 44	District 46
Life expectancy (years)	79	77	81	82	80	76	83	81
Population more than one mile from a full-service grocery store (%)	0	0	0	0	0	0	0	0
Households receiving SNAP benefits (%)	7	9	8	3	8	14	8	4

Source: Centers for Disease Control and Prevention (2022)

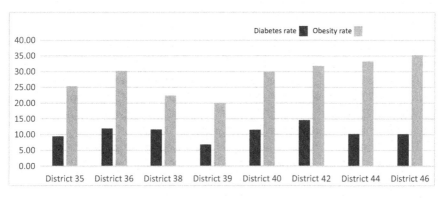

FIGURE 2.11 Percentage of Brooklyn's adult population with obesity and diabetes by district
Source: Centers for Disease Control and Prevention (2022)

the displacement that has already occurred. The borough is administratively organized into 16 districts—from District 33 in the north to District 48 in the south. Eight of these form part of this study, including those with the lowest and highest median household and per capita incomes. As with Chicago, districts with socio-economic and demographic profiles that mirror those of their immediate neighbors were disregarded. In terms of population, all of the borough's districts are fairly equal in size, ranging from just above 150,000 residents (District 40) to close to 180,000 (District 35). Median household incomes range from just above $44,000 (District 42) to close to $134,000 (District 39), while per capita incomes range from just above $22,500 to almost $68,000. Therefore, Brooklyn's median household income disparity is less than that of Chicago, and its per capita income disparity is less than those of Chicago, Atlanta, and Washington, DC.

Brooklyn has a relatively high percentage of children under 18 years of age across the 16 districts, although the proportions are especially high in its two lowest-income districts. This mirrors Washington, DC, where the two lowest-income wards also have very large under-18 populations. The borough's diabetes rates range from 6 to 14 percent, while its obesity rates range from 20 to 35 percent. While these disparities are significant, they are not as large as those in either Chicago or Atlanta. Life expectancies range from 76 to 83 years, indicating that disparities in life expectancy are also less pronounced than those in other cities, including Chicago and Atlanta. Predictably, the lowest-income districts have the highest percentages of SNAP recipients (14 percent in District 42), and vice versa (3 percent in District 9). Overall, though, the percentage of SNAP recipients is rather low, which may reflect a high rate of undocumented immigrants who may be reluctant to register for a government-run program such as SNAP.

Oakland, CA

Oakland is located on the West Coast of the United States in the San Francisco Bay Area of California. It is the largest city in Alameda County and the county seat. With a population of over 440,000 in 2020 (United States Census Bureau, 2023), it serves as the Bay Area's trade center and economic engine (California Port Authority, 2023). The city's port is the busiest in northern California and the fifth busiest in the country.

The earliest-known inhabitants of Alameda County were the Huchiun, who belonged to a linguistic grouping later known as the Ohline (meaning the "Western People"). At the time, the area was covered by coastal terrace prairie, oak woodlands, and coastal scrub. Oakland became part of the colony of New Spain in the late eighteenth century, was ceded to the United States following the Mexican–American War, and was incorporated as a town in 1852. There was an abundance of oak and redwood timber in the surrounding area, and the fertile soil enabled the region to become a major agricultural center. Consequently, in the 1860s, Oakland was selected as the western terminal of the transcontinental railroad.

The town grew quickly during the gold rush of the 1850s and 1860s as land became too expensive in neighboring San Francisco. Most notably, it experienced particularly rapid growth of its Asian population as laborers from China migrated to the United States to escape the Opium Wars and work on the railroads. However, there was considerable hostility toward these immigrants and Chinese settlements were burned down on several occasions. Further expansion and unprecedented investment in housing stock and infrastructure following the catastrophic San Francisco earthquake of 1906, as many of the survivors relocated to Oakland. Another major earthquake struck the Bay Area in October 1989, causing significant damage to many of Oakland's buildings, the double-decker portion of Interstate 880, and the San Francisco–Oakland Bay Bridge. Two years later, a massive fire swept down from the Berkeley and Oakland Hills, destroying nearly 4,000 homes. At the time, this was the worst urban firestorm in US history in terms of both economic cost (estimated at $1.5 billion) and loss of life. However, the wildfires of 2017 and 2018 wrought even more damage.

In the 1990s, Oakland initiated a large-scale urban redevelopment and renewal program that went some way to revitalizing the downtown area, the port, and the airport. However, it suffered disproportionately from the COVID pandemic, which continues to have a detrimental impact on the city's economic recovery.

Administratively, Oakland is organized into seven districts of roughly equal size. Districts 1 and 4, which have predominantly white populations, have the highest average household incomes, the highest per capita incomes, and the lowest unemployment rates. District 2 has a predominantly Asian population, while Districts 5, 6, and 7 are majority Hispanic. The latter three districts have the lowest household and per capita incomes.

Interestingly, food-related illnesses in Oakland do not entirely follow the familiar pattern. While, as in other cities, the highest-income district has the lowest obesity and diabetes rates, District 2 has the second-lowest obesity rate, even though it ranks in the middle in terms of both household and per capita income. This suggests that the dietary habits of the majority Asian population of District 2 may have a positive impact on food-related health

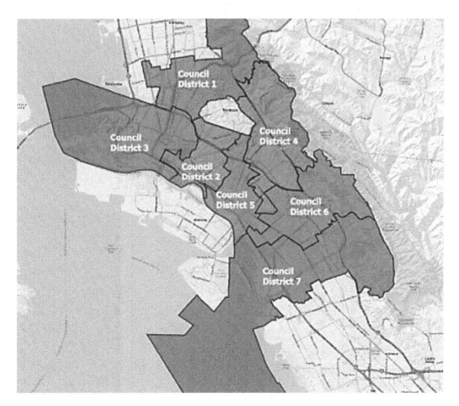

FIGURE 2.12 The seven districts of Oakland, CA
Source: BondGraham (2022)

TABLE 2.12 Socio-economic and demographic characteristics of Oakland, CA

Demographics	District1	District 2	District 3	District 4	District 5	District 6	District 7
Total population	64,962	61,194	59,033	65,321	59,618	69,622	57,750
Children under 18 (%)	15	16	13	20	23	24	15
People over 65 (%)	13	14	14	19	12	11	11
Non-Hispanic black (%)	17	13	29	11	17	35	30
Non-Hispanic white (%)	52	30	31	51	12	15	8
Hispanic (%)	11	18	15	12	47	37	53
Asian (%)	11	33	18	16	20	9	4
Native American (%)	1	1	0	2	1	1	1
Household income ($)	116,604	89,593	82,996	150,787	63,358	81,775	70,545
Per capita income ($)	70,735	53,817	55,586	76,769	27,276	37,435	27,839
Unemployment (%)	5	6	9	5	8	7	6

Source: United States Census Bureau (2023)

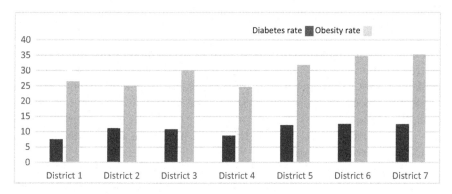

FIGURE 2.13 Percentage of the Oakland, CA, adult population with obesity and
diabetes by district
Source: Centers for Disease Control and Prevention (2022)

TABLE 2.13 Health indicators across the seven districts of Oakland, CA

Health indicators	District 1	District 2	District 3	District 4	District 5	District 6	District 7
Life expectancy (years)	80	81	80	78	78	77	76
Population more than one mile from a full-service grocery store (%)	0	0	11	10	0	5.9	11.8
Households receiving SNAP benefits (%)	3	5	6	1	5	4	4

Source: Centers for Disease Control and Prevention (2022)

outcomes. District 2 also has the highest life expectancy (81 years), even
though 5 percent of its households receive SNAP benefits—the second-highest
percentage across all seven districts. However, Oakland's SNAP recipient rates
are uniformly low, ranging from 1 percent to 6 percent.

Summary

This brief overview of the socio-economic and demographic characteristics of six
US cities illustrates their diversity in terms of age, race, ethnicity, and income.
Only 4 percent of the oldest Chicago district are under the age of 18, whereas 36
percent of the youngest Brooklyn district are in that age bracket. Similarly, in
some of Chicago's wards, only 4 percent of the residents are over the age of 65,
whereas Albuquerque has districts where the figure is as high as 23 percent. All
six cities have majority white districts or wards, but other areas may be predominantly non-Hispanic black (Atlanta, Brooklyn, Chicago, Washington,

DC), predominantly Hispanic (Albuquerque, Brooklyn, Chicago, Oakland), or predominantly Asian (Oakland).

Per capita income disparity also varies considerably, from the relatively narrow margins of 1 to 2.2 (Albuquerque) and 1 to 2.8 (Oakland) to the gulfs of 1 to 5.1 (Atlanta) and 1 to 5.5 (Chicago). Size alone cannot explain these differences. While the smallest city and the smallest metro area in our sample (Albuquerque) is the least unequal, the largest (Brooklyn) ranks in the middle, with a ratio of 1 to 3 for both per capita income and median household income disparity.

Disparities in food-related health outcomes are evident in all six cities, and indeed across all geographic areas of the United States from north to south and east to west. Yet, the picture of food insecurity and food-related illnesses appears to be more complex than commonly used social determinants of health might suggest. While racial, ethnic, and socio-economic factors obviously have significant impacts on the food-related health outcomes of US city dwellers, other important factors emerge in cultural, historical, and personal narratives. These complex factors are not easily captured in raw statistical data, so the following chapter tries to unpack some of them by presenting the stories of those experiencing food insecurity and those committed to addressing it.

References

Anderson, J., Ferguson, S., Karounos, D., O'Malley, L., Sieling, B. and Chen, W.J.J. (1980). Mineral and vitamin status on high-fiber diets: long-term studies of diabetic patients. *Diabetes Care*, 3(1): 38–40.

Anderson, J.W. and Herman, R.H. (1975). Effects of carbohydrate restriction on glucose tolerance of normal men and reactive hypoglycemic patients. *American Journal of Clinical Nutrition*, 28(7): 748–755.

Anderson, S. (1990). Core indicators of nutritional state of difficult-to-survey populations. *Journal of Nutrition*, 120(11): 1555–1598.

Atlanta Civic Circle. (2021). Atlanta City Council map. https://atlantaciviccircle.org/2021/07/19/atlanta-city-council-map/.

Bockman, J. (2016). Home rule from below: the cooperative movement in Washington DC. In: Hyra, D. and Prince, S. (eds.), *Capital Dilemma: Growth and Inequity in Washington DC*. New York: Routledge, pp. 66–85.

Bodor, J., Rose, D., Farley, T., Swalm, C. and Scott, S. (2008). Neighbourhood fruit and vegetable availability and consumption: the role of small food stores in an urban environment. *Public Health Nutrition*, 11: 413–420.

BondGraham, D. (2022). Deadline blown, Oakland's Redistricting Commission hopes to adopt a final map soon. *The Oaklandside*, 18 January. https://oaklandside.org/2022/01/18/deadline-blown-oakland-redistricting-commission-final-map/.

Broady, K., Macklin, M. and O'Donnell, J. (2020). Preparing US workers for the post-COVID economy: higher education, workforce training and labor unions. https://www.brookings.edu/articles/preparing-u-s-workers-for-the-post-covid-economy-higher-education-workforce-training-and-labor-unions/.

California Port Authority. (2023). Port of Oakland. https://californiaports.org/ports/p ort-of-oakland/.

Caswell, J. and Yaktine, A. (2013). *Supplemental Nutrition Assistance Program: Examining the Evidence to Define Benefit Adequacy.* Washington, DC: National Academies.

Center for Disease Control. (1971). *Ten-State Nutrition Survey in the United States, 1968–1970.* Report to Congress. https://eric.ed.gov/?id=ED057150.

Centers for Disease Control and Prevention. (1995). *National Health and Nutrition Examination Survey (1988–94).* https://wwwn.cdc.gov/nchs/nhanes/nhanes3/default. aspx.

Centers for Disease Control and Prevention. (2022). *Overweight & Obesity.* https:// www.cdc.gov/obesity/data/surveillance.html#NPAO.

Chicago Data Portal. (2013). Map of grocery stores. https://data.cityofchicago.org/ Community-Economic-Development/Map-of-Grocery-Stores-2013/ce29-twzt.

Chicago Historical Society. (2005). Grocery stores and supermarkets. In: *Encyclopedia of Chicago.* http://www.encyclopedia.chicagohistory.org/pages/554.html.

Chicago Metropolitan Agency of Planning. (2014). *Bronzeville Food Access Study.* www.cmap.illinois.gov.

Chun, Y., Haupert, T., Roll, S., Fox-Dichter, S. and Grinstein-Weiss, M. (2022). Did the pandemic advance new suburbanization? https://www.brookings.edu/articles/ did-the-pandemic-advance-new-suburbanization/.

City of Albuquerque. (2022). 2022 City Council Redistricting Process. https://www.ca bq.gov/council/projects/current-projects/2022-city-council-redistricting-process.

City of Chicago. (2022). Ward map of the city of Chicago. https://app.chicagoelections. com/Documents/general/Citywide%20Ward%20Map%202022.pdf.

Coleman-Jensen, A., Rabbit, M., Gregory, C. and Singh, A. (2021). *Household Food Security in the United States in 2020.* Report No. ERR-298. Washington, DC: United States Department of Agriculture.

Combs, G. (2005). History of Interdepartmental Committee on Nutrition for National Defense: course of events and nutrition methodology in typical surveys. *Journal of Nutrition,* 135(5): 1263–1265. https://doi.org/10.1093/jn/135.5.1263.

Cronquist, K. (2021). *Characteristics of Supplemental Nutrition Assistance Program Households: Fiscal Year 2019.* Washington, DC: United States Department of Agriculture, Food and Nutrition Service, Office of Policy Support. http://www.fns. usda.gov/ops/research-and-analysis.

Crowe, J., Lacy, C. and Columbus, Y. (2018). Barriers to food security and community stress in an urban food desert. *Urban Science,* 2(2): 46. https://doi.org/10.3390/urba nsci2020046.

DeWitt, L. (2010). The decision to exclude agricultural and domestic workers from the 1935 Social Security Act. *Social Security Bulletin,* 70(4): 49–68. https://ssrn.com/a bstract=1646367.

Dutko, P., Ver Ploeg, M. and Farrigan, T. (2012). *Characteristics and Influential Factors of Food Deserts.* Economic Research Report No. 140. Washington, DC: United States Department of Agriculture Economic Research Service.

Eisinger, P. (1998). *Toward an End to Hunger in America.* Washington, DC: Brookings Institution Press.

Feeding America. (2021). Help end hunger today. https://give.feedingamerica.org/ LKFEsahLjEu3nPhcOQEmKQ2?s_.src=Y23XP1H1Y&s_subsrc=c&s_keyword=fe eding%20america&gad=1&gclid=Cj0KCQjwi46iBhDyARIsAE3nVrbjXEL2hlBRm uiffS0C5XNjbKouPWA4lad9RaNpzcCmHx8d5EGdbwaAlGfEALw_wcB&gclsrc= aw.ds.

Field, A. (2008). The impact of the Second World War on US productivity growth. *Economic History Review*, 61(3): 672–694.

Food and Agriculture Organization. (1996). *Rome Declaration on Food Security and World Food Summit Plan of Action*. https://www.fao.org/3/w3613e/w3613e00.htm.

Food and Agriculture Organization. (2010). *Food Security and Nutrition: Building a Global Narrative towards 2030*. https://www.fao.org/3/ca9731en/ca9731en.pdf.

Foodbank News. (2023). Top 300 food banks by revenue. https://foodbanknews.org/top -300-food-banks-by-revenue/.

Francis, G.A. (2021). *Just Harvest*. Brentwood, TN: Forefront Books.

Frey, W. (2018). *Early Decade Big City Growth Continues to Fall off, Census Shows*. Washington, DC: Brookings Institution.

Garrison, T. (2018). Cherokee removal. In: *New Georgia Encyclopedia*. https://www.georgiaencyclopedia.org/articles/history-archaeology/cherokee-removal/.

FRED. (2022). Total Gross Domestic Product for Chicago–Naperville–Elgin, IL–IN–WI (MSA). https://fred.stlouisfed.org/series/NGMP16980.

Goodwin, D. (2001). The way we won: America's economic breakthrough during World War II high growth needn't require a war. *American Prospect*, 19 December.

Gregory, J. (1989). *American Exodus: The Dust Bowl Migration and Okie Culture in California*. New York: Oxford University Press.

Hodges, R.E. *et al.* (1978). Hematopoietic studies in Vitamin A deficiencies. *American Journal of Clinical Nutrition*, 31(5): 876–885.

Horowitz, J., Igielnik, R. and Arditi, T. (2020). Most Americans say there is too much economic inequality in the US, but fewer than half call it a top priority. Pew Research Center. https://www.courthousenews.com/wp-content/uploads/2020/01/pew-inequailty.pdf.

Huff Stevens, A. (2021). Transitions into & out of poverty in the United States. Center for Poverty and Inequality, University of California, Davis. https://poverty.ucdavis.edu/policy-brief/transitions-out-poverty-united-states.

Interdepartmental Committee on Nutrition for National Defense. (1957). *Manual for Nutrition Surveys*. Washington, DC: Interdepartmental Committee on Nutrition for National Defense.

Jarosz, L. (2014). Considering sovereignty, care ethics and policy in food politics. *Dialogues in Human Geography*, 4(2): 229–232. doi:10.1177/2043820614537162.

Jones, W. (1972). Supermarket era closes cooperatives. *Washington Post*, 13 November.

Kennedy, J.F. (1961). President Kennedy's special message to the Congress on urgent national needs. https://www.jfklibrary.org/archives/other-resources/john-f-kennedy-speeches/united-states-congress-special-message-19610525.

Kleinman, R., Murphy, J., Little, M., Pagano, M., Wehler, C., Regal, K. and Jellinek, M. (1998). Hunger in children in the United States: potential behavioral and emotional correlates. *Pediatrics*, 101(1): E3. doi:10.1542/peds.101.1.e3.

Kolak, M., Bradley, M., Block, D., Pool, L., Garg, G., Kelly, C., Kyle Boatright, T., Lipiszko, D., Koschinsky, J., Kershaw, K., Carnethon, M., Isakova, T. and Wolf, M. (2018). Chicago supermarket data and food access analytics in census tract shapefiles for 2007–2014. *Data in Brief*, 21: 2482–2488. https://doi.org/10.1016/j.dib.2018.11.014.

Kuemmerlin, A. *et al.* (1974). *Three Decades of Endeavor: A Bibliography: 1944–1974*. Denver, CO: US Army Medical Research and Nutrition Laboratory.

Lee, J. and Gill, T. (2015). Multiple causes of wind erosion in the Dust Bowl. *Aeolian Research*, 19: 15–36.

Long, J. and Siu, H. (2016). *Refugees from Dust and Shrinking Land: Tracking the Dust Bowl Migrants*. National Bureau of Economic Research Working Paper No. 22108. http://www.nber.org/papers/w22108.

Mitchell, T. (2003). Trade reforms and food security: conceptualizing the linkages. Food and Agriculture Organization. https://www.fao.org/documents/card/es/c/bca b5bfe-a5d9-5c78-9c74-7f5fbf7be2be/.

National Academies. (2006). *Food Insecurity and Hunger in the United States: An Assessment of the Measure.* Washington, DC: The National Academies Press. http s://doi.org/10.17226/11578.

National Archives. (2001). *The Homestead Act of 1862.* https://www.archives.gov/. milestone-documents/homestead   act#:~:text=The%20Homestead%20Act%2C% 20enacted%20during,plot%20by%20cultivating%20the%20land.

National Weather Service. (2023). The Black Sunday Dust Storm of April 14, 1935. https://www.weather.gov/oun/events-19350414.

New York City Districting Commission. (2023). Brooklyn. https://www.nyc.gov/assets/ districting/downloads/pdf/20221006-Final-Plan-Brooklyn-Districts-c.pdf.

Nikolaides, B. and Wise, A. (2017). Suburbanization in the United States after 1945. https://oxfordre.com/americanhistory/display/10.1093/acrefore/9780199329175.001. 0001/acrefore-9780199329175-e-64.

Norton, P. (2016). Infrastructure: streets, roads, and highways. https://oxfordre. com/americanhistory/display/10.1093/acrefore/9780199329175.001.0001/acrefore-9 780199329175-e-139.

O'Hara, S. (2001). Urban development revisited: the role of neighborhood needs and local participation in urban revitalization. *Review of Social Economy,* 59(1): 23–43.

O'Hara, S. (2018). *The Five Pillars of Economic Development: A Study of a Sustainable Future for Wards 7 and 8 in Washington DC.* University of the District of Columbia. https://docs.udc.edu/causes/Five-Pillars-DC-Final-05-2018.pdf.

O'Hara, S. and Toussaint, E. (2021). Food access in crisis: food security and COVID-19. *Ecological Economics,* 180. https://doi.org/10.1016/j.ecolecon.2020.106859.

O'Neill, A. (2022). Urbanization in the United States 1790 to 2050. https://www.sta tista.com/statistics/269967/urbanization-in-the-united-states/.

Ori, R. (2023). Despite headquarters defections, Chicago keeps title as top spot for investment. *CoStar News,* 1 March. https://www.costar.com/article/203048637/desp ite-headquarters-defections-chicago-keeps-title-as-top-spot-for-investment.

Patel, R. (2013). "Food sovereignty" is next big idea. *Financial Times,* 19 November.

Radimer, K., Olson, C. and Campbell, C. (1990). Development of indicators to assess hunger. *Journal of Nutrition,* 120(11): 1544–1548. doi:10.1093/jn/120.suppl_11.1544.

Radimer, K., Olson, C., Greene, J., Campbell, C. and Habicht, J.-P. (1992). Understanding hunger and developing indicators to assess it in women and children. *Journal of Nutrition Education,* 24(1), Supplement 1: 36S–44S. https://doi.org/10. 1016/S0022-3182(12)80137-3.

Richardson, J., Mitchell, B. and Franco, J. (2019). *Shifting Neighborhoods: Gentrification and Cultural Displacement in American Cities.* National Community Reinvestment Coalition. https://ncrc.org/gentrification/.

Roberts, S. (2010). Listening to (and saving) the world's languages. *New York Times,* 29 April. https://www.nytimes.com/2010/04/29/nyregion/29lost.html?smid=url-share.

Ruffing, K. (2013). "Gini Index" from census confirms rising inequality over four decades. Center on Budget and Policy Priorities. https://www.cbpp.org/blog/gini-in dex-from-census-confirms-rising-inequality-over-four-decades.

Sandstead, H. (2005). Origins of the Interdepartmental Committee on Nutrition for National Defense, and a brief note concerning its demise. *Journal of Nutrition,* 135: 1257–1262.

Saunt, C. (2020). Creek Indians. In: *New Georgia Encyclopedia*. https://www.georgia encyclopedia.org/articles/history-archaeology/creek-indians/.

Semega, J. and Kolla, M. (2022). *Increase in Income Inequality Driven by Real Declines in Income at the Bottom: Income in the United States 2021*. Report No. P60–276. Washington, DC: United States Census Bureau.

Union of Concerned Scientists USA. (2020). National soil erosion rates on track to repeat Dust Bowl era losses eight times over: scientists say farmland degradation to worsen with climate change. https://www.ucsusa.org/about/news/national-soil-er osion-rates-track-repeat-dust-bowl-era-losses-eight-times-over.

United States Census Bureau. (2020). Census demographic profile. https://www.census. gov/data/tables/2023/dec/2020-census-demographic-profile.html.

United States Census Bureau. (2022). Income inequality. https://www.census.gov/top ics/income-poverty/income-inequality.html.

United States Census Bureau. (2023). Data. https://www.census.gov/data.html.

United States Department of Agriculture Agricultural Research Service. (2020). History of Western Human Nutrition Research Center (WHNRC). https://www.ars. usda.gov/pacific-west-area/davis-ca/whnrc/docs/history/.

United States Department of Agriculture Economic Research Service. (2022). Measurement. https://www.ers.usda.gov/topics/food-nutrition-assistance/food-security-in-the-u-s/ measurement/.

United States Department of Agriculture Food and Nutrition Service. (2010). *A Short History of SNAP*. https://www.fns.usda.gov/snap/short-history-snap.

United States Government. (1964). *The Foodstamp Act of 1964*. Public Law 88–525. https:// www.govinfo.gov/content/pkg/STATUTE-78/pdf/STATUTE-78-Pg703.pdf#page=1.

United States Government. (1968). Committee on Labor and Public Welfare, United States Senate. Hearings before the Subcommittee on Employment, Manpower, and Poverty. S. Res. 281.

US President's Task Force on Food Assistance. (1984). Executive Order 12439: President's Task Force on Food Assistance. https://www.reaganlibrary.gov/archives/speech/execu tive-order-12439-presidents-task-force-food-assistance.

Varley, B. (2021). Chicago food deserts: where are they and who do they affect?https:// storymaps.arcgis.com/stories/ae5fb33c466d46c4a5ded10805b9d7c8.

Wikipedia. (2023). Boroughs of New York City. https://en.wikipedia.org/wiki/Bor oughs_of_New_York_City.

Zenk, S.N., Lachance, L.L., Schulz, A.J., Mentz, G., Kannan, S. and Ridella, W. (2009). Neighborhood retail food environment and fruit and vegetable intake in a multiethnic urban population. *American Journal of Health Promotion*, 23(4): 255–264.

3

WHO IS FOOD INSECURE AND WHO IS NOT?

The story of too much and not enough food in US cities

This chapter shines a light on the people behind the data presented in Chapter 2. First and foremost, it does this by hearing from those who struggle with food insecurity—the people who cannot get enough food on the table or cannot afford the food they would like to buy for themselves and their families. In addition, it gives voice to those who are trying to alleviate these problems through food pantries and food banks. The goal is not to cover every aspect of food insecurity by collecting and presenting so much information that we reach a point of data "saturation" (Strauss and Corbin, 1998; Morse et al., 2002). Instead, the intention is to provide some sense of the scope of food insecurity in the United States and the wide range of people it affects. If we are to address what might be called the "pandemic" of food insecurity in the midst of plenty in cities across the world's largest economy, it is essential to listen carefully to the people involved and the differences and commonalities in their stories.

The six stories presented here are largely based on interviews conducted between January and May 2023, although some also contain information obtained during earlier conversations. While they reflect the unique voices of six individuals and the organizations they represent, they also exemplify various aspects of food insecurity that can be found in the six cities described here, and in other cities across the United States.

Scarcity in the midst of plenty: a food pantry in Washington, DC

The food pantry we run here, in one of the most affluent neighborhoods of the city, is somewhat of a surprise to people. The city started to issue housing vouchers to low-income residents to address the severe housing shortage. So, people who had not previously lived in this neighborhood moved into some

DOI: 10.4324/9781003322399-3

of the apartment buildings in the area. This meant that they had a roof over their heads, but they no longer had access to other services they had in their previous neighborhoods. They got a housing voucher and moved here either from another neighborhood or from a shelter or the street. They were basically in an empty apartment, and while they now had some degree of security in terms of housing, they had no other wraparound services, and many of them have tremendous needs. They need furniture and household items; some have children and need school supplies; some have mental-health needs; and, of course, they need food. They are also not necessarily welcome in their new apartment. Often they don't exchange a word with their new neighbors, but they can tell that they are not welcome. So, now, they also lack the networks that they had in their old neighborhoods (to the extent that they had them): networks of church, extended family, a familiar walk-in clinic, and so forth.

We opened our doors in May 2021, during the COVID pandemic. The pantry grew out of my previous volunteer work with a mutual-aid group that shopped for people during the pandemic. So, here we were in one of the most affluent neighborhoods of the city, and my assigned task was to get food for about 30 families. For many of them, I was their dedicated shopper and would pick up groceries once a week. Many of my clients didn't have a car. Since we were paying retail prices for these groceries, we didn't get very far and I grew frustrated because you could spend your entire time doing the grocery shopping for these families and never be able to do enough for them. We also didn't have a lot of leeway to shop for items that were on sale, or for items the clients wanted but that were not approved items. Also, our funding was based on donations, and I just grew frustrated with the fact that we were facing this tremendous need with no ability to make even a dent. So, that's when I started to look into the possibility of starting a food pantry.

One of the interesting things about our pantry is that this neighborhood is used to doing charity work. People here are used to writing a check or giving donations. But we usually take these donations across the river to another part of town; this is the first time for many of us that we have really seen the needs of people right here in our own neighborhood. They are now our neighbors. So, we see their needs right in front of our eyes, and we see that the needs are really quite significant. Our pantry serves around 180 households a week. Almost half of them live in our own neighborhood. We have a number of refugees, including teenagers who came here without a parent. We have several Afghan refugees, for example. We also have some really young teens from Central and South Asia and some from Central America. I haven't yet talked to them about how they got here, but I suspect they are asylum-seekers or associated with some of the embassies in town. It's really sad, but there are plenty of people who work but don't get benefits, and if anything goes wrong, they can't make it on their own. It's very expensive to live in this city. Many of our clients also don't speak English. One family told me they have been desperately trying to find affordable medical insurance and they can't find anything. Some of them get no support other than what little we can give them at the pantry. A good 40 percent of our clients are senior citizens, but we have not formally surveyed them yet, so this is an estimate. At least 10 percent have some kind of disability. It's hard to say exactly how many because they're not necessarily physical disabilities you can see, but we talk to people waiting to get food and they tell us about their mental health challenges or anxiety disorders. We see a lot of that. Most of our clients are individuals. We don't serve a lot of families with children. I think this makes our pantry somewhat different. I would say at least half of our clients live in single-person households, but many of them also have family members who cycle in and out of their household, including children, grandchildren, nieces and nephews, and so forth. I have met several women in particular who find themselves taking care of their grandchildren unexpectedly, but they're not getting any benefits for them since there is no legal recognition of their status as caregivers. I often find these things out by accident when they ask for a particular food item, for example because they are taking care of grandchildren. I think it's a pretty big problem among our clients. The benefits they receive are small enough as they are, then they have to take care of other family members and it just becomes impossible to make ends meet. Sometimes I also wonder about schooling. Most of the people I meet who are in these caregiving situations tell me that their grandchildren go to their old school across the city, despite what you read in the newspapers about the crowded conditions in the schools. I'm not sure how many people are sending their kids to the neighborhood schools where they now live. So, some of these kids are taking the bus, or a parent or grandparent may take them over there, even though the schools are better over here. But I suppose it's easier to stick with the old school they are familiar with. It adds to the burden on the household, though. That's definitely a situation where I feel the pantry makes a difference for people because we are filling in where people have no other place to turn since their eligibility criteria do not align with the realities of their lives.

There is no way that we are addressing the needs of these families, though. Many come to us because we don't require any paperwork. If you are willing to stand in line on a Sunday afternoon to get food, then we figure you must need it. No one does this if they don't have a need. We don't even ask for proof of residence in DC, although most other pantries will require that. Most of our clients are on SNAP or other benefits. We know that some of them make the rounds to other pantries, and they are quite knowledgeable about who offers what, when their opening hours are, what kind of proof of eligibility they require, and so forth. That's no small matter, because information about opening hours, available services, and eligibility criteria is often hard to find. But some people figure it out and they know exactly who offers what, when, and where.

Occasionally, there's a tense moment when someone is standing in line for someone else and others feel they are taking away from what should be going to them. But for the most part people are quite peaceful and they actually tell us that our pantry is peaceful and feels safe. Then they'll tell stories about standing in line at other pantries where things can be quite tense sometimes. Then again, some of those pantries are much bigger than ours. Some serve something like 2,000 people a week and they've been open for almost 30 years. Some of them are very impressive operations. Most require some kind of eligibility and we see some of our clients on their rosters.

We also fill another gap because we try to provide a lot of fresh produce and protein whenever possible. We are of course very dependent on donations, but we have a dedicated cadre of volunteers who will drive to some of the high-end grocery stores in the area to pick up produce and chicken and whatever other items they have for us. We also glean from the farmers' market across the street during the market season. The farmers are quite generous. Sometimes we also get fresh produce from a community garden across the street, which is great. We try to assemble the food boxes for our clients in such a way that everybody gets what they need to prepare several healthy meals. We are lucky to have a very good donor network in addition to getting discounted food from the area food bank. Our clients tell us that they look forward to the fresh produce, and most of them prepare home-cooked meals. Our Asian and Hispanic clients know what to do with dried beans and lentils and so forth, but of course everyone is happy to take a chicken. Although everyone loves it when we have prepared meals from some of our grocery stores. We also have a small number of clients who live in a shelter, so they have no kitchen facilities, and that certainly limits the choice of food they can take. But, regardless of whether people have a kitchen or not, the prepared meals are very popular because they save people time. When you work and you have family obligations, and then you have to stand in line to get enough food for your family, that takes a lot of time. Sometimes we are drowning in macaroni and cheese, though, which seems to be a favorite thing for people to donate. We don't need any more of that! We need spices, olive oil, the kind of things you would use in your own kitchen to make a meal not just good but delicious. We also offer cleaning supplies and hygiene products, but we are not supplying anywhere near enough of what these households need.

Most of our clients get to us by public transportation. We are fortunate to be located right next to a metro station and several bus stops. A few have cars, and they may then come with several others for whom they provide transportation, but most come by bus. Since we are only open on Sundays, it can be quite a long trek for them since not all of the bus lines are running on Sundays, but then again, almost half of our clients live right around here.

I think COVID added a lot of people to the long list of those in need of food. We have a sizeable workforce here in low-paying jobs. Many of these jobs were lost during COVID, and that placed a lot of people in a very precarious situation, at least temporarily. But I think that at least half of our clients have been food insecure for some time ... and long before COVID. When we first started the pantry, I did not expect to see so many working people coming here. Many of them come during the second half of the month because their paychecks just cannot tide them over. Toward the end of the month, we'll see some of our largest crowds at the pantry. Sometimes we also hear from a teacher who makes us aware of children who may not participate in the school lunch program because their family may be worried about getting on some kind of government list. Some also find it a stigma to apply for a free school breakfast or lunch program, or they may be just above the eligibility threshold. During COVID, we received food boxes from the area food bank. In fact, for a while, we were drowning in food boxes. Now that they are gone, we miss them terribly and we now have to buy some foods to make up for the COVID boxes.

It's a whole patchwork of organizations and strategies we work with, and of course we couldn't do this without our volunteers. We have about 40 regulars who pick up food, sort, pack, and distribute every weekend. I'd say our total roster of active volunteers is about 80 people, and that includes DC public school students who have to do volunteer hours. We've also received a couple of grants that help us stretch our budget. But that can also be incredibly frustrating because some of the grants come with a lot of strings attached: for example, you may not be able to spend the grant money on cleaning supplies; or we need another refrigerator, and it turns out you can't spend it on that.

The gardeners across the street have offered to include our clients in their community garden in addition to donating some of the food they grow, but I think very few of our clients would consider gardening as an option. Many of them are older, and while some may find it therapeutic to grow some of their own food, it is also time-consuming and hard work. So, I don't think that's very feasible for most of our clients. But I wish we could offer our clients more choices. If we gave people some kind of stipend and offered them discounted food so they could buy it directly and make their own choices, that would be a big step in the right direction; and if the working people we see at our pantry could be paid just a little bit more, that would make it possible to reduce their dependence on the pantry. That would be another big step in the right direction.

Working families in search of food: managing a food bank in Atlanta

Our food bank serves 29 counties in metro Atlanta and north Georgia, which accounts for approximately 65 percent of the state's population. We distribute food through a network of nearly 700 community-based, nonprofit organizations who, in turn, distribute food to those in need. The majority of these partners are food pantries operated by faith-based organizations, primarily churches, but also synagogues and mosques. Others are operated by civic organizations, senior centers, after school programs, shelters and soup kitchens, healthcare facilities and more. We also organize over 1,000 mobile pantries each year, often in partnership with our partner organizations.

Food insecurity varies across our service area with higher degrees of food insecurity concentrated in the most urban counties, Fulton, DeKalb, and Cobb, that straddle the city's boundaries. However, several of our rural counties also have high percentages of food insecure households. Our partner organizations naturally are concentrated in the more heavily populated and better resourced communities of our service area. This leaves some of the suburban and rural communities with fewer hunger relief organizations. We are constantly looking to onboard new, reliable partners who can serve some of these underserved communities. When local resources can't meet the need we are taking a more hands-on approach. We have begun to stand up our own retail food distribution centers in communities where the need exceeds the local resources. We currently have two such food centers and plan to open several more in the coming years to fill the gaps across our service network.

Through our network of partners, we serve a full spectrum of people who are food insecure. We refer to the people we serve interchangeably as either clients or neighbors; we use these terms because they reflect the service-orientation of our work. Nearly half of the population we service are working families with children. Those families have many structures, from the more traditional two-parent households to single-parent and multi-generational households, where grandparents care for their grandchildren. Beyond families, we also serve seniors, veterans, and disabled people, and even college students through campus food pantries at several of the area's major universities.

We know that anyone experiencing food insecurity is usually forced into making tough choices between buying food and paying for other necessities such as medicine, utilities, rent, and transportation. Metro Atlanta currently suffers from an affordable housing shortage so rent for many people consumes a majority of their living expenses. This leaves little money for anything else, including food. While we don't track health, disability, or mental health issues, we are certainly aware of them. We know that juggling financial tradeoffs and living in crisis mode can cause trauma, and we are working with our partners to make them aware that addressing food insecurity requires a lot more than handing out food.

Food banking has evolved through the years and, despite the enormous disruptions caused by COVID to our distribution models, it has helped us to be more efficient. For instance, shifting to more mobile pantries allowed us to move perishable foods faster, getting it into the hands of those who needed it rather than waiting for our partner agencies to pull it through our inventory system. Over the years we have greatly increased the amount of fresh and frozen perishable foods we distribute such as produce, meats, and dairy. Perishable food now comprises more than half of all the food we distribute. New and evolving partnerships with farm cooperatives, as well as some government programs to connect local farmers to food banks, have made a big difference and have contributed greatly to the quantity and variety of fresh produce we can offer to our partner organizations and our neighbors. Atlanta is a sanctuary city, so we have people from all over the world who live here and who come from different food cultures. We try to have at least a few food items that are familiar to these clients and a popular part of their food cultures.

How our partners distribute food to those in need has evolved as well. Early on, visitors to food pantries would receive boxes or bags of food which pantries tried to compose with a good variety of what was available. This left many recipients with unfamiliar foods or foods they didn't like. Many conducted trades in the parking lots or simply shared the unwanted items with their neighbors. Over time we worked to move our system to offer more "client choice" by implementing a grocery store model that allows visitors to our food pantries to "shop" for the foods they like from a selection available at the pantry. Some items are limited by family size, but generally this choice model allows families to get what they want or need. And by offering our families a greater degree of choice and allowing them to select their own items, we also offer them the dignity they deserve. When we looked at the numbers, we also realized that when people were allowed to select their own food items, they often took less food than what we were putting into those pre-packed boxes and bags!

The pandemic forced us all to innovate food distribution once again. We had to adopt a new, contactless distribution model where people stayed in their cars and pantry staff would place boxes and bags into their trunks or back seats. While it reversed the gains we made with the "client choice" model, it allowed us to keep serving neighbors under the social distancing protocols of the pandemic. However, many time-crunched neighbors actually preferred the curbside model even after the pandemic protocols ended. Today, many of our pantries, including our own food centers, are operating a hybrid of distribution models, including client choice and curbside. Many now also are utilizing scheduling systems to better manage visitor volume in the pantry while offering the neighbors a more streamlined experience.

For many years, food banking was focused on merely getting the food out to those who needed it. We relied on the generosity of food donors with less control over what was donated—often we'd find ourselves with too much of some items and not enough of others that would round out a suitable pantry. Donations still are a significant percentage of our food procurement, but today we have better partnerships with our donors, and we work together to ensure our inventory is more diverse, and more of what families need and want for better nutrition. We also are spending more to buy food through wholesale channels. Originally, this was due to supply chain issues among our donors during the pandemic, as well as their own financial strains; but now, we need to purchase food just to keep up with the increased demand across our pantry network.

One of the biggest challenges for people experiencing food insecurity is access. By access, we refer broadly to a person's ability to obtain the foods they want or need at times that meet their unique schedules. For most of us, we can go to a nearby grocery store between 7 a.m. and 11 p.m., seven days a week, and be assured that the shelves will be stocked with the items we know and love. For our food insecure neighbors who rely on the charitable food network it is a different story. Most of the pantries are operated by a limited number of paid staff members, and most rely heavily on volunteers. Most of them also have very limited opening hours, just one or two times a week. Some pantries limit the number of times a neighbor can visit within a week or month, and the food that will be available will likely change from visit to visit. All this limits access to food.

To address these access issues, we are undertaking a number of initiatives that will transform the neighbor's experience across our food pantry network. Working with our partners we are focused on making access to food more convenient, consistent, frequent, and equitable. We will work to expand opening times, for example, reduce or eliminate restrictions on how frequently our clients can visit a pantry, and strive to have a more predictable inventory of food. We also invest in technology to expand scheduling and pre-ordering, and we are exploring more home delivery options. These are just a few of the things we can do to improve access to food in the charitable food network.

We estimate that most people who come into the food pantry system do so for limited periods of time. On average, our clients stay for about eight months. A typical pattern we see is for someone to visit a food pantry at the end of a month as a last resort after they have exhausted their other resources, whether it be cash reserves or SNAP benefits. Several years ago, we conducted a pilot program and research project, working with two partner pantries, whereby we invited neighbors to come to the pantry as often as they needed to meet all their food needs. Our research showed that after a few months of not having to stress about finding enough to eat, people were able to achieve better outcomes in other aspects of their lives, such as securing a job, for example. The results of this study helped inform the initiatives we are now undertaking to expand access.

In addition to food distribution, we offer a number of other programs to neighbors who visit food pantries. Of these, the most impactful is the assistance we provide in helping people gain access to federal or state food assistance programs such as SNAP or WIC. We are certified to pre-screen and submit applications for benefits on behalf of neighbors in need. We take applications over the phone and through field-based, traveling staff members who maintain a presence at our various partner agencies. The SNAP program can provide many more meals to families in need than what we can do through the food pantry system. SNAP also has the added benefit of providing neighbors the dignity of shopping at grocery stores on their own schedule and choosing their own foods (certain SNAP program restrictions notwithstanding).

Our nutrition program is another important element of our hunger relief efforts. We offer cooking classes to help people prepare inexpensive, simple, nutritious meals from pantry staples or items they may receive from a local food pantry. Our nutrition team also supports our partners in stocking healthy food items and provides advice on making healthy food options attractive and easy to choose.

Official food insecurity estimates have been declining for the past decade. An improving economy following the 2008 recession has been a factor, despite the interruption caused by COVID. But, during that decade, we quadrupled the volume of food we distribute, improved the quality and consistency of the food we distribute, and improved our service offering overall. Unfortunately, the number of people visiting our network of food pantries is at near record numbers—almost as high as during the pandemic. This has many causes: an uneven economic recovery, the lingering effects COVID has on the workforce and the economy, the end of pandemic-era relief programs, and the rising prices we currently experience. Food and energy prices are rising especially fast and inflation is at a 20-year high. But we also believe that the improvements we've made to our service offerings have contributed to greater reliability and trust among those who rely on the charitable food network to make ends meet. Food banks are an integral part of our nation's food supply chain—we need to continue to improve our services, expand access, and eliminate the insecurity too many people have about their ability to put food on the table.

Food insecurity among seniors: the story of a 64-year-old woman in Brooklyn

The food pantry here is a life-saver for me. The people are really nice. I haven't lived here very long. I moved to this neighborhood from just a few bus stops away, but it's a lot quieter here than where I used to live. I like it here, though I'd like to move into another apartment within my building, but I'm not sure that's possible. If I move, I will have to come up with another downpayment for the new apartment, and I don't have that kind of money. But everything is convenient here. I'm next to the bus stop and close to the subway.

Right now, I'm on disability. I have arthritis, and I can't stand up or sit for long. Things are a little easier now that I'm eligible for retirement, though. I live by myself now, mostly anyway. I took care of my mom for more than 15 years when she got very sick and she needed constant care and supervision. She was always such a strong woman, but then she developed dementia and became very frail. That was tough. I had to quit work because she just could not be left alone. When I worked at a grocery store, I had most of what we needed. It wasn't full time, but they called me in for enough hours, and my mom worked until her retirement too. So, things were alright then.

It was hard to get a housing voucher to move here, though. I waited for years to get into the apartment where I live now. But whatever I do, I'll never go back to the shelter. It's a terrible place to be. You can't open the windows, and you can't cook in there, and you can't leave anything or people steal you blind. So, I'm really happy to have this apartment now. I like to cook, and sometimes I have a few family members over, like my nephew, for example. He stays with me sometimes and I like to feed him. It's nice to have the company, and he's always so appreciative and tells me how much he likes my cooking.

I love to cook. My father was a great chef and I mostly learned from him, but also from my mom. My father was a great handyman, too. He could fix anything. He also knew how to stretch our budget. So, I learned from a young age how to manage. You need to be smart about how you shop. So, every week, I go to the food pantry. It helps a lot, and I love that they have a lot of fresh vegetables there. Especially greens. I love mustard greens, for example. They are really good for you and cleanse your blood and your inner organs. That's my biggest issue with the stores around here. I've asked them about it and they said they would get some mustard greens for me, but they rarely have them. It's strange that they don't get them here, but they used to get them at the grocery store where I used to work. Sometimes, during the spring and summer, some of the vendors have fresh greens and I go there and get some of their greens. Most of the vendors are nice. When I get there just when they are packing up, I get a lot of things from them. I use the greens mostly for smoothies, so I don't care if they are a little wilted. They are still good. It used to be easier where I lived before, though. We had a market there where things were a lot cheaper and they also took food stamps. Nowadays, everything has gotten so expensive and the prices for some of the things are outrageous. I still go to my old market sometimes to do some of my shopping, but everything has gotten more expensive there, too. The one problem I have with the pantry is that it's hard to get spices and herbs there. None of the food pantries seem to have them and buying them is kind of expensive. So sometimes, when things are on sale, I will buy herbs and I'll dry them myself. When I got my income taxes back I ordered myself a dehydrator. It is so nice to have that and I use it for all kinds of things. That way I can buy fresh fruits and vegetables when they are on sale.

So, here is what I do: when things are on sale, like chicken thighs, for example, I will buy a whole family-size tray of them and cook them up and put them in my freezer. I do that with all kinds of meats whenever they are on sale. It's tough to do with lamb, though. You have to be careful with lamb. It has to do with the fat. You have to cook it pretty good. I learned at my church that the best way to cook it is to use lime juice, garlic, and rosemary. I freeze things in portion sizes and then when I run low on things, I can just take things out of the freezer one meal at a time and add to it. You'd be amazed what you can do with a few added ingredients and how you can turn that into a great meal. That way, I rarely use canned or frozen foods. Those are my last go-to. One time, I cooked a whole leg of lamb when it was on sale. That was so good; it was so tender you could cut it with a fork. My favorite is chicken, though. I made a great chicken salad the other day with a lot of vegetables and some fruit in it. My nephew said he couldn't believe how good it was.

When I was young, we raised a few chickens and we grew a lot of our own vegetables. Maybe we'll have to learn that again because we may be facing some tough times. It's written in the scriptures that we will face a shortage of everything, and some of the movies prepare us for what's coming too. Times will be tough and we will have to defend ourselves against evil. Money keeps losing its value, too. We see that already and it will only get worse. That's why I try to save and preserve things and store them as much as possible.

You also have to manage carefully with things other than food, like toilet paper, soap, and those kinds of things. I don't buy any of those things unless they are on sale. But I still run out of money toward the end of the month, and sometimes I run out of food. I get less than $50 a week for food. It's hard to manage on that. It was a little more during COVID, but that's over now and everything has gotten more expensive. I'm really relieved that COVID is over, though. It was difficult when I couldn't get out and so many of my neighbors here were very sick; some died, too. But at the end of the day, I always rely on prayer. When I think there's no way I'll make it this month, the Lord will hear my prayer and something will happen. Like the other day, when the good people at the food pantry gave me a bag of cat food. That was such a help. You can't use food stamps for cat food. It's not allowed.

Once in a while, I get something special for myself. I love fried or grilled chicken, so when they have that on sale, I sometimes splurge a little and get some fried chicken. But because I used to work at a grocery store, I know what to look for. Sometimes they leave the chicken in too long, and then it's not good. So, I know who is working that day and who is paying attention to the chicken. When it's the right person, I can tell that it's done right and I will buy some chicken. But some people don't pay attention and that's a waste of my money. By the way, you also need to make sure when you get bananas that you take the bunch apart—that way they will ripen better. When you leave them in the bunch some turn brown when they are not even fully ripe. So, don't store your bananas in a bunch, always take them apart.

It would be nice if I could have just a little bit more money, though. The first thing I would buy is fish oil. I'm sometimes worried that I will have the same problems that my mom had with not being able to remember things and getting lost and just wandering off somewhere. They have this fish oil at the organic market—not the tablets, but the one that comes in a bottle. That's really good for you, but it's not cheap. It's almost $30 for the bigger bottle and the small bottle isn't worth it. I feel I can tell the difference when I'm taking the fish oil. It would really help me, I know.

I've sometimes thought about helping out at the pantry. Maybe they'll need someone. I've also heard that there is a community garden somewhere close by. I haven't done any gardening in a very long time, but it would be nice to try, although my arthritis is bad, so I'm not sure how much I could do. But maybe I'll try sometime. It could help me stretch my budget a bit further. That would help a lot.

Temporary food insecurity in times of crisis: the story of a 56-year-old immigrant in Oakland

I'm grateful for the food pantry. One of my neighbors told me that they don't want to see any identification, so I thought I would try it. I used to teach English as a second language part time to other immigrants. I really liked it, but when they asked me to apply for a full-time position I didn't feel comfortable doing that. I'd rather do contract work. If I ever want to go back home, I think it's better if I don't work for any organization related to the government. I stopped working when my mother got sick and I had to take care of her, then COVID happened and teaching was suspended for a while. My sister's husband was also out of work during COVID. He is also self-employed. But we are doing better now and my brother-in-law has work again. Things were difficult these past two years. My mother passed away a few months ago. So, now I live with my sister. Maybe one of these days I can teach again. I would like that. But in the meantime, we have relied on the food pantry to tide us over.

My sister-in-law has sometimes gone to the food pantry with me, but I mostly cook for everyone. It started when my mother became very sick and someone had to stay home and take care of her, so that fell to me and I like to cook, so that's fine. We all prefer our own food, so I like to go to the local markets so I can shop for the ingredients we are used to and like. I also like to go to the farmers' markets in the area. We don't get prepared food very often and we almost never go out. I usually take my sister-in-law's car to get our groceries. Taking public transportation would be too risky. I was always worried about taking the bus with my mother when she was so sick. We couldn't take the risk of exposing her to COVID or something else that she would not be able to fend off. So, during that time, I simply got out of the habit of taking the bus.

I mostly go to the pantry toward the end of the month, but it really depends. Our family does contract work, so it depends when we get paid. Sometimes, when we don't have a lot of work, it can be difficult to get food on the table. That's been hard for me to accept. There have been only a few times during my life when I've not had enough money to get food. We are lucky to have a roof over our heads, but that's because we live together, and there's always room for one other person. But when you don't have work things can catch up with you very quickly and you just run out of money to pay the rent, pay your electricity, water, and so forth, and still have enough left for food. Also, when my mother was so sick, we had medical bills to pay and that can burn through your money very quickly.

What's nice about the pantry here is that they have some fresh vegetables. That's what we mostly eat—vegetables and sometimes chicken—but not a lot of meat generally. We love carrots, zucchini, peppers, broccoli, all kinds of greens, cabbages, or whatever may be affordable. That varies during the year, of course. We also love herbs like basil, cilantro, and parsley. Sometimes I get nuts or different beans and, of course, rice. I can buy that in big bags, which is cheaper. We also like all kinds of fruit. One of our neighbors has a fig tree, which is wonderful, and she gives us some figs sometimes. But mostly we eat vegetables and a lot of greens. We don't eat a lot of sugar. When I first came to America I fell in love with jellybeans, but I have to be careful with that. It's too much sugar and I have to watch my health. I can't afford to get sick.

I can see how easy it is for people to run out of money and even to be homeless. You can really see it right now. Everything has gotten so expensive, and you can really see what's going on with all the homeless people by the bridges next to the road. There are almost like villages of homeless people living in tents or makeshift sheds or in front of some of the buildings where there is an overhang. You can see more and more people living there. We are lucky, though. We all went to school and we can usually find a way to find work, but I am grateful for the food pantry to tide us over.

Eventually, I'd love to go back to teaching. Or maybe I'll work in an office where they need someone with language skills. Some people may need help with their English. Also, a lot is happening in this area and around the world with weather catastrophes and wildfires and all kinds of things, so sometimes translation services are needed so that everyone is informed about what's going on and how to find help and so forth. I'd love to work in that kind of a position. I love to teach and I love to work with computers, too. When I was working, I would always do twice as much as what people expected of me. One of my dreams is that Google will hire me. I would love it if they gave me a job to come up with a better translation program for some less frequently spoken languages. I guess, for some languages, the computer translations are now pretty good, but for some they are still very bad and they might need help in coming up with a better way to translate some of those languages. I would even work for little money as long as I would have good insurance. That would be great. In the meantime, I hope that maybe later this year I might not need the help from the pantry anymore and someone else might get the food who needs it more than I do. But it's still a great help right now.

Working to make ends meet: the story of a 38-year-old mother of four in Chicago

We come to the food pantry at least once every month. When the children are in school, things are a bit easier. The two older ones get lunch at school. We also get SNAP, but that's not much. I took a course once where they taught us how to cook healthy meals on a budget. That helped some, but honestly, it takes a lot of time to cook like that. I try to plan ahead, and get things at the store that are on sale, and that I know I need in order to cook a few meals; but then something comes up and I just have to get some food on the table, especially toward the end of the month when we run out of everything. And everything is so expensive now it's hard to manage. I can't always say no to my kids when they want things. They like chicken, and burgers and fries, of course. My oldest is a teenager now and he is constantly hungry. I also have another daughter. She doesn't live with us. She is in Woodlawn and still comes sometimes, which helps with the kids in a way, but then I feed four of them instead of the three younger ones. Although, sometimes she brings things too, which is nice. I'm in a program now to get myself a better job. I've had work here and there but not really enough, and of course everything fell apart during COVID.

Childcare is also hard to find here, at least the spots that are free or not so expensive. If you don't qualify, you have to pay almost $1,000 a month for childcare. Who can do that? So, it always feels like you can't win. When I have part-time work, it's hard to find good childcare because they'd rather have someone whose child comes every day. But when I work full time and I can't find a spot for free or low-cost childcare, then I don't make enough money to pay for the childcare and the bus and everything else. That's actually something I've been thinking about: I'd like to start a childcare place out of my apartment. It seems like something I'd like to do and I know there are others like me who need it. But it's expensive to start that. I've looked into it. You need to have a good space, and take all kinds of training, and get insurance, and a license. So, it's not really realistic, but I kind of like the idea.

Also, my youngest needs special daycare. They tell me she's behind where she should be and I can see the difference myself. My older daughter, who is in elementary school now, would just do things. This one doesn't: she just sits and she doesn't talk, either. I need to fill out an application to get her into a Head Start program so she can hopefully catch up before she starts kindergarten.

My problem right now is not only money, but also time. I get up early, get myself ready, get the kids ready for school, and then we catch the bus to take my youngest to daycare. Then I go to my job training. After that, I pick up my youngest, the other two stay for their after-school program, so they don't come home alone, then I get home from the bus stop almost the same time my other two get home from school. So, sometimes, I just pick up burgers and fries or fried chicken on my way home from the bus. The kids like it, and it's a quick dinner. There is no grocery store around here, so when I need to get to the store, I mostly do that on weekends. My oldest is pretty good about doing his homework, but now he's telling me he wants to get a job. Maybe this summer, but I don't want him to get behind on his schoolwork.

Sometimes on the weekends I go to the store and also to the food pantry when I don't have enough money to get everything from the store. I usually go with one of my neighbors. She has a car and her daughter can watch the kids, but sometimes we take them with us. I like the food pantries where we can get fresh things, and where they let you pick things; then I get some greens or apples, grapes, and bananas. We also get milk and bread, and sometimes I get the toddler diapers that are like training pants. There is also a Salvation Army store where we can get clothes, and one of the pantries at the church also has clothing. The kids grow so fast, it seems every time you turn around they need new clothes or shoes. The shoes are expensive, and now my daughter doesn't want just any kind of sneakers; they have to be the right kind.

You asked whether I'd want to join a community garden and grow some of our own food and maybe meet people who can teach me to do that. It sounds nice, but I don't know when I would do that. I know people say it's also good for the children to get out there and learn about where your food comes from, but I don't know that mine would want to do that—like, get into the dirt. And where would we do that anyway? I don't know a garden anywhere near here, and even if we had a garden close by, I don't know that I'd want my kids to go there, at least not by themselves. And I would want to know who's running things there, to make sure it's safe. It sounds nice, though.

Connecting the dots between farm and food security: a story from New Mexico

I work for a social justice nonprofit organization called the American Friends Service Committee. It was started in 1917 by Quakers as a way of putting their faith into action by supporting social justice projects around the world. I am in Albuquerque, New Mexico, but I work in many places around our state. Our program here is turning 15 years old next year. The idea is to support people who have always lived on the land—that is, primarily indigenous and Indo-Hispanic people—but whose traditional way of life has been disrupted because they lack access to water and land and other resources that make it possible for them to stay on the land. There is a lot of pressure on these communities to give up their traditional way of life and to move into the wage economy. We have a large military presence here in New Mexico and also a lot of extraction industries, like oil and gas, so these communities are under a lot of pressure to give up their traditional way of life. The idea is, I guess, that they should make money instead of growing their own food. The problem is, though, that when they don't make enough money and can't afford any good food, then the downward cycle starts.

My first project when I came on staff almost 16 years ago was to work with a farmer whose family had been farming a small piece of land, roughly three acres, for over 400 years. He saw everyone around him being pushed off the land and falling into these unhealthy lifestyles, so he wanted to create a training program for small growers so they could stay on the land and maintain their traditional farming methods and feed their families and their community. I came out of a community-organizing background, he came out of a farming background, so we decided to put the pieces together and create a training program that would pass down the knowledge of growing food on small parcels of land to the next generation. We raised money to be able to pay people a stipend, so everyone who went through this year-long training program to learn how to grow food during every season of the growing cycle would get a small stipend. Otherwise, it would be impossible for people to afford to go through a year-long training program. The program was designed to be offered three days a week, and on the other two days program participants could farm and grow their own food or sell it, or work in another job. Anything people earned in addition to the stipend would of course go to them, and we designed the program in a very hands-on way so that people could already start to grow food during the training, and basically have a small working farm or large garden once they completed the program.

The program was very successful and helped incubate 15 small farms in Albuquerque, plus a few others that we did not launch, but we helped them to transition to a more successful model of farming. During the course of the program, we also built close to 40 passive solar cold frames to make sure that people could grow year-round at a higher level of productivity even during the colder months.

One of the reasons we focused on Albuquerque was because it's the largest city and metro area in the state, and the area has traditionally seen quite a bit of farming and gardening. We also wanted to connect more urban and rural folks, and help these small growers to succeed by linking them to reliable consumer markets. The program covered 15 different areas of training, from soil health to crop production, business planning, how to run a farm stand and interact with customers, to creating relationships with institutional customers like schools. Once the program was successful and we knew it could be successfully replicated, we turned it over to the community to run the program themselves. Our model is always to put ourselves out of business and to hand things over to the communities we serve so that our programs become community owned and the community can run things themselves.

This idea of community ownership is very important in our region, not only when it comes to farming, but also when it comes to the natural resources that are necessary for farming. The most important one, of course, is water. We live in an arid area and water is very precious. It is also a necessity when it comes to growing food. No water, no food. The acequia water rights are a way to organize water for irrigation, animal husbandry, and other needs in a community-operated way. Historically, the acequias were engineered canals that carried snow run-off from the mountains and river water to distant fields and gardens for irrigation. The acequias benefit the local ecosystems and crop production, and maintain ground-water levels. These traditional ways of managing water rights have also proven to be an effective way of managing a scarce and essential resource like water during times of climate change. They are totally integrated with life in the Rio

Grande Bosque in the Albuquerque area. The acequias mean that water is managed as a commons here; water as something any one person owns privately would be hard to imagine. Of course, managing water as a commons has become more challenging in this time of climate change. Farmers are the first ones to experience the impact of climate change. When you and I garden to supplement what we buy at the store or the market, we may experience that our tomato harvest is down and our greens are shriveling up due to lack of water, but we can compensate for these losses by buying more from the market. Farmers don't have that kind of buffer, and neither do low-income households who rely on their homegrown food. When their fields and gardens dry up and they lose their harvest, they can't go to the store and buy food, or anything else for that matter; they simply have to take that loss and suffer the consequences of a declining income and even hunger. New Mexico has had some tough years. Last year we had a massive drought and also some unusually cold temperatures that wiped out entire citrus crops. This may seem like a contradiction, but it is not. There is a cold phase called La Niña followed by an unusually warm phase called El Niño. Beside the temperature differences, these two phases also have very different pressure patterns that influence weather patterns in different ways, and some fluctuations can last for some time, so those who live off the land have a difficult time adapting.

This is the problem with our current system of farming. It is an extremely unjust system that makes it really difficult for small farmers who do the right thing to stay viable. Our current system does not fund food; it funds feed. And it does not fund farming that protects natural resources like our water and soils and protects against climate change; it funds farming that exploits our natural resources and exacerbates climate change. That's the challenge we face: how do we divest from agriculture that supports monopolies and supports climate change, and invest in agriculture that supports small-scale, diverse food production and counteracts climate change? We need to work on the next Farm Bill right now to shift things in the right direction. That $5 meal at McDonald's that all Americans buy every day is actually very expensive. The only reason it is so cheap is because we are subsidizing the wrong things. For one thing, farmers are buying things at retail prices and are expected to sell at wholesale prices, while subsidies are going to ethanol production and animal feed instead of food.

After our initial farming training program was turned over to the community, we transitioned to a new phase of our work. Two of our most important new programs are the Farm to Food Bank Program and the Farm to Early Childhood Program. One of the farmers who graduated from the farmer training program was very creative, very innovative. He was able to build relationships with a diverse range of customers, including individual households, retailers, schools and other institutional clients, restaurants, and so forth. Then COVID happened and we were told to shut down our office until further notice. When I put up a sign on our office door, that farmer just happened to stop by. When I asked him how he was doing, he told me that he was afraid of losing his farm. I was taken by surprise because my assumption had been that we will need food, no matter what. But, for him, COVID meant that he lost all of his markets. All the restaurants shut down, the farmers' markets shut down, the schools shut down; he lost all his markets in one fell swoop. He told me that he had no revenue coming in and not enough money to harvest his fields. At the same time, our local food bank—the "Road Runner"—was experiencing its own crisis. The grocery stores experienced panic buying and they were running so low on food that they had nothing to donate to the food bank. And so many people had lost their jobs that the food bank and the food pantries experienced unprecedented demand. So, I thought why not create a win–win and link farmers that have food with food banks and food pantries that need it? In the Quaker community, we believe in the Spirit moving, and that's what it felt like. We have an annual event we sponsor every March in honor of the community organizer, Hugo Chaves. The event was cancelled due to COVID, so I suggested that we shift the money from the event to buy food from our farmers. Before we knew it, we had all kinds of food pantries participating, indigenous food pantries, immigrant programs, faith-based programs, and we matched them with our farms. Our farmers loved the idea that their food would go to the people who needed it most; and since we bought their food, they had a guaranteed revenue stream through the Farm to Food Bank Program. At the same time, the food banks loved the food from our farmers.

Food banks are not uniformly happy about donations of fresh food. For example, one of the food banks got a whole pallet of cauliflowers from a grocery-store chain that wanted the donation to be a tax write-off. When a food bank receives a donation, it takes volunteers a considerable amount of time to go through the donation and throw out what's spoiled and salvage what can be saved. In the case of that cauliflower donation, it was almost completely rotten. The food that our local farmers brought didn't need any sorting. It was just beautiful food with no waste at all, and no time at all for the volunteers to sort through anything.

We also have a program focused on proteins where we work with a local egg farmer. A year into the program, I was interviewed by National Public Radio and suddenly we were receiving money from California, Iowa, DC, Baltimore, and so many others who wanted to support the program. All these communities who heard about the program felt like this was a great strategy to support local agriculture. The State of New Mexico is now taking over the program to scale it after we ran it successfully for two years. It will be interesting to see how the program evolves from here.

The other program we started is the Farm to Early Childhood Program. This program is so important because we know that we develop our palates as children from the time we are born to about age ten. So, we know we need to work with early childhood programs like Head Start to get children to learn to like fresh food. The program is into its sixth year now. We received some funding from the Kellogg Foundation to reach children at a very young age and get them to eat vegetables, and to get local farmers to provide food for the program. The preschool program in Albuquerque is a great fit for our local farmers. They can meet the program's demand for weekly food deliveries, but the program still needs to be subsidized. Buying from local farms is a big change for our schools and preschools. They are accustomed to buying from large box-store suppliers. So, the prices that our farmers need to charge to make their businesses viable are higher than what they are used to. Also, offering beautiful local food to our kids isn't all that's needed to get them to like it. Our children are used to eating things covered in ranch dressing or cooked with a lot of salt and fat. So, it takes some time to get children to like fresh vegetables from a local farm. We came up with programs like the Carrot Crunch, Give Peas a Chance, and the Cherry Tomato Hunt. Each program is developed around one vegetable, and the children learn how it is grown, harvested, prepared, and what it tastes like. Once a child tastes the vegetable, they get a sticker. One of the great elements of our program is that we link the children and their teachers directly to the farmers. They come to the schools and the children get to ask them any question they come up with. And they come up with fabulous questions, including questions about how food grows. That's a great step in the right direction because we know that when people become interested in gardening, they also begin to eat healthier.

This may be what our programs are ultimately about: they are about building relationships. People need healthy food and they need to be exposed to it from a young age and at affordable prices. Farmers need a living wage and they need to be able to pay a living wage to their workers. This is also why we incubate cooperatives among our farmers. Even when our farmers don't form a formal cooperative, we facilitate informal collaborations between them to stop the race to the bottom they usually face. We have been successful at helping our farmers coordinate their efforts. For example, small farmers have a tough time taking on big customers like an entire school district. But when multiple farmers go in together, they can successfully serve a large customer as one of them will produce, let's say, tomatoes, and another greens, and a third strawberries. If they collaborate, they can also maintain a decent price point instead of being pitted against one another and bidding their prices down in the process.

We are also very cognizant of the difference between local farming and sustainable farming. A farm may be local, right here in your community, but not farming in wholesome, healthy ways. They may use conventional farming methods, with a lot of pesticides, and no crop rotation, but because they are local, they may get a contract with a local school district. For us to connect a farmer with our local Farm to Early Childhood Program, being local is not sufficient. We want to know how they grow their food and that they are committed to healthy growing methods and to treating their farm workers fairly.

We are also very cognizant of the difference between conventional farming and traditional farming. Conventional farming is what the majority of American farmers do. Traditional farming is what our tribal farmers do. Some of them have been farming for a thousand years using traditional farming methods. We can learn a lot from them. One of those things is that land and water cannot be owned by any one person or group. It belongs to all of us, including the animals. This may be one of the keys to taking our food system back and to making sure that farmers get a just price for their food and that the food they grow improves people's health and the health of our planet. Healthy food must be for everyone.

Concluding thoughts

The insightful stories presented in this chapter reflect the voices of six unique individuals, yet they also represent the stories of countless people and organizations in cities across the United States. They represent the people who seek help at local food pantries: the elderly, those with children, and those who fall through the cracks of the government's main nutrition assistance program either because they earn just above the eligibility threshold or because they are reluctant to check whether they are eligible. They also represent those who are committed to reducing food insecurity, and who recognize it not as a stigma but as a systemic problem. All six interviewees speak articulately about the many pressures food-insecure households face, and their smart and determined efforts to overcome them. All are well aware of the benefits of fresh food and healthy eating, yet they recognize that time constraints and tight budgets may make it difficult for the food insecure to adopt a healthier lifestyle.

Those who address the needs of food-insecure households believe that food-assistance programs could be improved, not only by providing more nutritious diets but also by treating those in need of assistance with greater dignity. All of the assistance providers are also keenly aware of the systemic issues that are blocking the path toward a more sustainable and just food system. The example from Albuquerque also highlights some of the connections between food consumers and food producers. These will be explored further in Chapter 5.

References

Morse, J.M., Barrett, M., Mayan, M., Olson, K. and Spiers, J. (2002). Verification strategies for establishing reliability and validity in qualitative research. *International Journal of Qualitative Methods*, 1(2): 1–19.

Strauss, A. and Corbin, J. (1998). *Basics of Qualitative Research: Techniques and Procedures for Developing Grounded Theory*. Thousand Oaks, CA: Sage.

4

FOOD IS MORE THAN FOOD

Connecting the dots between food and green cities

The new urban food landscape

US cities are not renowned as places to grow food. Yet, as consumer demand for local food has grown steadily, city dwellers have been leading the charge. This was especially true during the recent COVID pandemic. However, it turns out that interest in growing more food locally during times of crisis, including in cities, has a bit of a history in the United States. For instance, city dwellers turned to urban food production during the flu pandemic of the 1890s, World War I, the Great Depression of the 1930s, and World War II (Lawson, 2005). During all these crisis events, urban food production was viewed as a strategy to improve food access and the health of local populations. The concern for fresh, healthy food is consistent with surveys of today's consumers, who mention freshness, improving their own health and that of their families, and more transparency about where their food comes from as some of the main motivations for seeking out local food options (Birch et al., 2018; Low et al., 2015; Stagl and O'Hara, 2002). This does not imply that large numbers of consumers are concerned about the quality of the food sold in the United States. Yet, reports about remnants of growth hormones in milk, antibiotics in meat, and e-coli on lettuce have certainly caused a growing number of consumers to ask questions about where their food comes from and how it is produced. In addition, concerns about food-related health conditions like obesity, diabetes, and heart disease have raised questions about food that has "empty calories" and little nutritional value.

In response to these concerns, the United States Department of Agriculture (USDA) launched its "Know Your Farmer, Know Your Food" initiative in 2009, and invested over $1 billion in local and regional food projects (United States Department of Agriculture, 2009; Low et al., 2015). Know Your Farmer, Know

DOI: 10.4324/9781003322399-4

Your Food was by no means the first time the USDA focused on urban food systems. The department established its first urban conservation district in 1962; the Urban Garden Program and the Farm to Consumer Direct Marketing Act were both passed in 1976; the Urban Resources Partnership was established in 1994; and the Farmers' Market Promotion Program was launched in 2002. However, none of these initiatives was widely known or well funded.

By 2012, Know Your Farmer, Know Your Food had established a local food working group, which launched the Local Food Compass, a website that features stories, photographs, and video footage of local and regional food system initiatives. It also includes an interactive map that features USDA-supported local food activities in all 50 states and enables both producers and consumers to share information about initiatives in their areas (United States Department of Agriculture Agricultural Marketing Service, 2020b). By 2018, Know Your Farmer, Know Your Food had morphed into an internal USDA working group—Local and Regional Food—which was tasked with developing a framework for transforming the nation' s food system and strengthening connections between local farms and local consumers, known as "Farm-to-Table" linkages (United States Department of Agriculture, 2022). "Local food" was defined as any product that is marketed "less than 400 miles from where it was produced, or in the State in which it was produced" (United States Congress, 2008). Reports from Cooperative Extension offices across the country, as well as subsequent research, confirmed that demand for locally produced food, including meat, poultry, and dairy products, soared during the COVID pandemic, while the established, highly centralized supply chains collapsed (United States Department of Agriculture National Institute of Food and Agriculture, n.d.; Richards and Vassalos, 2021; Balagtas and Cooper, 2021; Marchesi and McLaughlin, 2022).

The Farm-to-Table initiative also encourages the USDA's 17 agencies to invest both independently and collaboratively in local and regional food options. Moreover, while much of the interest in local food systems comes from consumers, the USDA appears to be at least equally focused on the producers. For instance, Know Your Farmer, Know Your Food views local food systems as engines of innovation and entrepreneurship that can drive job growth and efficiency gains, particularly on small farms. The initiative is also careful not to devote all its attention to urban and peri-urban agriculture; it also stresses its support for small rural communities in urgent need of economic development. As a result, in addition to promoting US farm products to US households, the Agricultural Marketing Service (AMS) provides US farmers with market data that will help them expand into new markets (United States Department of Agriculture Agricultural Marketing Service, 2022b). Especially since the 2018 Farm Bill, the USDA and the US Congress have added ever more tools to the local food systems toolbox. The Farmers Market and Local Food Promotion Program, the Local Agriculture Markets Program, the new Office of Urban Agriculture and Innovative Production, and the newly reorganized Local Agriculture Markets Program (LAMP) are all intended to strengthen local and regional food systems. For example, LAMP is currently in the process of issuing its first grants to regional food business centers and regional food system partnerships (United States Department of Agriculture Agricultural Marketing Service, 2020a).

One of the consequences of the growing interest in Farm-to-Table was the rapid revival of farmers' markets across the United States. Fewer than 2,400 farmers' markets were still in operation in 1990, due primarily to the seemingly inexorable rise of full-service grocery stores. However, that number increased to 5,000 by 2010, and more than 8,000 by 2020. The AMS defines a "farmers' market" as two or more farm vendors selling agricultural products directly to customers at a consistent location and on a consistent schedule. It maintains a directory to provide customers with easy access to information about the markets' locations, hours of operation, product offerings, and accepted forms of payment (United States Department of Agriculture Agricultural Marketing Service, 2022b). According to the USDA, over 147,000 of the United States' 2 million farms produced and sold food locally in 2020, generating about $9 billion in revenue (United States Department of Agriculture National Agricultural Statistics Service, 2022). Notwithstanding the recent growth in farmers' markets, 8,000 seems like a rather modest number for a country with a population of 330 million, certainly when compared to the estimated 10,000 farmers' markets in France, which has a population of just 68 million. This relatively low figure may be due to the fact that, despite leading the world in urbanization, the United States remains a country of small towns. Almost three-quarters of all incorporated municipalities have populations of less than 5,000, and home gardens are the norm. Meanwhile, fewer than 800 US cities have populations of more than 50,000. The three states that led the way in direct food sales in 2020 were California ($1.4 billion), Pennsylvania ($600 million), and New York ($584 million), which rank first, fourth, and fifth in population size, respectively. Most of the farms that sold directly to consumers in 2020 operated on-farm stands, and almost 80 percent of vendors operated within 100 miles of their farms. However, even though farmers' markets are generally regarded as outlets for locally grown food, not all of them meet that standard. Some urban farmers' markets do not make it a requirement for the vendors to be food producers, or even to source from local and regional farms. As a result, some vendors source their produce from wholesalers.

Community-supported agriculture groups (CSAs) provide more of a guarantee that the food they sell is either locally or regionally grown. Although unknown in the US food system prior to the 1980s, they have since grown rapidly, with almost 7,500 farms supplying them in 2020 (United States Department of Agriculture National Agricultural Statistics Service, 2022; see also Woods et al., 2017; NC State Extension, 2022). CSAs link consumers to growers with the goal of providing the former with fresh, locally grown produce while strengthening the local food economy and supporting small farmers (Barham, 1997; Ostrom, 1997). Instead of buying food by the pound or by volume, consumers buy a "share" of freshly grown produce that is supplied to the CSA by local farmers. In return for this annual subscription, member households receive freshly harvested vegetables, fruits, herbs, and flowers throughout the growing season. Deliveries are typically scheduled weekly, although the size varies according to time of year and abundance of the harvest. As a result, some of the risks of farming are shifted from the farmer to the consumer. Shares are generally bought before the start of the growing season to provide the farmers with a guaranteed revenue stream. In return, consumers have opportunities to become actively involved in production decisions affecting their own food supply. Linking consumers to local producers in this way vastly reduces the need for cold chains and long-distance food transportation. CSA consumers only receive food that is in season and can be stored or processed in their own households. As a result, they tend to become more knowledge about food preparation, processing, and preservation. A survey of CSA members in Madison, WI, found dramatic improvements not only in their eating habits but also in their awareness of food in general (Ostrom, 1997). This increased awareness compelled the members to question a range of issues about the prevailing food system. Another survey, this time of CSA members in Troy, NY (about two and a half hours north of New York City), found that, while their top priorities were food quality and health-related issues, broader social and environmental factors also motivated them to join the group (O'Hara and Stagl, 2001). For instance, although "improve health," "getting fresh vegetables," and "getting organically grown vegetables" were identified as the top-three reasons, respondents also considered "wanting to be supportive of local farming," "eating vegetables in season," and "knowing where my food comes from" as either "very important" or "important." The latter factor may well reflect CSA members' distrust of the prevailing, distant, industrial-scale food system (Kane and Lohr, 1997; Cooley and Lass, 1998; Ostrom, 1997). The Troy survey also found that CSA members' education levels and median household incomes were some 33 percent above the state average, and that they were more concerned about pesticides, where their food was grown, and how it was produced than non-members in the same region. While they did not spend any more time on food preparation than non-members, they did spend more time collecting their food, as it had to be retrieved from a designated pickup station at a specified time. This lack of flexibility and a lack of choice in the food received were cited as the biggest drawbacks to CSA membership (O'Hara and Stagl, 2001). The distribution costs associated with delivering produce to members on a weekly basis can be considerable. While CSAs in densely populated urban and metropolitan areas with numerous multi-family apartment buildings may seem to offer a promising solution to the distribution cost problem, the mismatch between the demographics of CSA member households and affluent city dwellers may pose limits (see the DC example in Chapter 5).

A specific market niche for locally produced food are farm-to-school programs. These direct marketing schemes are typically initiated by municipalities to supply their local schools with fresh food that is higher in nutrients and lower in sugar, salt, and fats. In other words, the main goal is to improve the diets of school-aged children. Like the CSAs, the farm-to-school movement began in the 1990s when a handful of schools started to push back against the prevalence of processed foods in their cafeterias. Since then, it has grown exponentially: by 2020, almost 40 percent of schools nationwide had implemented some form of farm-to-school program on behalf of almost 25 million students (United States Department of Agriculture Food and Nutrition Service, 2022; National Farm to School Network, 2022). The USDA began supporting the idea of farm and school partnerships in 1997 through its Small Farms to School Meals Program, which was later renamed the National Farm to School Program. In 2007, the National Farm to School Network (NFSN) was launched to share best practices and provide leadership in support of farm-to-school programs at the state, regional, and national levels. The NFSN's goal is to increase access to local food and nutrition education and thereby improve the health of America's children while also strengthening local farms. In 2017, after reviewing its first decade in operation, the NFSN launched its *Strategic Plan 2017–19* (National Farm to School Network, 2017). This outlined the network's aim "to articulate a distinct role for NFSN to institutionalize farm to school in the future and to identify refinements to existing processes and structure to ensure sustainability." Three years later, it provided $9 million in grant support to help farmers and food-service directors develop win–win collaborations. However, this seems like a paltry amount, given that more than 40,000 farms sold food directly to schools and other institutions in 2020, generating roughly $4 billion in revenue. By way of comparison, on-farm stores and farmers' markets generated about $2.9 billion, while direct sales to retailers generated about $1.9 billion nationwide.

Food hubs are another means of localizing and decentralizing the US food system. According to the AMS, a food hub is "a business or organization that actively manages the aggregation, distribution, and marketing of source-identified food products primarily from local and regional producers to strengthen their ability to satisfy wholesale, retail, and institutional demand" (Barham et al., 2012: 4). This definition emphasizes the benefits accruing from the distribution and market aggregation aspects of food hubs. Yet while, in principle, US policy supports the concept of short, direct-to-consumer food supply chains to ensure that smaller producers can participate in the marketplace, the challenges associated with scaling the benefits of food hubs have also been recognized (Dumont et al., 2017). As one food hub director pointed out:

Food Hubs are competing in one of the world's most cutthroat businesses, often operate on net margins of less than 1 percent, and they are trying to return more money to the farmers, operate on smaller scales, and provide additional social and environmental services ... [T]he reality is that there is no way to challenge the economies of scale of industrial food production, which is propped up by subsidies, kickbacks, and money-saving environmental short cuts.

(Dimiero and Mayfield, 2014: 6)

Some food hubs expand on the market aggregation and distribution aspects of food hubs by emphasizing their relational aspects and offering networking events and educational programs for both producers and consumers. For example, a survey of 50 food hubs conducted in 2022 found that over half offered a variety of educational and training programs (Shariatmadary et al., 2023). Therefore, they may be considered as important elements in a less centralized, more localized food system that has the potential to alter, or at least complement, long food supply chains (Lees et al., 2020). Like CSAs and farmers' markets, food hubs can also provide more detailed information on where and how food is produced and handled throughout the supply chain (Fonte, 2008). The aforementioned study of 50 food hubs found that all of those surveyed were either "committed" or "very committed" to offering workshops and training events for consumers on healthy eating habits and lifestyles; meanwhile, 20 percent were "committed" or "very committed" to offering workshops and capacity-building events for the producers who supplied their networks (Shariatmadary et al., 2023).

The urban food hubs of the University of the District of Columbia (UDC) in Washington, DC, broaden the AMS's definition still further. Each hub consists of four components: food production, food preparation, food distribution, and closing the loop through waste and water management (O'Hara, 2017). This comprehensive approach not only stresses the hubs' education and networking roles but expands on them to build capacity across and beyond the food system. The capacity-building programs focus on innovative food production, health and wellness, new models of food distribution, and enhancing the links between food production, green infrastructure, and urban resilience. At the same time, the UDC model bridges to other critical sectors. For example, the cutting-edge technology of soil-less hydroponic and aquaponic systems links food production to water- and energy-saving technology by utilizing a unique aerator that is based on molecular spin rather than compressor systems. Meanwhile, the food-processing component links the model to the hospitality and food retail sectors, while nutrition education in the form of recipe sheets and cooking classes helps to reduce food-related health problems by changing participants' eating habits through culturally appropriate diets. Finally, the waste and water management component links to a host of green infrastructure and green building sector initiatives, from mitigating flooding by reducing storm-water run-off and increasing permeable surfaces to reducing the effects of heat islands by growing food on green roofs, improving soil health through composting, and using bio-digesters to generate energy from organic waste. Taken together, the four components of the UDC model demonstrate that food systems are complex and can generate multiple social and environmental benefits when they are decentralized and adapted to specific social and environmental conditions. This highlights urban food systems' potential to provide the spark that is needed to trigger the economic redevelopment of entire regions (Stuiver and O'Hara, 2022).

Since its inception almost ten years ago, the USDA's Farmers' Market and Local Food Promotion Program has provided an average of $18 million annually in grants in support of local food system initiatives. By contrast, over the same timeframe, total agriculture subsidies exceeds $200 billion, and ballooned to almost $50 billion in 2020, largely as a result of COVID-related initiatives in support of US agriculture. Although funding levels declined to $27 billion in 2021, they still made up over 20 percent of total farm incomes in that year (Schechinger, 2021; United States Department of Agriculture Agricultural Marketing Service, 2022a; United States Department of Agriculture National Agricultural Library, 2022).

Urban gardens: the link between food access and urban agriculture

Urban gardens are situated between the production and consumption side of urban food systems. They typically produce flowering plants as well as food, not for commercial purposes but for local households who want to supplement store-bought products with their own home-grown produce. Urban gardens come in all shapes and sizes. Some are squeezed into small spaces between buildings, while others may extend to ten acres or more. Some operate on public land made available to local residents who want to grow their own vegetables and flowers, while others are operated by non-profit organizations and neighborhood committees. Some operate on privately owned land with the permission of the property owner, while others are vigilante gardens run by self-appointed groups of residents. Some are arranged as large community plots, while others are collections of small individual plots, possibly with some shared resources, like tools or watering facilities. Some charge membership fees, while others provide free access. In most cases, after signing up for their plots, residents grow vegetables and other plants for their own use, but some also grow produce for neighbors experiencing food insecurity, school cafeterias, or rehab facilities. The American Community Gardening Association (ACGA) defines a community garden as an urban, suburban, or rural space where individuals or a community grows flowers, vegetables, and fruits. A community garden may also be considered as a community-managed open space where a group of individuals determines how to design and manage the space (American Community Gardening Association, 2022; LaManda, 2014). Clearly, this is different from a public park or playground, where another entity, typically a municipality or a private landowner, ultimately determines what the space should look like and how it should be managed, even though they may seek input from the surrounding community.

Like farmers' markets and CSAs, community gardens have recently grown in leaps and bounds. By 2020, there were almost 30,000 of them in the 100 largest US cities alone, up from 15,000 only 20 years earlier. This represents an impressive turnaround, given a significant decline in the number of community gardens in the 1980s and 1990s. Their impact has been impressive, too. They have been linked to an increase in property values of between 3 and 9 percent in the surrounding area; crime and safety concerns have been found to decrease significantly, as have concerns about food insecurity; community gardeners eat 37 percent more fruits and vegetables than non-gardeners; and they are 40 percent less likely to be overweight than their neighbors (Litt et al., 2011; McCormack et al., 2010). The most common reasons for participating in community gardens are increased access to fresh foods, health benefits, enjoying nature, and connecting with others, but researchers have found that those in low-income neighborhoods benefit the local community in other ways, too (Milburn and Brooke Adams, 2010). For example, they provide open spaces for community gatherings, bring together neighbors of different ages, cultures, races, and ethnic backgrounds, and offer educational opportunities by enabling senior citizens who may have grown up in rural farming communities to share their knowledge with children and young adults who may never have picked spinach or seen a carrot grow. Several studies also established links between the lifestyle benefits of community gardens and the physical and mental/emotional health of gardeners during the COVID pandemic, especially when social-distancing mandates were in place (O'Hara and Ivanic, 2022; Dooley, 2022; San Fratello et al., 2022; Schoen et al., 2021; Rutgers University Office of Public Outreach and Communication, 2020).

In response to the growing demand for gardening space, the 2018 Farm Bill expanded the USDA's ability to support community and urban gardens. It also directed the Secretary of Agriculture to establish the Office of Urban Agriculture and Innovation Production (OUAIP), which was tasked with promoting urban, indoor, and other agricultural projects, including urban and suburban rooftop farms, green walls, vertical production sites, greenhouses, and controlled environment agriculture (CEA) facilities utilizing hydroponic, aeroponic, and aquaponic techniques. To date, the OUAIP has funded 237 urban agriculture projects totaling $52 million. However, this is barely a drop in the bucket compared with the $47 billion in agricultural subsidies allocated in 2020, and there is much room for improvement.

Given the recent surge in urban community gardens, they may seem like a recent phenomenon. Yet, their history dates back well over 100 years. During the 1893 flu pandemic, the Mayor of Detroit, Hazen S. Pingree, formed a committee to identify vacant lots that residents could use to grow their own food. A year later, almost 1,000 families were growing potatoes, beans, squash, cucumbers, and other produce on what became known as "Pingree's Potato Patches." Two decades later, during World War I, so-called "war gardens" grew a substantial amount of produce. Relief and subsistence gardens also helped feed an estimated 23 million US households during the Great Depression. And in World War II, close to 20 million "victory gardens" produced almost half of the country's produce (Gowdy-Wygant, 2013). While these figures are impressive, they represent subsistence, as opposed to commercial, production. Yet, subsistence agriculture can free up financial resources for other needs. A study conducted in Brooklyn, NY, estimated that if the Brownsville neighborhood's vacant land were converted to vegetable production, as much as 45 percent of its annual demand for dark green vegetables, including broccoli, collard greens, kale, leaf lettuce, mustard greens, and spinach, could be supplied locally. Moreover, if similar projects were launched on available public land, close to 50 percent of local households' total demand for produce could be met through urban food production (Ackerman et al., 2014). These figures are even more remarkable when one considers that the study was conducted in New York City, where the relatively short growing season creates less than ideal conditions for urban food production.

Despite these encouraging estimates, no one would suggest that urban gardening and urban agriculture can meet all of urban consumers' demand for fresh produce. However, they could make a meaningful contribution, in part by reducing urban communities' vulnerability to shock events. The key is to prioritize crops that are highly perishable (and would therefore deteriorate during transportation in long supply chains) as well as nutrient dense, such as dark greens, baby greens, and herbs.

One of the challenges facing most urban gardeners and food producers is that space tends to be in short supply in US cities. There are exceptions to this rule, most notably in the so-called Rust Belt cities of Buffalo, NY, Detroit, MI, and Cleveland, OH. These urban areas have all experienced flat or declining land values, with entire neighborhoods abandoned by many of their residents. In such places, urban gardens and farms are plentiful, not least because startup costs are low. These projects are viewed as ways to stabilize declining neighborhoods by removing dilapidated and abandoned buildings and making room for food production.

By contrast, land values are soaring in the majority of US cities, meaning that urban food producers face incessant pressure from urban developers. Some recent initiatives have sought to provide assistance to urban growers in this regard. In Washington, DC, for example, the 2019 Urban Farming Land Lease Amendment Act (DC Law B23-390) proposed the allocation of land leases of "5 years ... not to exceed 14 years" to eligible applicants with "experience in agricultural production." However, this scheme may be limited in its effectiveness: it does not prioritize low-income growers, places no restrictions on where or to whom the produce is sold, and makes no mention of the capacity-building initiatives and training that potential growers in distressed neighborhoods will need if they are to succeed in a competitive urban environment. Rather, by establishing a private marketplace for urban farms via tax incentives, the DC Urban Farming Act and similar laws have sought to privatize public land while ignoring the socio-economic factors that disadvantage distressed communities. The tax credits associated with using land for food production sustain the narrative of the American Dream, which insists that everyone can pull themselves up by their own bootstraps, irrespective of the structural barriers that hinder the advancement of marginalized citizens and low-income communities (Figueroa, 2015; Silver, 2019). In addition, such laws limit the liabilities associated with the environmental risks of urban farming for the public sector, with the Urban Farming Land Lease Amendment Act stating unequivocally that nothing "shall be construed to create governmental liability ... related to the safety of food produced on land leased from the District." The same law also waives soil-testing requirements for farmers who employ food production methods that do not require the use of potentially contaminated soils, such as growing in raised beds rather than local soil, growing hydroponically and aquaponically, growing on rooftops, and using vertical agriculture techniques. In its *Urban Agriculture Toolkit*, the USDA estimates the average startup cost for a typical urban community garden or farm at around $200,000 (United States Department of Agriculture, 2016). However, startup costs for high-tech, soil-less projects are far higher, making them unfeasible for low-income residents in distressed neighborhoods.

Therefore, what are needed are new approaches that recognize the full potential of urban food production, beyond its purely economic benefits. One such approach is based on the Social and Solidarity Economy (SSE) framework (Toussaint, 2018; Hossein, 2019), which draws on insights from ecological economics, feminist economics, and critical legal scholarship. SSE focuses on the specific community context, seeks to empower people-centered organizations, and implements participatory democracy strategies. It has already been used successfully in the development of land banks, community land trusts, and cooperatives. Yet, prior to exploring these alternative means of leveling the playing field of land access in high-value urban communities, we must first address the multifaceted potential of urban food production, including its potential for improving food access.

Food production: rethinking cities and metro areas

The recent interest in urban agriculture has brought the farm to the city. However, the type of farming that is possible in land-poor, densely populated urban spaces is very different from the conventional farming methods of land-rich, population-poor rural areas. In addition, urban agriculture must not only determine how food can be grown in cities but how it can be grown *sustainably*. As a growing number of cities establish their own sustainability goals, urban agriculture must contribute to, rather than find itself in conflict with, urban sustainability and resilience objectives. Therefore, its focus must extend beyond farming to a comprehensive food system approach that takes its cue from the circular economy movement. Urban agriculture must be both resource and waste conscious, and it must adapt to the diverse urban and peri-urban environments in which it is located.

Some urban food production can take place on the ground, in natural soil, but city soils are often low in organic material and heavily compacted. To increase their productivity, they usually require the addition of topsoil and compost, and they must be given sufficient time to recover between growing seasons. This runs counter to restrictions that frequently limit the availability of land for urban farming to between five and fifteen years. This is barely long enough to restore soil quality to a decent level of productivity. In addition, where soil contamination is an issue, food production may have to take place in raised beds. These require a mixture of imported topsoil and compost on a membrane above the natural soil layer. Yields can be increased by growing plants in clusters in bio-intensive raised-bed gardens, but such schemes are expensive, at least initially, until soil fertility and contamination issues have been addressed.

Food can also be grown on rooftops, either in engineered soil or in hydroponic and aeroponic systems to reduce weight. Engineered soils are typically lower in organic materials than standard garden soils to reduce the weight of the soil. Hydroponics is a method of growing plants in nutrient-enriched water, rather than soil, with nutrient levels maintained by adding liquid fertilizers. Since the water can be recirculated, some hydroponic techniques use a fraction of the water needed by conventional growing systems. Aeroponics moistens the roots of plants with nutrient-rich mist. It uses even less water than hydroponics. Both of these soil-less systems can produce substantial amounts of food in very small spaces, including indoors. For example, greens can be grown in vertical gutters in a standard shipping container. This turns the inside of the container into the equivalent of two to three acres of horizontal growing space. A wide variety of vegetables and fruits can be successfully grown in these soil-less systems, including herbs, micro-greens and sprouts, greens like lettuce, spinach, and kale, tomatoes, peppers, cucumbers, beans, okra, squash, and strawberries. Since no soil is required, hydroponics can also be used in areas where contamination is an issue. Retrofitting a roof to enable food production may, however, require careful calibration of the roof's weight-bearing capacity. Once this is done, the perimeter and interior may be planted with different species that can tolerate different root depths. For instance, tomatoes, peppers, beans, okra, eggplant, and even berry bushes could be grown around the perimeter, with leaf lettuce, micro-greens, and herbs in the shallower interior of the roof structure (O'Hara and Hare, 2017).

Aquaponics is a soil-less food production technique in which plants are grown hydroponically in water that is fertilized with fish excrement. It uses only 10 percent of the water needed for conventional food production, generates less waste, and virtually eliminates the need for commercial fertilizers. Similar systems were utilized by ancient civilizations such as the Aztecs and the Babylonians, and eighteenth-century Dutch sailing ships used a form of hydroponics to feed their crews. The more recent innovation of aeroponics was pioneered on the Mir Space Station. While all three systems are becoming increasingly energy efficient, they are not yet energy neutral: that is, the energy needed to grow the plants is higher than the kilocalories of energy harvested. This is because the energy provided by sunlight to power photosynthesis is still superior to any artificial lighting alternatives.

Since experience with food production may be limited in urban communities, ease of installation and maintenance of urban farms are important considerations. The USDA published its first *Urban Agriculture Toolkit* in 2016. It explains the financial, technical, and organizational aspects of starting an urban farm. Costs can vary widely, depending on soil condition and preferred growing method, but upfront investment is often substantial. Moreover, the agricultural, technical, and business skills required may be limited in an urban setting. Urban growers frequently indicate that one of the barriers to expanding their businesses is a shortage of qualified workers who are familiar with harvesting and packaging herbs and vegetables, and repairing even basic equipment. These are commonplace skills in agriculture, but they are foreign to those accustomed to urban environments. This highlights the need for more education and training. The newly established OUAIP and the 17 Urban Agriculture Committees have an opportunity to take a lead on this. Their capacity-building efforts must encompass every aspect of the food system, including cultivation, product aggregation, processing, distribution, and marketing of agricultural products in urban and suburban communities. Training events will have to focus on bio-intensive soil-based growing methods, soil-less food production, integrative pest management, food safety, age-appropriate nutrition, food preservation, composting, and water management, as well as the intersection between urban agriculture and green infrastructure. Meanwhile, the OUAIP should continue to advise the Secretary of Agriculture on the development of policies relating to urban, indoor, and other emerging agricultural practices. For instance, two of its pilot programs—the Compost and Food Waste Reduction Program and the Urban Agriculture and Innovative Production Program—are still in their infancy. So there is opportunity to shape them in such a manner that they will be able to address the multi-layered capacity deficits of disadvantaged communities in cities and metro areas.

US municipalities' growing interest in urban sustainability and resilience will play a key role in these programs. There is increasing recognition that cities and metro areas cannot sustain their high population densities simply by relying on surrounding suburban and rural areas as compensatory spaces. Such spaces not only supply urban areas with the majority of their resources but also receive the bulk of their emissions and waste. As cities continue to grow and sprawling suburbs continue to encroach on previously open space, the result is a steady loss of both compensatory spaces and arable land. Cities must therefore become more sustainable, in part by maximizing the potential of urban agriculture. For example, urban food production intersects uniquely with urban storm-water management and waste-reduction goals (O'Hara et al., 2017). Green roofs and urban farms and gardens increase the acreage of permeable surfaces in the urban landscape, reducing the pressure on storm-water systems that are already at full capacity in many US cities. Therefore, they can help municipalities to mitigate the impact of increasingly erratic weather patterns, including unprecedented precipitation levels.

Likewise, green roofs, garden spaces, and trees help to cool the urban landscape (Taylor, 2007; Li et al., 2014; Ladan et al., 2022; Humaida et al., 2023). The term "urban heat island" refers to the inevitable temperature differential between a city and the surrounding area. However, a city's street pattern, the size of the buildings, the heat-absorbing properties of the building materials, ventilation, and the amount of green cover all play important roles in the severity of the heat island effect. According to the Environmental Protection Agency (2020), cities should adopt five strategies to mitigate the impact of their heat islands:

1. increase green cover, including tree canopies and other vegetative cover;
2. install green roofs;
3. install reflective or cooling roofs;
4. use permeable or reflective pavements; and
5. implement smart-growth practices that utilize natural ventilation and green spaces in the cityscape and improved conservation strategies to protect existing green space.

Urban agriculture can make valuable contributions to at least three of these strategies by increasing the amount of green cover, installing green roofs, and promoting smart-growth practices. The recommended strategies also highlight the need to consider where urban agriculture will be most beneficial. For example, cities should not rob Peter to pay Paul by turning public parks and other green spaces into urban gardens and farms. Only *new* green spaces will help in the fight to reduce the heat island effect.

Urban agriculture also has a significant role to play in reducing food waste. This involves much more than simple composting and other end-of-pipe waste-reduction initiatives. Indeed, the best solution would be a comprehensive redesign of the whole food system to avoid waste generation in the first place. This distinction is important because agricultural production relies on huge inputs of water, gasoline, fertilizers, labor, and so on. Therefore, composting the end product—food—should be considered as a last resort. The resources that foodstuffs contain are far more valuable than what can be recovered through composting or even in bio-digesters that turn food waste into methane. Hence, *preventing* food waste is far preferable to *recovering* it. Urban agriculture not only shortens the distance between farm and fork but eliminates the need for energy-intensive cold chains and cold storage. Moreover, about 20 percent of all food waste occurs on the farm because the produce falls below consumers' unrealistic expectations in terms of size, color, or shape. The apple with brown spots, the carrot with two legs instead of one, the asymmetrical tomato—all are perfectly healthy and nutritious foodstuffs that end up on the compost heap or are simply left to rot. Therefore, changing urban consumers' expectations by reacquainting them with their food and how it is grown could make a meaningful contribution to reducing food waste.

A less centralized food system consisting of a network of small, local food production sites is both less vulnerable and more resilient than a single large production facility. Absorbing storm-water run-off in multiple locations has a greater impact than doing so in just one location. Reducing heat islands across multiple neighborhoods is more effective than tackling a single heat island in one area. Similarly, better food security, nutritional health, job creation, water management, soil enhancement, and heat absorption are not separate but connected aspects of a more socially and environmentally sustainable food system.

The idea of strengthening local economies by replacing imports with the goods and services of decentralized local business networks is not new (Florida, 2005; Shuman, 2015; O'Hara, 2018). Known as "leak plugging" or "relocalizing," it consists of two main strategies: persuade businesses to relocate to the area; and help existing businesses to expand, chiefly through focused capacity-building efforts. In principle, urban agriculture can make a valuable contribution to both of these strategies. For example, urban and peri-urban food system businesses can address multiple social determinants of food insecurity and realize multiple sustainability objectives in the neighborhoods that are most in need of development. Such businesses might include a health-focused startup that maximizes nutrient yield and offers health assessment and nutrition counseling; an urban farm that grows micro-greens and herbs for high-end restaurants; an ethnic crop garden that supplies local niche restaurants and grocery stores; green roofs that provide food production and event spaces; and a nursery that supplies urban parks with native plant seedlings (Royte, 2015). This type of urban business cluster will undoubtedly require training and technical support, as well as financial assistance. However, it will likely repay this investment many times over through its social, environmental, and economic contributions to the local community.

This brings us to restorative urban agriculture (O'Hara and Stuiver, 2022). Based on the concept of sustaining production (O'Hara, 1997; 2016), this adds several critical dimensions to local and sustainable urban agriculture. In addition to the familiar notion of production efficiency, restorative urban agriculture focuses on sink capacities: that is, an ecosystem's ability to absorb, process, and ameliorate harmful substances. It thus addresses one of the chief failings of conventional agriculture, which for too long has acted as if it operates independently of the social and environmental systems that provide its resources and receive its emissions and waste by-products. For example, producing vegetables requires labor, water, fertilizer, and soil minerals or nutrient-rich water. As Chapter 1 pointed out, most of the focus in agriculture has been on producing ever-higher crop yields with the same or fewer inputs, and especially with less labor. Agriculture has been wildly successful in this respect, freeing up workers and enabling them to enter other economic sectors. Over the past 50 years, a secondary focus has been on reducing both nutrient run-off from fertilizers and pesticide residues on food plants. Yet, only recently has attention started to shift from increasing efficiency and reducing emissions to the contributions that agriculture could make to improving ecosystems and the services they provide (O'Hara and Stuiver, 2022). For example, soil can sequester carbon and reduce carbon-dioxide emissions; increasing soils' capacity to absorb water can mitigate flooding; and maintaining biodiverse ecosystems can provide habitats for the pollinators that make crop production possible. These are all becoming increasingly important considerations in the era of climate change. Temperatures are rising as carbon dioxide continues to accumulate in the atmosphere, and as a result the hydrological cycles of evaporation and precipitation are becoming more erratic. This has massive implications for agriculture. Yet, there has been little or no interest in increasing the sink capacities of arable land or the watersheds it impacts. Resources have a price; sinks do not. Agricultural practices' ability—or inability—to absorb carbon dioxide is not reflected in either the cost of producing food or the final price paid by the consumer. No wonder, then, that sink capacities are declining at an alarming rate. When food production is viewed in this way, it is clear that we must adopt a different approach that prioritizes the maintenance of healthy ecosystems and their sink capacities.

As soon as the focus shifts from resource inputs to sinks, perceptions of the value of agricultural products and the way in which they are produced alter dramatically. Supposedly "costly" decentralized, smaller-scale urban food production methods—which increase permeable surface areas, sequester carbon, preserve biodiversity, mitigate flooding, and absorb heat—may turn out to be far cheaper than conventional farming techniques once their restorative side-effects are factored into the equation. Similarly, greens produced in ways that restore or maintain sink capacities will be far more valuable than those that generate a host of negative by-products. And the costs of "expensive" green roofs and community gardens in public housing developments will be far outweighed by their positive impact on the health of residents as well as the extra green cover and permeable surfaces they provide. Sinks are not only environmental but social and personal. While the soil absorbs harmful substances, our communities absorb the negative side-effects of illness and stress, and our own bodies absorb pesticide residues, traces of antibiotics, and herbicides.

The four key principles of restorative agriculture are:

1. It redefines efficiency not as the ratio of output to inputs but as the efficient use of environmental and social assets.
2. It reduces emissions and waste by closing feedback loops as much as possible and reducing environmental and social burdens.
3. It increases sink capacities through social support networks that strengthen social equity and ecological resilience.
4. It redefines the value of food as restorative and dependent on its ability to maintain assets, reduce emissions and waste, and increase sink capacities.

Operationalizing these principles will require considerable effort and a new urban agenda that educates decision-makers about the neglected sink dimensions of our food system. Introducing the notion of sinks along with sources requires us to consider not only how much food we produce, but how we produce, distribute, and process it, and whether the end product is valuable, has no value, or even has negative value, since it is destructive. Without the explicit commitment to restoring the sink capacities of our food system, the rising cost of their decline may prove unaffordable, and future generations will be left with no options.

Urban agriculture in six US cities

The six cities introduced in Chapter 2, which are the focus of this book, are located in every corner of the United States, so, inevitably, they have very different growing seasons, ranging from year-round in Albuquerque to just six months in Chicago and New York. As a result, food production and storage conditions vary considerably, too.

The USDA began to publish data on different regions in 1965 so that those with similar climates and soil conditions could share information and make better production decisions. Almost half a century later, in 2012, it published its first Plant Hardiness Zone Map, which provides growers with recommendations of plants that thrive in particular regions. While this sort of basic information may be useful for gardeners and farmers who use conventional production methods, the USDA has seen no need to provide detailed demographic, economic, and cultural information that would give growers a better understanding of potential markets and revenue opportunities. Obviously, close proximity to a sizeable number of consumers can be an advantage for urban growers, but it may also present some challenges. For instance, those neighborhoods that are most in need of fresh food also tend to be the ones with limited purchasing power. This raises questions about food-insecure neighborhoods' ability to generate sufficient revenue to meet the costs of urban food production. Therefore, the latter may require nonprofit and/or public sector support.

The remainder of this chapter focuses on current urban agriculture initiatives in each of our six cities as a starting point for assessing their ability to meet urban food-security and sustainability needs.

Washington, DC

As mentioned in Chapter 2, the mid-Atlantic region is the most urbanized and densely populated region of the United States. This has already had a dramatic effect on the landscape, and the remaining agricultural land is now under intense pressure from developers. The conversion of farmland into developed land has also resulted in widespread erosion and stream contamination. The region's warm season lasts for about three and a half months, from early June to mid-September, during which the average high temperature can exceed 80°F (27°C). The cold season extends from December to March, during which the average high is below 52°F (11°C). The region is also known for its high humidity, especially during the summer months, with June typically the wettest month. The driest month is January. The hot and humid conditions make it possible to grow crops outdoors for close to nine months of the year, with heat-resistant species grown in the height of summer and hardy varieties cultivated during the colder months. However, pests and fungi also thrive in the summer months, which can make it difficult to farm without pesticides.

Washington, DC, has a vibrant urban food scene in which many different food cultures are represented, coupled with a strong commitment to using locally and regionally grown food. Hence, it is no surprise that it leads the United States in farmers' markets per 1,000 of the population. In 2014, Mayor Muriel Bowser established the DC Food Policy Council to oversee every aspect of the city's food system, from urban food production to waste management, health, energy, and sustainability.

DC is one of the greenest cities in the country, with the fourth-largest number of trees and the third-largest number of green roofs. Its commitment to sustainability is also reflected in its Sustainable DC plan, which was formally launched in 2012. This is DC's roadmap to becoming the healthiest, greenest, and most livable city in the United States by 2032. It covers a total of 13 areas—governance, equity, built environment, climate, economy, education, energy, food, health, nature, transportation, waste, and water—each with distinct goals, measurable targets, and proposed actions to achieve those targets. An annual report outlines the progress that has been made toward meeting the targets (Government of the District of Columbia Department of Energy and Environment, 2022). The plan's food-related goals include:

- making healthy, fresh food available and affordable for all DC residents to improve their health and well-being;
- building a thriving, community-driven food system, including community gardens, farmers' markets, and public spaces where neighbors can gather

to share growing tips and recipes, and access healthy food for themselves and their families;

- local grocery stores and restaurants that offer employment as well as fresh, healthy food options;
- ethnic foods that represent the city's diverse population;
- healthy school meals for all of the city's schoolchildren;
- reduced food waste; and
- a smaller carbon footprint.

According to the most recent report, DC has 134 active school gardens, 73 active community gardens, 18 urban farms, 71 healthy corner stores, and 40 full-service grocery stores (Government of the District of Columbia Department of Energy and Environment, 2022). In addition, a USDA database of local food initiatives indicates that the city has 7 farmers' markets that accept SNAP and WIC benefits, 14 CSAs, and 3 active food hubs (United States Department of Agriculture Agricultural Marketing Service, 2022b). In 2020, an estimated 9.4 percent of the city's population was food insecure, which is below the national average of 10.2 percent and considerably lower than the 12.2 percent average for households in the country's principal cities (United States Department of Agriculture Economic Research Service, 2023); see also Feeding America, 2023).

Albuquerque, NM

The State of New Mexico is characterized by high mountains and hot, dry lowlands, with sections of all four North American deserts—the Great Basin, Mohave, Chihuahuan, and Sonoran—on New Mexican territory. The Rio Grande is the only perennial river and therefore an indispensable source of agricultural and municipal water for an otherwise dry region. The average annual precipitation is less than 20 inches (500 millimeters), so crop irrigation is essential. Moreover, most of the rainfall occurs during high-intensity thunderstorms between July and September, which means the water evaporates quickly.

Temperatures can easily reach 95°F (35°C) during the summer, with the hottest month being July. Winter temperatures generally remain above freezing, and an average 310 days a year are sunny, making year-round food production viable. However, the hot and arid climate means soil erosion is a major concern. While some regions of the United States require winter shelters for livestock, Albuquerque needs watering structures. On the other hand, solar power is an efficient source of energy due to the year-round sunshine. The main crops in the area surrounding Albuquerque are pecans, peppers, corn, wheat, peanuts, cotton, and hay.

Since 2016, Albuquerque has been consistently ranked in the top-ten urban agriculture cities in the United States, and in 2020 it was ranked fourth in terms of number of community gardens (Schwab, 2020). The same year, it was selected as one of the 17 participants in the USDA's new Urban Agriculture Committee scheme. Given the year-round growing conditions, it is renowned for its bountiful harvests of vegetables, fruits, herbs, and spices, especially those that are not grown easily elsewhere in the United States. Albuquerque's urban farms and gardens are spread throughout the city and the surrounding area, and many use organic and sustainable growing practices that avoid pesticides and other chemicals. Many of them also offer educational programs on the importance of sustainable agricultural practices, farm-to-table options, and the benefits of eating organic and locally grown foods. Other social engagement and community activities include sustainable lifestyle workshops, cooking courses, and classes on age-appropriate healthy-eating practices. The farms also make a meaningful contribution to Albuquerque's thriving food economy: local produce is sold to restaurants, stores, and farmers' markets, creating both on- and off-farm jobs. In addition, the city has a Food and Agriculture Action Plan (Grow New Mexico and Thornburg Foundation, 2019) to coordinate its many urban agriculture and local food initiatives, address existing barriers, and support further expansions.

According to the USDA, Albuquerque has five farmers' markets and three CSAs within a ten-mile radius, along with just one food hub (United States Department of Agriculture Agricultural Marketing Service, 2022b), although the activities of the city's Urban Farm Collective (https://urbanfarmcollective.org) suggest that these figures may not tell the whole story. Despite the robust local food economy, an estimated 12.7 percent of Albuquerque's population were food insecure in 2020, which is above the national average of 10.8 percent but close to the average food insecurity rate (12.2 percent) across all US cities (United States Department of Agriculture Economic Research Service, 2023).

Atlanta, GA

Atlanta is located in the midst of a rich agricultural area characterized by cash crops, forests, and fertile piedmonts. The Chattahoochee River supplies 70 percent of the metro area's drinking water. The annual precipitation is close to 70 inches (1,800 millimeters), mostly in the form of rainfall, which is relatively evenly distributed throughout the year. Snow is a rare occurrence, and roughly nine months of the year are frost free. Summer temperatures can easily reach 95°F (35°C), with the hottest month being July. The abundant moisture and long growing season make outdoor agricultural production possible across at least nine months of the year. However, pest and fungus management is a challenge due to the hot and humid summers, regardless of whether crops are cultivated indoors or outdoors. The main crops in the area surrounding Atlanta are pecans, peanuts, tobacco, blueberries, and peaches.

The city has long been recognized as an urban agriculture hub, so it was no surprise when the USDA selected it as the location for an Urban Agriculture Committee in 2020. Indeed, it is rated the second-best city for urban agriculture in the United States, after New York (Bernardo, 2023). It also ranks second in terms of number of community gardens (with 120) and first in terms of local and regional garden clubs. Finally, it has the largest urban food forest in the United States, with over seven acres of fruit trees in one of the city's lowest-income neighborhoods.

According to the USDA, Atlanta has 33 farmers' markets (11 of which accept SNAP, WIC, or other food-assistance benefits) and 3 CSAs (United States Department of Agriculture Agricultural Marketing Service, 2022b). However, as with Albuquerque, these official figures likely underestimate the city's commitment to urban agriculture. A more accurate picture is probably presented by AgLanta (www.aglanta.org), a web portal maintained by the Department of City Planning and the One Atlanta Office, which shares information about collective urban agriculture projects with the goal of ensuring that a minimum of 85 percent of the city's residents live within half a mile of affordable fresh food. Some of these projects are consumer oriented while others are producer oriented. For example, the main aim of AgLanta Grown is to help producers build trust in their locally grown fruits, vegetables, and herbs in order to provide a boost to the local food economy and create more living-wage jobs in the farm sector. However, a welcome benefit is that the program also increases consumer access to locally grown, nutritious produce.

Another AgLanta project, Grows-A-Lot, is a capacity-building program that encourages food entrepreneurs from the private and nonprofit sectors to apply for five-year, renewable licenses to operate urban farms or gardens on vacant, city-owned lots. Other capacity-building programs offered by AgLanta's training academy enable urban framers to improve their farming skills, bookkeeping, or food-processing knowledge. Meanwhile, outreach efforts provide residents with information about local food options and available lots in their neighborhoods, and encourage them to buy locally to support urban farmers or become members of urban garden schemes themselves.

Similar to the Sustainable DC plan, many of AgLanta's projects are also characterized by a commitment to reduce food waste. For example, this is one of the principal goals of AgLanta Food Matters, which redistributes fresh, surplus food to the city's food pantries and shelters, and composts produce that is no longer edible. Atlanta's food-insecurity rate stood at 11.3 percent of the population in 2020, which is above the national average of 10.8 percent but below the average of 12.2 percent for principal cities (United States Department of Agriculture Economic Research Service, 2023).

Chicago, IL

Lake Michigan is the main source of both municipal and industrial water for the whole of the Chicago metropolitan area. The surface water is suitable for almost all uses, but it is very hard because of the region's limestone and dolomite geology, so it requires some treatment to make it suitable for agricultural purposes. The main crops in the area around Chicago are soybeans and corn, but some fruit is also grown near the shore of Lake Michigan, including apples and grapes. Because Chicago is located within a historic glacial system, the area's soils are generally low in natural organic matter. The average annual rainfall is less than 40 inches (1,000 millimeters), although the snowfall is close to 95 inches (2,500 millimeters). Chicago has a relatively short growing season of roughly six months, with the exception of some lakefront areas, which have a unique microclimate.

Despite these unfavorable growing conditions, the city has had an active urban agriculture movement for more than 20 years, which explains why the USDA selected it as the location for an Urban Agriculture Committee. In 2020, it was ranked third in the country in terms of number of community gardens, and it has consistently ranked in the top five for green roof coverage. Indeed, it has over 5 million square feet of green roofs, some of which are used for food production. In addition, it is twelfth on the list of most sustainable US cities (Maive, 2022).

According to the USDA, Chicago has 64 farmers' markets (6 of which accept SNAP or WIC benefits), 3 CSAs, and 5 food hubs (United States Department of Agriculture Agricultural Marketing Service, 2022b). Once again, though, these figures likely underestimate the city's urban agriculture activities. Building on its rich history of food processing, food and beverages continue to play a large role in the city's economy. Chicago's urban food production activities range from small community gardens to high-tech hydroponic farms and large, commercial roof farms. In 2011, the City Council amended the city's zoning ordinance to formalize urban farms and community gardens as approved land-use options. This spawned further land-use initiatives, such as the Green and Healthy Neighborhoods project, as well as city-wide policies, including Recipe for Healthy Places, which recommended the systematic development of public food production spaces throughout the city. Another city-wide program is Large Lots, a land-use stabilization initiative that enables property owners and nonprofit groups to purchase city-owned plots in certain neighborhoods for just one dollar, on condition that they turn the plots into growing spaces or use them for beautification. To date, over 1,000 plots have been sold as part of this scheme. Meanwhile, the Department of Planning and Development has collaborated with partners such as the nonprofit land trust NeighborSpace to develop community gardens and urban farms in many of the city's neighborhoods.

Another notable initiative is the Urban Growers Collective (www.urbangrowerscollective.org), a black- and women-led nonprofit farm that aims to challenge the inequities and structural racism of the conventional food system (Ruppenthal, 2018). Its stated mission is to cultivate nourishing environments that support health, economic development, healing, and creativity through urban agriculture. The group offers capacity-building and training programs for farmers, and mitigates food insecurity by increasing access to affordable, culturally affirming, and nutritionally rich food. It cultivates eight urban farms on eleven acres of land, predominantly in the south side of the city. At 10.9 percent, Chicago's food insecurity rate was close to the national average in 2020, and below the average for principal cities (United States Department of Agriculture Economic Research Service, 2023).

Brooklyn, NY

New York City has been the top-ranked city for urban agriculture in the United States for more than ten years. Its average annual rainfall is less than 50 inches (1,300 millimeters), which is fairly evenly distributed throughout the year. Snowfall is moderate, too, despite the low winter temperatures. An average of 220 days are frost free each year, and several perennial rivers, lakes, and streams provide more than enough fresh water for drinking and irrigation purposes. New York's sandy soils drain easily and offer good growing conditions for a wide range of high-value vegetable crops and fruits, especially apples. The western part of New York State is also known for its high-quality wines. However, the region's high population density has resulted in significant soil contamination. Consequently, conservation practices are often essential to minimize erosion and soil degradation.

New York City has a total of over 750 community gardens, more than any other city in the country, despite its relatively short growing season of roughly seven months. It is rated America's best city for urban gardening (Bernardo, 2023) and the world's best city for urban agriculture (Laddha, 2023). Given its diverse population, there is demand for almost every imaginable type of produce.

The city's urban agriculture initiatives are supported by several agencies, including the Department of City Planning, whose stated mission is to make New York a better place to live; NYC Parks, which provides advice and material support to more than 550 GreenThumb community gardens across the five boroughs; and the Department of Small Business Services, which supports startups and job-creation. According to these agencies, urban agriculture provides multiple benefits to New Yorkers, including better access to healthy food, stronger community networks, improved environmental conditions, jobs, and educational opportunities. The city boasts numerous commercial farms, rooftop facilities, and even hydroponic and aquaponic farms. Partly as a result of these projects, it is ranked third in the country in terms of urban sustainability.

There has been especially strong interest in urban agriculture in the borough of Brooklyn, where several of the city's largest projects are based. This was one reason why the USDA chose it as the location for one of its 17 Urban Agriculture Committees. According to the USDA, Brooklyn is home to 117 farmers' markets (ten of which accept SNAP, WIC, or other food-assistance benefits), seven CSAs and three food hubs (United States Department of Agriculture Agricultural Marketing Service, 2022b). Nevertheless,

15.5 percent of the borough's households are food insecure, which is the highest rate among the six cities selected for this book (United States Department of Agriculture Economic Research Service, 2023).

Oakland, CA

The subtropical Oakland region is characterized by sloping valleys, rolling terraces, and low mountains that are rich in fruits and specialty crops. Indeed, it is one of the most productive agricultural regions in the United States and home to a wide variety of enterprises that produce everything from wine and table grapes to nuts, olives, greens, rice, citrus fruits, and avocados. Its warm summers and cool, wet winters are reminiscent of the Mediterranean climate. Evapotranspiration is high during the summer months, and water sources can be affected by carbonates and salts. As a result, crops generally have to be carefully managed. The average annual precipitation is less than 30 inches (700 millimeters), and temperatures are usually in the range of 45°F to 80°F (7°C to 27°C), although summer highs can reach 100°F (38°C). As winter temperatures rarely dip below freezing, the growing season is almost year-round (about 320 days, on average).

San Francisco is considered the most sustainable city in the country, one of the top-ten cities for urban agriculture, and number seven in terms of community gardens per 100 of the population, whereas Oakland does not feature anywhere near as prominently on these national rankings and does not show up at all on any international rankings (Statista Data Service, 2022; Maive, 2022). Yet, the USDA selected the latter rather than the former as the location for one of its 17 Urban Agriculture Committees. This decision may be explained by the fact that the region has long been associated with the alternative food movement and, by extension, urban agriculture. Indeed, Oakland's urban agriculture community dates back almost 20 years, and its initiatives have been supported by a range of public policies and regulations, including the Energy and Climate Action Plan and the Oakland General Plan's Open Space and Conservation provisions. Both of these plans were developed in consultation with residents, urban farmers, and community organizations. The city's urban agriculture regulations, which were adopted in 2014, include zoning for crop cultivation as well as new definitions of community gardens and agricultural land use based on production intensity. Both bee keeping and animal husbandry, such as raising chickens and small grazing animals, are also permitted under these regulations.

Over 20 plant species native to the Bay Area are grown on Oakland's impressive green roofs, several of which supply produce to local eateries. Meanwhile, other urban agriculture projects have made it their mission not only to improve food security but also to increase food justice. For example, the Planting Justice nursery cultivates more than 1,500 different species of fruits and vegetables in a low-income, predominantly black and Latino neighborhood. However, the plot once belonged to the indigenous Ohlone people, so Planting Justice is now working with a local trust to return the land to its original owners. Once this is done, Planting Justice intends to lease the plot and continue to operate in much the same way as it does now, providing jobs and access to locally grown produce at affordable prices to neighborhoods in need of both.

According to the USDA, Oakland has 30 farmers' markets (ten of which accept SNAP, WIC, or other food-assistance benefits), five CSAs, and three food hubs (United States Department of Agriculture Agricultural Marketing Service, 2022b). Its food insecurity rate is a relatively low 9.1 percent of the population, which is well below the national average and the lowest among our six cities (United States Department of Agriculture Economic Research Service, 2023).

Summary

As this brief overview of urban agriculture initiatives in US cities illustrates, the ease with which food can be grown is not necessarily a predictor of the level of urban agriculture activity. For example, Brooklyn and Chicago are both highly active and experienced at adapting to their relatively short growing seasons. They also have the two largest consumer markets in our sample, which is obviously advantageous, especially for commercial operations.

Meanwhile, Albuquerque and Oakland stand out in terms of their advantageous, year-round growing seasons. Both cities also have distinctive food cultures. For instance, Albuquerque, with its predominantly Hispanic neighborhoods and relatively high Native American population, prides itself on its long history of traditional agricultural practices. There is a strong

TABLE 4.1 Urban food production and distribution in six US cities

City	Albu-querque	Atlanta	Brooklyn	Chicago	Washin-gton, DC	Oak-land
Farmers' markets per 1,000 residents	0.1	0.7	0.47	0.25	0.46	0.65
CSAs per 1,000 residents	0.06	0.06	0.03	0.02	0.21	0.12
Community gardens per 1,000 residents	1.9	6.1	1.4	2.35	0.94	12.8
Farms in the city	22	50	16	68	18	15
Green roofs (square feet)	N/A	N/A	1 million	5.56 million	5.05 million	N/A

Sources: United States Department of Agriculture Agricultural Marketing Service (2022b); United States Department of Agriculture Economic Research Service (2023); see also Feeding America (2023)

Hispanic presence in Oakland, too, but also a significant Asian population. As the interviews in Chapter 3 indicate, these groups' food cultures shape the demand for locally grown produce. At the same time, the range of food-insecurity rates in the six selected cities cannot be fully explained by their growing conditions, their urban agriculture activities, or even commonly cited social determinants. This speaks to the complexities of food and food systems that make it difficult to establish a direct link between urban food systems and food security.

All six of our cities have proactive municipalities that have supported urban agriculture through forward-thinking zoning regulations, grants, and capacity-building initiatives at both the commercial and the individual household level. Unfortunately, up to now, it has been difficult to gather precise data on the success or failure of the programs, or even on the number and types of urban agriculture operations they seek to target. This also accounts for some of the data gaps in Table 4.1. However, the USDA's newly created Urban Agriculture Committees should go some way to rectifying this problem by providing detailed information on both subsistence and commercial urban agriculture enterprises. As the next chapter will demonstrate, these enterprises are committed to improving both food security and sustainability.

References

Ackerman, K., Conrad, M., Culligan, P., Plunz, R., Sutto, M.-P. and Whittinghill, L. (2014). Sustainable food systems for future cities. *Economic and Social Review*, 45 (2): 189–206.

American Community Gardening Association. (2022). About us. https://www.comm unitygarden.org/about.

Balagtas, J. and Cooper, J. (2021). *The Impact of Coronavirus COVID-19 on US Meat and Livestock Markets*. Washington, DC: United States Department of Agriculture Office of the Chief Economist. https://www.usda.gov/sites/default/files/documents/covid-impact-livestock-markets.pdf.

Barham, E. (1997). Social movements for sustainable agriculture in France: a Polanyian perspective. *Inchiesta*, 27: 84–91.

Barham, J. and Diamond, A. (2012). *Moving Food along the Value Chain: Innovations in Regional Food Distribution*. Washington, DC: United States Department of Agriculture Agricultural Marketing Service.

Barham, J., Tropp, D., Enterline, K., Farbman, J., Fisk, J. and Kiraly, S. (2012). *Regional Food Hub Resource Guide*. Washington, DC: United States Department of Agriculture Agricultural Marketing Service. https://www.ams.usda.gov/sites/default/files/media/Regional%20Food%20Hub%20Resource%20Guide.pdf.

Bernardo, R. (2023). 2023's best cities for urban gardening. *Lawnstarter*, 3 April. https://www.lawnstarter.com/blog/studies/best-cities-urban-gardening/.

Birch, D., Memery, J. and Kanakaratne, M. (2018). The mindful consumer: balancing egoistic and altruistic motivations to purchase local food. *Journal of Retailing and Consumer Services*, 1(40): 221–228.

Cooley, J. and Lass, D. (1998). Consumer benefits from community supported agriculture membership. *Review of Agricultural Economics*, 20: 227–237.

DC Food Policy Council. (2019). *Food System Assessment 2018: The District's Efforts to Support a More Equitable, Healthy, and Sustainable Food System.* https://dcfoodpoli cycouncilorg.files.wordpress.com/2019/06/2018-food-system-assessment-final-6.13.pdf.

Dimiero, E. and Mayfield, C. (2014). *A Guide for Scaling up Food Hubs.* https://nesfp. org/sites/default/files/resources/worldpeas_scalingupguide.pdf.

Dooley, E. (2022). *People Turned to Gardening for Stress Relief, Food Access during Pandemic: A Survey.* https://www.ucdavis.edu/food/news/survey-people-turned-garde ning-stress-relief-food-access-during-pandemic.

Dumont, A., Davis, D., Wascalus, J., Wilson, T., Barham, J. and Tropp, D. (eds.). (2017). *Harvesting the Power of Regional Food System Investments to Transform Communities.* Washington, DC: Federal Reserve Bank of St. Louis.

Enthoven, L. and Van den Broeck, G. (2021). Local food systems: reviewing two decades of research. *Agricultural Systems*, 193: 103226. https://doi.org/10.1016/j.agsy. 2021.103226.

Environmental Protection Agency. (2020). Heat island cooling strategies. https://www. epa.gov/heatislands/heat-island-cooling-strategies.

Feeding America. (2023). Hunger in America. https://www.feedingamerica.org/hunger-in-america.

Figueroa, M. (2015). Food sovereignty in everyday life: toward a people-centered approach to food systems. *Globalizations*, 15(4): 1–15.

Florida, R. (2005). *Cities and the Creative Class.* New York: Routledge.

Fonte, M. (2008). Knowledge, food and place: a way of producing, a way of knowing. *Sociologia Ruralis*, 48: 200–222. doi:10.1111/j.1467-9523.2008.00462.x.

Government of the District of Columbia Department of Energy and Environment. (2022). *Sustainable DC Plan 2.0.* https://sustainable.dc.gov/sdc2.

Gowdy-Wygant, C. (2013). *Cultivating Victory: The Women's Land Army and the Victory Garden Movement.* Pittsburgh: University of Pittsburgh Press.

Grow New Mexico and Thornburg Foundation. (2019). *Albuquerque Food & Agri- culture Action Plan.* https://www.cabq.gov/sustainability/documents/albuquerque-food-and-agriculture-action-plan.pdf.

Hess, D.J. (2009). *Localist Movements in a Global Economy: Sustainability, Justice, and Urban Development in the United States.* Cambridge, MA: MIT Press.

Hossein, C.S. (2019). A black epistemology for the social and solidarity economy: the black social economy. *Review of Black Political Economy*, 46(3): 209–229. https:// doi.org/10.1177/0034644619865266.

Humaida, N., Saputra, M., Sutomo, H. and Hadiyan, Y. (2023). Urban gardening for mitigating heat island effect. *IOP Conference Series: Earth and Environmental Science*, 1133. https://iopscience.iop.org/article/10.1088/1755-1315/1133/1/012048.

Kane, D.J. and Lohr, L. (1997). *Maximizing Shareholder Retention in Southeastern CSAs.* Athens, GA: University of Georgia.

Ladan, T., Ibrahim, M., Ali, S. and Saputra, A. (2022). A geographical review of urban farming and urban heat island in developing countries. *IOP Conference Series: Earth and Environmental Science*, 986. https://iopscience.iop.org/article/10. 1088/1755-1315/986/1/012071.

Laddha, D. (2023). Top ten cities for urban ag. https://www.agritecture.com/blog/2021/ 2/23/top-10-cities-for-urban-ag.

LaManda, J. (2014). *Start a Community Food Garden: The Essential Handbook.* Portland, OR: Timber Press.

Lawson, L. (2005). *City Bountiful: A Century of Community Gardening in America.* Los Angeles: University of California Press.

Lees, N., Nuthall, P. and Wilson, M. (2020). Relationship quality and supplier performance in food supply chains. *International Food and Agribusiness Management Review*, 23(3): 425–445. doi:10.22434/IFAMR2019.0178.

Li, D., Bou-Zeid, E. and Oppenheimer, M. (2014). The effectiveness of cool and green roofs as urban heat island mitigation strategies. *Environmental Research Letters*, 9 (5). https://iopscience.iop.org/article/10.1088/1748-9326/9/5/055002/meta.

Litt, J., Soobader, M., Turbin, M., Hale, J., Buchenau, M. and Marshall, J. (2011). The influence of social involvement, neighborhood aesthetics, and community garden participation on fruit and vegetable consumption. *American Journal of Public Health*, 101(8): 1466–1473.

Low, S., Adalja, A., Beaulieu, E., Key, N., Martinez, S., Melton, A., Perez, A., Ralston, K., Stewart, H., Suttles, S., Vogel, S. and Jablonski, B. (2015). *Trends in US Local and Regional Food Systems*. Washington, DC: United States Department of Agriculture Economic Research Service.

Maive, S. (2022). 2022's most sustainable cities. *Lawnstarter*, 21 April. https://www.lawnstarter.com/blog/studies/most-sustainable-cities/.

Marchesi, K. and McLaughlin, P. (2022). *The Impact of COVID-19 Pandemic on Food-Away-from-Home Spending*. Working Paper No. AP-100. Washington, DC: United States Department of Agriculture Economic Research Service.

McCormack, L., Laska, M., Larson, N. and Story, M. (2010). Review of the nutritional implications of farmers' markets and community gardens: a call for evaluation and research efforts. *Journal of the American Dietetic Association*, 110(3): 399–408.

Milburn, L. and Brooke Adams, V. (2010). Sowing the seeds of success: cultivating a future for community gardens. *Landscape Journal*, 29(1): 71–89.

National Farm to School Network. (2017). *Strategic Plan 2017–19*. https://www.farmtoschool.org/resources-main/national-farm-to-school-network-2017-2019-strategic-plan.

National Farm to School Network. (2022). *Annual Report*. https://www.youtube.com/watch?v=QgmAwLyfgFE.

NC State Extension. (2022). *Community Supported Agriculture (CSA) Resource Guide for Farmers*. https://growingsmallfarms.ces.ncsu.edu/growingsmallfarms-csaguide/.

O'Hara, S. (1997). Toward a sustaining production theory. *Ecological Economics*, 20 (2): 141–154.

O'Hara, S. (2016). Production in context: the concept of sustaining production. In: Farley, J. and Malghan, D. (eds.), *Beyond Uneconomic Growth*, Vol. 2: *A Festschrift in Honour of Herman Daly*. Burlington: University of Vermont, pp. 75–106.

O'Hara, S. (2017). The urban food hubs solution: building capacity in urban communities. *Metropolitan Universities Journal*, 28(1): 69.

O'Hara, S. (2018). *The Five Pillars of Economic Development: A Study of a Sustainable Future for Wards 7 and 8 in Washington DC*. https://docs.udc.edu/causes/Five-Pillars-DC-Final-05-2018.pdf.

O'Hara, S. and Hare, W. (2017). *Urban Food Production: An Exploration of Production Methods and Target Markets in Washington DC*. Washington, DC: College of Agriculture, Urban Sustainability and Environmental Sciences, University of the District of Columbia.

O'Hara, S. and Ivanic, M. (2022). Food security and lifestyle vulnerabilities as systemic influencers of COVID-19 survivability. *Medical Research Archives*, 10(8). https://doi.org/10.18103/mra.v10i8.2989.

O'Hara, S., Jones, D. and Trobman, H. (2017). Building an urban food system through the UDC urban food hubs. In: Hampton-Garland, P., Burtin, A. and Flemming, J.

(eds.), *Changing Urban Landscapes through Higher Education.* Hershey, PA: IGI Global, pp. 144–169.

O'Hara, S. and Stagl, S. (2001). Global food production and some local alternatives: a socio-ecological economic perspective. *Population and Environment*, 22(6): 533–554.

O'Hara, S. and Stuiver, M. (2022). Restorative economics: food hubs as catalysts of a new urban economy. In: Stuiver, M. (ed.), *Symbiotic Cities.* Wageningen: Wageningen University & Research Academic Press, pp. 187–204.

O'Hara, S. and Toussaint, E. (2020). Food access in crisis: food security and COVID-19. *Ecological Economics*, 180(2021): 106859.

Ostrom, M.R. (1997). Toward a community supported agriculture: a case study of resistance and change in the modern food system. Ph.D. thesis, University of Wisconsin–Madison.

Richards, S. and Vassalos, M. (2021). COVID-19 and consumer demand forlocal meat products in South Carolina. *Journal of Agriculture, Food Systems, and Community Development*, 10(3): 31–36. https://doi.org/10.5304/jafscd.2021.103.004.

Royte, E. (2015). Urban agriculture is booming but what does it really mean? The benefits of city-based agriculture go far beyond nutrition. *ENSIA Magazine*, 27 April.

Ruppenthal, A. (2018). Urban farming program marks 10,000 customers served. *WttW News*, 22 August. https://news.wttw.com/2018/08/22/urban-farming-program-marks-10000-customers-served.

Rutgers University Office of Public Outreach and Communication. (2020). The importance of gardening during the COVID-19 pandemic. https://sebsnjaesnews.rutgers.edu/2020/04/the-importance-of-gardening-during-the-covid-19-pandemic/.

San Fratello, D., Campbell, B.L., Secor, W.G. and Campbell, J.H. (2022). Impact of the COVID-19 pandemic on gardening in the United States: postpandemic expectations. *HortTechnology*, 32(1): 32–38. https://doi.org/10.21273/HORTTECH04911-21.

Schechinger, A. (2021). Under Trump, farm subsidies soared and the rich got richer. https://www.ewg.org/research/updated-ewg-farm-subsidy-database-shows-largest-producers-reap-billions-despite-climate.

Schoen, V., Blythe, C., Caputo, S., Fox-Kämper, R., Specht, K., Fargue-Lelièvre, A., Cohen, N., Poniży, L. and Fedeńczak, K. (2021). "We Have been part of the response": the effects of COVID-19 on community and allotment gardens in the Global North. *Frontiers in Sustainable Food Systems*, 5. https://doi.org/10.3389/fsufs.2021.732641.

Schwab, N. (2020). The top 10 cities for urban farming. https://www.redfin.com/blog/best-cities-for-urban-farming/.

Shariatmadary, H., O'Hara, S., Graham, R. and Stuiver, M. (2023). Are food hubs sustainable? An analysis of social and environmental objectives of US food hubs. *Sustainability*, 15(3): 2308. https://doi.org/10.3390/su15032308.

Shuman, M. (2015). *The Local Economy Solution: How Innovative, Self-financing "Pollinator" Enterprises Can Grow Jobs and Prosperity.* White River Junction, VT: Chelsea Green Publishing.

Silver, J.S. (2019). The toll of American exceptionalism on American justice. *Intercultural Human Rights Law Review*, 14: 201–208.

Stagl, S. and O'Hara, S. (2002). Motivating factors and barriers to sustainable consumer behaviour. *International Journal of Agricultural Resources, Governance and Ecology*, 2(1): 75–88.

Statista Data Service. (2022). Cities with the largest number of community gardens per 1,000 residents in the United States. https://www.statista.com/statistics/1034254/number-of-community-gardens-per-10-000-residents-by-city-in-the-us/.

Stuiver, M. and O'Hara, S. (2022). Envisioning the future symbiotic city: narratives of Washington DC and the Netherlands. In: Stuiver, M. (ed.), *Symbiotic Cities*. Wageningen: Wageningen University & Research Academic Press, pp. 65–88.

Taylor, D. (2007). Growing green roofs, city by city. *Environmental Health Perspectives*, 115(6): A306–A311. doi:10.1289/ehp.115-a306.

Toussaint, E. (2018). The new gospel of wealth: on social impact bonds and the privatization of public good. *Houston Law Review*, 56: 153.

United States Congress. (2008). Food, Conservation, and Energy Act, H.R. 2419. http s://www.congress.gov/bill/110th-congress/house-bill/2419#:~:text=The%20House% 20and%20Senate%20passed,the%20trade%20title)%20as%20H.R.

United States Department of Agriculture. (2009). Know Your Farmer, Know Your Food. https://www.usda.gov/media/blog/2011/07/08/know-your-farmer-know-facts.

United States Department of Agriculture. (2016). *Urban Agriculture Toolkit*. Washington, DC: United States Department of Agriculture.

United States Department of Agriculture. (2022). USDA announces framework for shoring up the food supply chain and transforming the food system to be fairer, more competitive, more resilient. https://www.usda.gov/media/press-releases/2022/ 06/01/usda-announces-framework-shoring-food-supply-chain-and-transforming.

United States Department of Agriculture Agricultural Marketing Service. (2020a). Local Agriculture Markets Program (LAMP). https://www.ams.usda.gov/services/ grants/lamp.

United States Department of Agriculture Agricultural Marketing Service. (2020b). Local Food Compass. https://www.ams.usda.gov/local-food-sector/compass-map.

United States Department of Agriculture Agricultural Marketing Service. (2022a). *Farmers Market Promotion Program*. https://www.ams.usda.gov/services/grants/ fmpp. United States Department of Agriculture Agricultural Marketing Service. (2022b). Local Food Directories. https://www.ams.usda.gov/services/local-regional/ food-directories.

United States Department of Agriculture Economic Research Service. (2023). *Food Security in the US: Key Statistics and Graphics*. https://www.ers.usda.gov/topics/ food-nutrition-assistance/food-security-in-the-u-s/key-statistics-graphics/.

United States Department of Agriculture Food and Nutrition Service. (2022). *Farm to School Census and Comprehensive Review*. Washington, DC: United States Department of Agriculture Food and Nutrition Service.

United States Department of Agriculture National Agricultural Library. (2022). Agricultural subsidies. https://www.nal.usda.gov/economics-business-and-trade/agricultura l-subsidies.

United States Department of Agriculture National Agricultural Statistics Service. (2022). USDA releases local food marketing practices data. https://www.nass.usda. gov/Newsroom/2022/04-28-2022.php.

United States Department of Agriculture National Institute of Food and Agriculture. (n.d.). *Cooperatve Extension System*. https://www.nifa.usda.gov/about-nifa/how-we-work/extension/cooperative-extension-system.

Woods, T., Ernst, M. and Tropp, D. (2017). *Community Supported Agriculture: New Models for Changing Markets*. Washington, DC: United States Department of Agriculture Agricultural Marketing Service.

5

FINDING THE FRIENDS OF FOOD SECURITY

The diverse faces of new urban and regional food system innovators in US cities

This chapter introduces the food system innovators who are active in urban and peri-urban America. In addition to providing detailed accounts of their urban agriculture and food systems innovation activities, they challenge our assumptions about what constitutes a "local," "regional," "costly," "viable," or "valuable" food system. As the past few years have demonstrated, food systems innovators operate in challenging environments where mainstream assumptions about economic viability (or the lack thereof) clash with notions of environmental sustainability and social justice. While their stories are as diverse as the people themselves, they point to some common—and, crucially, viable—solutions. Each of the six food system innovators introduced here has a unique story to tell about the organization they created, but each of them also represents different aspects of the innovations taking place in the six cities discussed in this books and in cities across the United States and elsewhere.

The following stories are largely based on interviews conducted between January and May 2023, although some also contain information obtained during earlier conversations.

Farming in the southwest: the story of Chispas Farm

Chispas Farm is located in the South Valley of the Rio Grande. We are on unseated Tiqua territory, only about ten minutes from downtown Albuquerque. I am really honored to be cultivating this land, which was named after its former owner, Mr. John Chispas. We are a very diverse community, with people from all kinds of ethnic backgrounds, including various indigenous communities. New Mexico is known as a minority majority state. A lot of people have been here for many generations. My neighbor across the street, for example, was born in the house he lives in. So, I am very fortunate to be

DOI: 10.4324/9781003322399-5

surrounded by wonderful people who are very generous in sharing their knowledge of the area and the land with me. I haven't been here anywhere nearly that long. This is my 12th growing season on this land. I'm 33 and most of the people on my team are also in their 20s or 30s, although we have a couple of people in their 50s, too. That's pretty young compared to many of the other farmers in the state, although I think people working in this space have gradually become younger over the years. Most of my crew comes from Albuquerque and definitely from New Mexico, and we give priority to local people if possible.

We have a team of eight. Some of them are full time, at four and a half days a week, and some part time, at two or three days a week, plus we have close to 200 volunteers. Some come regularly, and we really couldn't do all we do without them, and some come for one or two specific projects. We also have school groups visit us and help with a project. So, there are a lot of volunteers coming through here. The farm is four acres large, or some would say four acres small. We are a soil-based, regenerative-striving, small-scale farm that grows over 120 varieties of heirloom fruits and vegetables in addition to keeping a herd of milk goats, a small flock of meat sheep, meat rabbits, ducks and geese, and a flock of about 100 hens. What I mean by "regenerative striving" is that we constantly strive to improve our production methods to become more and more regenerative. We were organic certified for some time, but I opted not to go for organic recertification since New Mexico no longer offers in-state organic certification and a lot of what we do as a farm is very relationship based. So, people can come here and see how we do things. It's all very transparent. They see the regenerative production methods we use, and that we use our animal waste as fertilizer. We use predominantly no-till methods to continuously improve the health of our soils, and to close as many loops in our production process as we can. So, I didn't think we needed formal organic certification.

Economically, it's actually been very cool to see the impact of our regenerative practices. We've been able to transition from purchasing a number of resources, like compost and fertilizer and so forth, to generating the nutrients we need for our soil right here on our farm. This means that we have been able to invest more resources to increase the wages of our crew and create more sustainable workplaces. Some of our highest-cost items have been infrastructure investments. When I took over the farm, a lot of things needed attention. We needed storage, shade structures, and a number of other facilities that make our work easier. Of course, labor is costly, but I realized that we really had to invest more in labor. During the first six years or so, I really exploited myself and a few others on my team, and I don't ever want to do that again. We really need to create sustainable workplaces, and it's been really rewarding to see how our regenerative farming practices have allowed us to shift more resources to create more restorative workplaces as well. It's interesting how these two things go hand-in-hand. Now our primary costs are labor, as it should be. Of course, training is always an issue as well. I actually love to train people like me who had no agricultural background when they decided to go into farming. That's not an easy journey, but it's very rewarding.

Our market is almost built in. We are so close to downtown Albuquerque and we sell at the local farmers' market, which is a pretty large one. We also have a CSA of 100 members and an on-farm farm stand where people just stop and buy food directly from us. We also accept food stamps at the farm stand, and our CSA members come mostly from middle to low socio-economic backgrounds. That's intentional. I come from that kind of background myself and I didn't go into farming to grow top-quality food for people who can already afford everything anyway. Given our climate, we can grow almost year-round and we can produce a full diet, including eggs, some meat, and of course all kinds of greens, tomatoes, peppers, eggplant, you name it. We also grow herbs, including some for teas, and a few medicinal plants. More recently we've also started to grow some grains, like blue corn, for example, and we've been exploring regionally appropriate wheat varieties. One of our part-time crew members is also a baker, and he's used some of the wheat we grow to make the best bread I've ever tasted. So, this year, we are growing a bit more wheat. We also sell to some local restaurants, and host a ton of events where people use our food. But I've decided that I'm only selling to restaurants where I can afford to eat. If their prices are too high for me to eat there regularly, then they can't have my food. We occasionally sell to a grocery store in the region or to a wholesaler, for example when we have an over-abundance of produce. Invariably, we hit a period during the growing season when we harvest over 1,000 pounds of tomatoes a week. We will then contract with a wholesaler in the region or a local processor to make sure our food doesn't go to waste. But they are not our focus. We focus mainly on the end consumer.

During COVID, I learned how lucky we are that we have a number of different outlets for our produce. That diversity of markets helped us a lot, and we didn't really slow down during that time. We also started to sell to some of the area food pantries who saw an enormous increase in the need for food. I really like the fact that my beautiful food goes to families who really need it and who can also benefit from the quality of the food. Healthy food makes us healthy. On the whole, I consider myself a regional specialist. We grow locally and we sell locally. My whole farm is built on local relationships. I know the people who live here and who know the history of this land. I love that about this work. Last year, we grossed just over $90,000, which is pretty good. The first year it was less than $40,000, so we've doubled what we make on the same amount of land, largely because we've diversified our operation and become more regenerative in our farming practices. So, I'm feeling pretty good about where we are and I don't intend to expand further. But I would like to create an even more egalitarian workplace for the people I work with and also for myself. The way we farm is based on reciprocity. What we receive, we must also return. We cannot farm successfully over the long run based on an extractive mindset. That's not only true for the land, but also for those of us who farm and those who farm with us. We must find more socially sustainable ways of farming where we restore our own health and creativity and allow ourselves to live as whole persons. I have seen too many people who are deeply committed to this work of restorative farming burn themselves out and lose who they are as whole people. I am committed to working on a model that changes this and includes not only the land but also the people who work the land in this idea of reciprocity.

This region is a wonderful place to explore these things. It is one of the longest-standing agrarian areas in America. It has been farmed continuously for longer than any other area in the country. I love hearing stories about this land from my neighbors, like who used to live here and what they grew. We stand on the shoulders of giants here and everything that we do now has consequences for the future. That's a powerful thing. So, I don't plan to expand my farm, but I want to get to a place where I can create an even more egalitarian workplace for my crew and myself, so that I can reinvest what we take and create a truly sustainable workplace with enriching relationships both on and off the farm.

One of the ways I'm exploring that might support this idea is the possibility of creating a network of socially sustainable farms. During COVID, we started to create a loose network of collaboration among eight farms. Some of us had worked together before and we knew that we had similar interests and that we might be able to complement each other. We used our network to significantly scale our CSAs as we faced such high demand for locally grown food. We also found out quite by accident that we already shared some of our crew members—some of the guys who work part time for me also work part time for one of the other farmers. So, we see a number of opportunities for further collaboration and for coordinating our efforts more intentionally. This might include some value-added cooperation in addition to the bakery. I also want to take a sabbatical and turn more responsibility over to my crew during my time away. I think it will be good for them and for me. This may not be how most people would think about expanding my operation, but I think these are exciting opportunities for expansion and growth in a qualitative way.

Planting Justice: more than urban agriculture in the Bay Area

Planting Justice grows more than food. Our mission is to empower people impacted by social inequities and incarceration by equipping them with the skills they need to create food sovereignty, economic justice, and healing for themselves and their communities. We translate these three goals of food sovereignty, economic justice, and healing into three core activities that we summarize in the tagline of Planting Justice: grow food, grow jobs, grow community.

The reason these three belong together for us is that we see the structural inequalities embedded in our current food system. For any effort to transform our food system to be effective, all three must be addressed. There is the lack of access to fresh, nutritious food in low-income communities and especially in communities of color; then there is the systemic exploitation of food system workers, especially the undocumented farm and kitchen workers who get low wages and no benefits; and third, there is our over-reliance on packaged, processed food that is killing our bodies and our environment. All three aspects are part and parcel of our current food system and all three contribute to illness rather than health. So, all three must be addressed to transform our food system.

We started to operate in the Bay Area 14 years ago to transform these three interrelated, destructive aspects of our food system one garden at a time. Over a 14-year period, we built over 600 edible gardens throughout the Bay Area and empowered hundreds of people to grow at least some of their own food through our community garden program. In addition, we started several urban farms and training centers in order to scale our work and create green jobs that pay a living wage while we build a local, sustainable food system. By creating living wages for our workers, we believe that we can reinvigorate our local economy and improve the health of our people and the planet at the same time. If we introduce people to healthy food and provide fair wages and benefits so they can make a decent living and actually buy healthy food for themselves and their families, then we begin to transform the entire food system as well as the lives of people who have always been mistreated by an economic system that intentionally exploits them and excludes them from any opportunity to succeed. The food system can then become the spark plug for creating a thriving local and regional economy even beyond food.

The economic engine of Planting Justice is our organic, permaculture plant nursery. This is the largest permaculture nursery in northern California and one of the largest in the US. Our nursery offers over 1,500 varieties of plants, including many rare and heirloom varieties. People from all over the country shop online at our nursery and we ship plants to the 48 continental states as sustainably as possible. That is important to us. We are fortunate that demand for some of our plants, and especially for some of our fruit trees, is always high. In fact, we could sell three or four times as much as we are currently able to produce.

We have a staff of 55 people who work across all of our programs, which currently include a 2-acre nursery, a 4-acre "Mother Farm" where we produce organic produce and propagation material, and our 3-acre aquaponics farm, which is currently under construction. A "pay-what-you-can" café, with a retail nursery, commercial kitchen, and community center called The Good Table is also currently under construction. We also run a youth education program, and a holistic reentry program for formerly incarcerated people.

All of our staff members get full health/dental/vision benefits for themselves and their families, and the average wage at Planting Justice is $25 an hour. This puts our staff in a position to make a living wage. Also, many of our staff members and trainees tell us that they start to eat healthier when they work here, and they feel better and more energetic. Whenever we hire, we make every effort to hire people from the community, including people who have come through our training program. We always have community members on our hiring committees to make sure their perspective is represented.

Our education and training programs are key to what we do. They take place at high schools, in prisons and juvenile detention facilities, on our 4-acre farm in El Sobrante, at our 2-acre nursery in East Oakland, and in partnership with community organizations across the Bay Area. All of our programs are hands-on and focus on skills development in a wide range of areas, including ecological design, nutrition education, multimedia arts, social justice literacy, and holistic wellness. Our trainees and workshop participants practice these skills by transforming un- and under-used community spaces into edible gardens that provide fresh and highly nutritious food to the neighborhoods where we work. Since our staff come from the communities we serve, they are able to develop important mentoring relationships with our trainees and workshop participants. Our training programs are always free to low-income participants. A great example of our approach is our Plant! Cook! Organize! curriculum, which we developed in collaboration with our community staff and our workshop participants. It will also be available online soon.

The key for us is to provide training and skills development that can provide the basis for a living-wage job. When people have been incarcerated, their self-worth is often at rock bottom. We try to give them their dignity back by building their skills and then calling on them to share their expertise with others. We need people who know how to propagate, transplant, craft, cultivate, harvest, package, maintain our websites, you name it. We need all kinds of skills, and our success speaks for itself. We have had only one person out of 75 who ended up returning to prison. That's a recidivism rate of 2 percent, compared to the 60 percent recidivism rate here in California. In other words, when we train people and give them a job where they earn a living wage and feel valued, they succeed, and stay at home with their families where they are needed most, instead of going back to prison. And wouldn't that be money so much better spent than the average $60,000 a year we pay for every person we keep in prison? And that doesn't even include the secondary costs that are created when a wage earner is incarcerated and his or her family must now figure out how to make a living and how to hold things together. The children of these families are at tremendous risk of ending up in prison themselves. It would make so much more sense to invest in healing people through dignified, living-wage jobs that also heal the land and our communities, so we can break these negative spirals and turn them into positive ones.

In 2017, we created a 4-acre edible food forest that now serves as the "Mother Farm" for our nursery collection. The forest has at least two plants of every plant variety and produces thousands of pounds of fruit for our community every year. All plants are planted close together and we keep our trees to 12 feet tall so we can reach the fruit from an 8-foot ladder. Between the shade from the trees, we plant perennial shrubs, groundcovers, and other flowering/edible understory plants to keep the weeds in check and bring in a huge diversity of pollinators and insects, to create ecological balance. We also planted a living fence along the edge of the orchard and installed barn-owl houses so the owls can help control the gopher population. We've dug a mile of water-harvesting swales just above each row of trees to catch and store all the rainwater that falls on the land, almost entirely eradicating storm-water run-off. This is how we use permaculture principles to run our orchards and farms; and, in the process, we seek to empower thousands of people in communities in the Bay Area and beyond to transform their own communities and become empowered producers rather than being dependent consumers.

The centerpiece of our operation is our perennial plant nursery in deep East Oakland. When we purchased the Rolling River Nursery in 2015, its former owners worked with us to ensure our community could build the skills to propagate and care for each plant in the collection. The nursery is located on a beautiful piece of land in Oakland's most economically depressed neighborhood and has an amazing collection of over 1,500 varieties of fruit trees and shrubs, including apples, apricots, avocados, blueberries, currants, elderberries, figs, feijoas, peaches, pears, plums, pomegranates, seaberry, quince, and many more. All plants are organically grown and certified, and they are for sale through our nursery. The nursery creates living-wage jobs, and we are now in the process of adding some value-added products like jams, pickles, pies, and so on for sale. This food-processing component fits well with some of our training programs and it will add revenue. We are already set up to ship our plants through our nursery, so adding value-added products made sense for us.

One of our newest projects is The Good Table café, which is a collaboration with the Good Table United Church of Christ. Through this collaboration, we purchased a historic Japanese nursery in El Sobrante to save it from being turned into a gas station. Now that the building has been completely renovated, we are starting to operate an incubator kitchen out of the space to create our new value-added products. Our new product line is run as a cooperative so that many small growers can contribute to it. The space also houses our new farm store. The Good Table operates as a "pay-what-you-can" café so that no one feels like they can't afford to eat here and enjoy the space, which also serves as a community gathering place and an arts venue.

We also operate six food hubs in North Oakland, West Oakland, East Oakland, downtown Oakland, at the South Lake Towers Garden, and at the Ashlands Apartment Garden. Recently, we have broken ground on an aquaponics incubator farm. This will be the culmination of a 12-year-long dream. The aquaponics farm site is in East Oakland, just 100 feet from our nursery, and the soil in that particular location is seriously contaminated since it was used for all kinds of industrial purposes. We figured that if we build a replicable and scalable model of sustainable food production under some of these harsh conditions here in East Oakland, with its polluted topsoil and hazardous environmental conditions, then it can be done anywhere. The aquaponics farm will demonstrate how to grow healthy food, and create living-wage jobs, using a fraction of the water needed for conventional food production. And most of the nutrients are built in too since the fish excrement serves as the fertilizer for the plants. Our incubator farm will be an anchor for other small aquaponics operations in the area, so we can train people to successfully own and operate an aquaponics farm on their own land. Our goal is to coordinate the produce production on these small farms so that everyone can gain efficiency by specializing, and collectively marketing and distributing what they produce. By empowering East Oakland residents to acquire their own small piece of land and run their own aquaponics farms, we plan to demonstrate that even an exploited neighborhood can gain food sovereignty, self-determination, and holistic wellness. This is what we must do in communities all over the country—heal the land and heal the people. Given the climate emergency that threatens food production in our area and all over the world, we consider this project a demonstration of what healthy food systems can look like even as growing conditions are becoming more challenging.

We have many additional plans and keep adapting them as our community members shape the direction of our work. But our three core principles are always the same: to achieve food sovereignty, create economic justice, and bring about healing.

From the soil to the roof: the success story of Gotham Greens

Gotham Greens started as a single rooftop greenhouse in Brooklyn, NY, and has grown to become one of the largest greenhouse lettuce producers in North America. We set out to innovate and differentiate the fresh produce supply chain by building and operating a decentralized network of hydroponic greenhouses across the United States. Gotham Greens produces and delivers fresh, longer-lasting, and delicious leafy salad greens, herbs, salad dressings, dips, and cooking sauces all year round.

When we started Gotham Greens, there were no commercial-scale urban hydroponic and vertical farms in the country. While traditional greenhouses have been used for centuries, sustainable greenhouses, such as hydroponic greenhouses and vertical farms, have only been in operation for a few decades. Yet they have been experiencing significant growth. Today, Gotham Greens operates 13 greenhouses across nine states: New York, Rhode Island, Maryland, Virginia, Illinois, Colorado, California, Texas, and Georgia. We're continuing to grow our brand footprint nationally through our regional network of greenhouses in cities across America in order to reach our goal of delivering the fresh produce Gotham Greens grows within a day's drive from our greenhouses to 90 percent of all consumers in the US.

For most parts of the US, it's difficult to get fresh, locally grown produce all year round since 98 percent of the lettuce grown in the country comes from California and Arizona. So, by the time it reaches other parts of the country, it loses its quality, taste, and nutritional value and has a much shorter shelf life. This can result in many consumers feeling disconnected from the food they eat and contributes to food waste, too. Indoor farming—and specifically greenhouse farming—provides a consistent and proven way of growing food closer to where people live year-round, regardless of the season and temperature outside. Since our company's founding in 2009, we have been committed to conserving vital resources through innovative and sustainable technology. We aspire to be a part of the agricultural industry's solution to the increasingly visible impacts of climate change.

Gotham Greens is also a Certified B Corporation™. B Corps meet the highest possible standards of social and environmental performance, public transparency, and legal accountability. By using hydroponic growing systems in renewable-electricity-powered greenhouses, Gotham Greens' farms use up to 95 percent less water and 97 percent less land compared to conventional open-field farming. In fact, our unique irrigation techniques use less than one gallon of water to grow a head of lettuce, compared with up to ten gallons used in conventional farming. Additionally, Gotham Greens produces around 30 times more lettuce per acre of land than conventional farming. Unlike vertical farming, which primarily relies on artificial lighting, at Gotham Greens we use direct sunlight and renewable electricity to power our greenhouse facilities. This is one way in which we continue to illustrate the best environmental and economic model of indoor farming.

Ultimately, our produce isn't the best because of how we grow it, it's the best because of who grows it. Our greenhouses are built upon the collective values, talents, and energy of our diverse team. While our technology has redefined urban agriculture, our dedicated farmers are the real secret to producing and delivering delicious fresh food, from seed to store. In addition to providing stable and enjoyable year-round jobs, we are dedicated to urban renewal and becoming permanent fixtures in the regions where we are located. Many neighborhoods where we have greenhouses have historically experienced higher than average rates of unemployment, resulting in poverty and long-term unemployment. Through partnerships with local workforce development organizations, Gotham Greens hires residents from surrounding neighborhoods. We support continuing education and foster a culture of upward mobility within the company; for example, previous entry-level employees are now plant managers and directors helping to "seed" and lead new greenhouse facilities.

By partnering with local schools, community leaders, and nonprofits, Gotham Greens also helps to put better food on the table through environmental, educational, and community initiatives. These programs are rooted in the communities surrounding Gotham Greens' facilities, but the impact extends beyond the borders of our neighborhoods. In 2022, for example, we gave back to our communities by donating more than 44,000 pounds of food to families in need and providing 27,000 seedling donations for community gardens and educational purposes. We're especially grateful to our local community partners, who help distribute, pack, and deliver goods to our deserving neighbors. We have forged meaningful relationships with and provided financial support for community and nonprofit partners across the country.

We want people to put more greens at the center of the table, and we remain committed to bringing consumers the best-tasting, most flavorful fresh foods on the market. We hope that consumers can sense our commitment to taste, quality, and sustainability in every bite. Every product that makes it to your plate is the result of a cumulative effort from our dedicated team members. By taking small steps like buying locally grown produce, we can work together to create a brighter future. As we look to what's next, we will continue to explore new additions to our fresh food portfolio that celebrate plant-based ingredients as the main hero and inspiration. Most importantly, knowing that plant-based diets offer many health benefits and can positively impact carbon emissions, we are committed to bringing more fresh, local, and sustainably grown leafy greens and plant-based foods to consumers' plates across the country.

Farming in Atlanta: the story of Ponics

Ponics is an urban hydroponics company committed to growing healthy food in neighborhoods that need it; and we also grow jobs in the process. About ten years ago, we became more and more fascinated with the idea of growing crops not in soil but indoors with no soil, no sunlight, and enormous water savings compared to conventional agriculture. There is so much waste in our current food system, in terms of both the resources we waste to grow it and the actual product we waste when we distribute it over very long distances. For example, if we recycle the water we use, we can save over 90 percent of it; and when we grow food close to where people live, we save energy and get fresher food to people without having to cool and store it. So, that sparked my interest and, from there, I went on to develop our first greenhouse. We couldn't afford any land, so we decided to buy a container—you know, one of those standard shipping containers that you see on the back of a flatbed truck—and turned that into a farm. Our first experiment was pretty spectacular. With no farming background, we were able to grow almost 1,000 pounds of food. We initially experimented with fruiting plants, like tomatoes and peppers, but decided to stick mostly with greens. So, we built our first prototype and spread the word that we were doing this. One of the first trade shows we attended was in Syracuse, NY, in the middle of February, with snow on the ground. Here were all the big tractors, and gigantic harvesters, and all this other agricultural machinery, and right next to it was our box—this shipping container that looked like nothing. But when we opened the doors somewhat so that the growing lights from inside the container could be seen, it was like magic. People could see our growing lights shining on all these fabulous-looking greens in the dead of winter in Upstate New York. We let everyone inside and it felt a bit like touring an airplane. Our first sale happened that day—a farmer from Maine wanted to buy our container right then and there. Maine has a really short growing season and he thought it was amazing that he would be able to grow year round. But we also had interest from farmers from warmer areas who just loved how healthy and clean the greens looked, and they could see selling this kind of product to restaurants and grocery stores and so forth.

Of course, there were detractors, too. Some people thought it was "unnatural" to grow food this way. But if you look at the science of it, you know that there is nothing unnatural about it. That's one of the reasons why I decided early on that we would work with educational institutions—so that people would be better informed about the science behind growing food hydroponically and why it can produce beautiful, healthy plants. You just need to feed the plants the nutrients they need by circulating nutrient-rich water through the system. We were using the same seeds that growers who grow outdoors use, and we were using a lot less water, and we were giving the plants exactly what they needed. Our system allows us to optimize all the inputs. The other reason why I thought education would be important is because there is an acute shortage of farmers. Conventional farming is not very attractive to young people. It is associated with a lot of hard work and dirt. Our kind of farming is much more interesting. It is fascinating to see food grow in a space like a shipping container that's associated with industrial production. And you can learn so much from farming, it's amazing. It's about innovation, engineers, biology, chemistry, business, computer science, and so much more. Hydroponics is a great learning platform for all these different subjects. So, we decided to create four prototypes of hydroponic systems, not just one. We have the "mini" for elementary schools, where younger kids can learn the science of growing food; the "future farmer" for middle schools starts to introduce the business aspects in addition to the science; the rack systems for high schools adds technology; and the container farm for the college level and the commercial market incorporates a lot more technology. We use a train-the-trainer model for the educational component of our prototypes so that one educator can train a group of students who can then train others to grow successfully using our curriculum and our turnkey systems. All of them are easily shipped in flat packages and then assembled on site. In our training materials, there are instructions for the hardware using simulations, guest lectures, videos, so the curriculum turns into on-the-job training, where the trainees wear goggles, lab coats, gloves, hairnets, and the whole nine yards from K to 12th grade and beyond.

We decided to make Atlanta, GA, our headquarters. The state is well known for its agricultural sector. It also has some population-dense areas that have very high rates of food-related illnesses. That makes it a great place for us to showcase the advantages of hydroponic production from both an environmental and a health perspective. Atlanta is hot and humid in the summer months, so there are a number of crops you just can't grow well here outside. We can grow these crops in our system year-round at a consistently high quality and with consistently high yields. And, of course, our systems are mobile and scalable and can be put anywhere.

We are motivated every day by the social mission of our product. We are committed to growing top-quality food, reducing food-related illnesses by improving eating habits, creating jobs, and jump-starting economic development in under-served communities. It's a challenging business model, no doubt, but we feel it can be done by selling to the high-end market so we can also sell to markets with lower purchasing power. We do need more help from the public sector, though. If we can nudge subsidies in the right direction and convince the public sector that we need to give subsidies to businesses that improve climate-smart agriculture and public health, our business model can become a lot more manageable. We are currently involved in a climate-smart initiative funded by the USDA where we collaborate with several universities to calculate the carbon offsets we can create by growing food hydroponically in cities. By optimizing production and reducing the resources we use, and cutting down on the food-distribution-related carbon footprint, we believe that we can considerably lower the carbon footprint of food production overall. That's the kind of food production that should be subsidized. On the other hand, industries with large carbon footprints should be charged for their carbon emissions in the form of carbon permits, for example, that they have to buy to get to emit the carbon they generate. If a hydroponic grower can show how much their production method reduces the carbon footprint compared to conventional agricultural production, then the carbon credits that carbon-emitting industries pay for can go to the low-carbon hydroponic growers. That would subsidize a low-carbon food production model and vastly improve the business model for hydroponic growers. In other words, carbon-emitting corporations can purchase carbon credits to offset their carbon footprints, and those funds can be transferred to agricultural growers who reduce the carbon footprint.

Right now, we are a team of ten at Ponics, plus a cadre of advisors who regularly work with us. We had to pivot a few times along the way to find our space and to figure out what we wanted to be in this emergent space of urban agriculture: farmers, tech company, or equipment company. We ended up in a unique in-between space of farmers and equipment company. We grow greens and we work with grocery chains and larger food distributors to use their existing networks to get our food in front of their customers in the retail space as well as the restaurant space. If chefs like our products, we can provide them with extremely fresh, high-quality food year-round. We sell our products with the roots, which extends the shelf life considerably. it also maintains the nutrient content of our food, since we don't harvest our products, technically speaking. They therefore do not suffer the typical post-harvest nutrient decline. In addition to selling our products year-round, we are launching a franchising program, where we license our technology to franchisees. And we sell our equipment to schools, universities, and other educational institutions. There is a pile of applied knowledge that is embedded in our systems. That's why it was important for us to launch the training program and the curriculum that outlines our operating procedure. It's also important to us that people don't think of our model as a David-versus-Goliath story or an either/ or story. I believe we need both hydroponic and soil production, and food production in both cities and rural areas. And we also try to make our systems—not only the food they produce—look beautiful so that the places where we operate look more attractive.

In addition to having a great team, I am fortunate to have a great group of advisors from all walks of life. They are engineers, inventors, chemists, water experts, farmers, marketing experts. It takes a whole network of expertise to make this work and be successful. In some ways, this diversity reflects my own background. I was always interested in science and engineering, but I'm also keenly interested in storytelling, public relations, and using data to tell stories effectively. I also really like to do things with my hands and build things. Maybe this is how I ended up in this innovation space that is about interdisciplinary and cross-disciplinary knowledge, and very much about applied knowledge. For knowledge to be meaningful, we must be able to use it to make a difference in people's lives and to make the world a better place. Ultimately, that's what it's all about.

More food systems innovations in Chicago: expanding the business model

Bubbly Dynamics is a for-profit social enterprise, so we are a for-profit business but with a social mission. Our focus is on reusing obsolete industrial space in our city by creating circular economies. All of our businesses are food related, and we work very hard to link them so that we can close loops, and use the waste stream of one business as the input stream for another as much as possible. In other words, we try to create synergies that small businesses would not be able to benefit from if they operated on their own. Sometimes the synergies are very advantageous and sometimes they are less obvious, but everyone benefits in some way from being co-located with other more or less like-minded businesses.

We actually started in 2011 as a nonprofit, but that turned out to be an unnecessary detour. Nonprofit boards tend to slow things down and sometimes they have mission drift, depending on where the money is. So, being a nonprofit became more of a bother and we turned it into a business, which we should have done in the first place. If we want our concept to be scalable, we have to prove that it works as a for-profit model.

We started Bubbly Dynamics by converting a former meat-processing plant that's been here since the 1860s. We own the building, so we are the landlord for the other businesses who operate out of our space. We offer them leases of varying lengths and take care of a number of other headaches, like negotiating vendor rates for items that all of them need and utility rates and so forth. In some cases, we can also point them in the right direction for permits and certifications. After all, we've done it a few times and might as well have others benefit from our experience. Most of our businesses are startups, but some are well-established businesses who just like the idea of being co-located with other cool businesses, and they want to support the concept of Bubbly Dynamics in general.

What we didn't know when we started to turn our very cool idea of reusing old commercial spaces and turning them into circular business clusters was that former slaughterhouses are just about the nastiest commercial spaces that you can convert. The clean-up effort was enormous, and getting the space certified for food production, and even for research, took a tremendous effort. But we did it, and we can now share the experience we've gained with others in the private, nonprofit, and public sectors who want to start something similar in their own city. If we can turn an old Chicago slaughterhouse into a food research laboratory, we can help others convert just about any space into a productive and innovative food business space. So, we are constantly expanding our business model and we are now offering consulting services. That's one of the newer tentacles we've grown. We also make use of some very short-term leasing opportunities when we can get them. Right now, for example, the space is being used for a movie. That's a great short-term revenue stream for us that benefits the whole building.

Some of our businesses have created pretty cool synergies. For example, the carbon dioxide from the brewery downstairs feeds the algae in the bioreactors upstairs, and it also goes into the growing rooms of our basil and microgreens producers to increase their yields. We also have a kombucha business, a coffee roster, a cheese maker, four farms that produce both indoors and outdoors on our premises, and we have some very cool food research businesses as well. For example, Back of the Yards Algae Sciences (BYAS) works on finding new uses for algae and mycelia as natural and sustainable ingredients for food products to enhance flavors and colors, and creates protein powders that can be used for plant-based products that can serve as substitutes for meat. They are also working on bio-stimulants to improve the yields and product quality of indoor farms. Very cool stuff. For us, they are an important partner because they inspired us to further upgrade our space to create food laboratories. That's a whole other level of building sophistication, to get lab space certified, but we did it. Now they rent lab space from us at a fraction of the cost they would have to pay if they rented elsewhere in Chicago.

Apart from the different products and services they create, our businesses are also quite diverse in terms of size and in every other way. One of the labs has a space of only about 400 square feet; our herb and micro-greens producer has a small growing room of about 3000 square feet, but everything is stacked vertically and they produce a lot of greens in there; one of the farms has indoor growing space of about 10,000 square feet plus some outdoor space. The whole building is just shy of 100,000 square feet, and we also have some outdoor space around it, so our total area is about three acres.

Some of our entrepreneurs are innovative young people fresh out of school, and some are probably my age or older—maybe pushing 70. For example, our cheese maker is very experienced and has been doing this for some time. More than 50 percent of our businesses are women-owned, and they also come from every imaginable background. Chicago is a very diverse city and we certainly reflect that diversity. We have African American, Mexican, and Filipino business owners and in general look and sound a bit like a mini-United Nations. The businesses also range from one- or two-person operations to about 50 employees, but most of them are on the smaller side. I think collectively we have the equivalent of about 110 full-time jobs. That's a lot of jobs, and we are located in the back yards of people who need jobs and are looking for jobs. When they work here they also see how food can be different than what they are used to. These neighborhoods are not just food and retail deserts; they are also education deserts. People who grow up with unhealthy eating habits don't choose to have these habits. They just haven't seen anything else. We find that when people start working here, they start eating differently, and they tell their friends that they shouldn't eat that fried, or salty, or sweet stuff all the time— try something else that's really good and good for you.

Over the years, some have moved out of our space when they've outgrown us. For example, one of our indoor farms has moved to a space that is much larger but is still located in a low-income, food-insecure neighborhood a bit north of us. They got a contract with a large grocery chain in our area and got too big to be here, and they employ a lot more people now. But they worked out of our space for six years, built their proof of concept for indoor food production, refined their production, and now they are a successful business. I consider that a great success story. We also had a couple of women who started to import saffron from Afghanistan. Both of them were veterans and one of them had been deployed in Afghanistan and made connections with women farmers in Afghanistan when she was over there. So, they started to import saffron and other high-quality spices, and they became so successful that they outgrew us and had to find another space. I'm very happy about these success stories. It's very rewarding to think that they got their start in our space and now they are successful companies. So, our businesses are doing pretty well.

They also have a range of different revenue streams. We are right here in the city, so they have their markets right in their own back yard. Some of them sell exclusively here in city, but others also contract with larger businesses in the region, like grocery stores and restaurants. Of course, things were a bit rough during COVID. The brewery lost a lot of its business, for example, when the restaurants and pubs shut down. We also have an ice company that's run out of our basement that had to shut down completely. But some of our other businesses were able to pivot to home deliveries of food, for example. We offered rent relief to everybody during that time until they were able to rebuild their revenue streams. But some of them actually didn't slow down much during the pandemic. We also hold community events—open houses where we give people a tour of the facility and explain what we do to let the neighborhood know that we are here and what our businesses are doing. Of course, it's always well received when we do that, especially when the brewery sells beer out of their tap room!

One of the things I like about our business model, apart from facilitating these very cool and sometimes unexpected synergies among our businesses, is that we have now created a proof of concept for some of our urban neighborhoods. Some of these neighborhoods were never affluent, even during their best days; others have seen a lot of ups and downs; and many have seen a variety of immigrant populations coming through here. They may have been bustling, but they were always poor and always on the edge. But just bringing in a developer, tearing everything down, and pushing everyone out or into cheap housing is not a solution. We have to do better than that. But creating the proof of concept for Bubbly Dynamics was not for the faint of heart. Yes, we got a good deal when we first purchased this facility, but I can't tell you how much money we've pumped into this place to convert a derelict meat-packing plant into the space you see today. I mean, the windows were ripped up and some of the floors were pitched so that the fluids from slaughtering the animals could easily drain; it was just a mess. For a while, we had groups of volunteers showing up every Saturday to help demolish things and shovel debris until we got to a point where we needed skilled contractors to do the electrical work and plumbing, for example. And now that things are working pretty well, the city wants a piece of the action. They just served us with a humongous tax bill. Where should we get that kind of money from? It's completely impossible. We do pay taxes, of course. We've also paid permitting fees along the way, and we paid any number of local businesses who worked for us to convert the space. We also pay our utilities. Occasionally, we get a grant from the city to help with some construction, but that's a very small percentage of what we put in. And now they want these huge sums in additional taxes from us? Where is that supposed to come from and how did they even come up with the numbers? Our lease contracts with our businesses are in place and usually for multiple years; and even if we could just increase the rent, we wouldn't want to, because that would put some of our folks out of business. It seems you just can't win. Everyone seems to like our concept and thinks it's very promising for multiple reasons: it reuses vacant space in a productive manner; it supports innovation; it creates jobs in low-income neighborhoods, where they are most needed; and it produces food and food-related innovations, which helps people who need better food; we are also a great circular economy model. But if you like all these things, then there has to be a financial structure in place that rewards a small incubator business like ours and doesn't penalize us for being a socially responsible for-profit operation.

Despite these challenges, we are working right now on launching another aspect of our business and another enterprise altogether that we refer to as the "Bubbly Expansion." The idea is to create a shared kitchen space. Kitchen space is very expensive here, so we are planning to build some shared washing, processing, and cold-storage spaces that will benefit a number of different food businesses. They can then get kitchen space at a fraction of the cost they would have to pay otherwise, and they can also benefit from potential synergies among their different businesses. If I had a magic wand, I would expand the number of our businesses and work with more micro-startups. We are getting a little bit stale and I'd really like to see an injection of new energy and new ideas into our space.

Businesses do best when they collaborate. It's a different form of competition—not competition to bid the price down, but to differentiate products, make them even better, and find compatible niches. That's great competition and great innovation. We are also continuing to push the envelope with our municipality and its office of planning. For example, we would love to expand into aquaponics so we can expand our indoor-farming operations. So far, we have not been able to get that approved, despite the fact that we are located on the site of a former meat-packing plant and next door to a former slaughterhouse. Despite the current hurdles, we hope to have organic fish here sometime soon. We are also providing space at no cost for a small local museum that documents the history of the Chicago stockyard and its rich diversity of immigrant communities and labor movements. We helped them develop the space and are very pleased to be a part of that project. It shows the proud and important past of this neighborhood, and we are committed to playing a role in building its proud and important future.

Linking profits, people, and planet in cities, suburbs, and rural communities of the DC metro area and beyond

4P Foods has been in operation for almost ten years now. We are a public-benefit for-profit corporation and consider ourselves a food systems innovator in the CSA and food hubs space. Scaling the CSA model is no small task. CSAs deliver fresh food to households, typically weekly, whereby the households buy their food delivery in the form of a CSA share and not by the pound or by volume. The food typically comes from local producers who want to contribute to a more localized and sustainable food system. The problem is that the CSA model can be a bit constraining since consumers don't have a lot of say in determining what their food delivery looks like. Most CSAs also don't operate during the winter months, which is not ideal for consumers who want a reliable delivery of food year-round. The added challenge is that the farmers who contribute to a CSA need to get a fair price for their produce so they can make a living. Yet, some of the consumers who are most in need of fresh produce may not be in a position to pay the prices the farmers need. This is a real dilemma, so the question we set out to answer is: how can we build a food system that addresses the needs of small farmers and consumers simultaneously? We think the answer lies in brokering as direct a meeting space between farmers and consumers as we can. Initially, we operated as a direct CSA model and attempted to scale the model by delivering primarily to households in high-density urban apartment and condo buildings. It worked okay, but it turns out that the CSA model is not a great fit for these kinds of households. Yes, we were able to deliver several CSA shares to the same building, which made the last mile of delivery more manageable. The problem is that people who live in apartment buildings are often smaller households who like to go out and don't cook at home all that much. So, a CSA share is a lot more food than they can handle.

So, we went back to the drawing board and rethought how we could scale the model. You see, I grew up in Hudson Valley and worked on the farm during my growing-up years. My dad worked in the grocery business his whole life, so I watched first-hand as our local food system was dismantled in the 1970s and 1980s. In the early days, my father would still buy apples or eggs and some dairy products from local farmers in our area, but eventually the whole system was centralized and you just had to buy everything from the large distributors or not buy at all. So, when I started 4P Foods, I wanted to re-envision how our food system works—namely, more like an ecosystem of regional food networks comprised of thousands of small farms and hundreds of regional aggregators—knowing full well that this would be an uphill battle. Our food system really rewards negative externalities, meaning that our farmers are forced to produce at the lowest possible price even if this means that they produce in ways that harm local ecosystems. Producing a better product in less harmful ways would mean that they couldn't cover their costs. Or if a farmer grows a large volume of commodity crops that needs to be shipped to foreign markets, they are eligible for subsidies even though they generate a big carbon footprint, whereas if they produce a small volume of vegetables for the local market, which requires less transportation and cold storage and therefore generates a much smaller carbon footprint, they will not be eligible for any subsidies. That's how we reward the negative externalities of conventional agriculture.

At 4P Foods, we try to upend this model by buying food from small farms that use sustainable, regenerative production methods, and we distribute that food to a range of consumers—both individual households and commercial customers. Our customers can go online to shop and we upload a new list of available items every week. We have two different cut-off times for customers to communicate their choices, depending on the delivery days. Every week a customer can pick from a menu and tell us what they want more of and what they do not want at all in their weekly delivery.

In 2019, we acquired a local food hub and with that we became a bit more of a hybrid model, whereby about half of our sales go to restaurants, healthcare providers, local grocery stores, and a lot of schools; the other half still goes to individual households. One of our commercial partnership models is Food Is Medicine. Through this program, we deliver fresh fruits and vegetables to households in under-resourced communities by way of hospitals and health clinics. The food is paid for by the health providers with whom we partner, and these providers take a holistic approach to the health of their patients. This means that they look at what their patients need to get healthy and stay healthy, including the food they eat. So, instead of prescribing pills from the pharmacy, they may prescribe fresh food, and we are the vehicle through which the patients get their delivery of that fresh food. This is a fairly high-touch delivery model since we may have to tweak what goes into the weekly grocery bags, and we also include recipe cards and instructions about how to fix the vegetables we deliver. Sometimes, the weekly delivery times may have to be adjusted, too.

We have also scaled up on the supply side, and now buy food from local and regional farmers in six states. We identify our farming partners not simply on the basis of distance between producer and consumer; ideally, we want farmers who aspire to building a restorative food production model that improves soil health, water resources, and the quality of the food. We want our producers to meet certain standards. It turns out that a food system works quite like a watershed—you need to improve practices in the entire watershed to improve the overall water quality. We draw the circle of our collaborators wider than, let's say, 100 miles. For example, we buy from a couple of farms quite a bit further south because they produce a high-quality heirloom grapefruit that we can't get anywhere further north. In total, we buy from about 200 small farms in Virginia, Maryland, Pennsylvania, and the Carolinas. We also try to optimize our transport routes: for example, we take apples from the north to the south and bring citrus back north. By buying sufficient volume to serve our markets in population-dense regions, we give our farmers from smaller rural communities access to larger markets and a reliable revenue stream. This allows them to invest in their operations and it allows us to expand what we can offer our customers. For example, one of our partners is the Piedmont Progressive Farmers Cooperative, which is a group of small, mostly African American farmers in a former tobacco-farming area of southern Virginia. We have such high demand for their eggs that they are now ready to expand their operation. So, they need access to capital, which made us aware of another problem in the local food ecosystem: namely, access to capital is not equally distributed. These small farmers had a really tough time securing loans for their operations. Having a larger network of partners and a larger-scale market that generates a reliable revenue stream year-round helped them gain access to capital.

For a while, we also delivered to office buildings so our customers could take their weekly food delivery home from work. It was a pretty popular program, but then COVID happened and all the office buildings shut down when everyone switched to working from home. It's still unclear what the future of this component of our market will look like. Overall, we now employ more than 60 people in addition to the people who work on our partner farms. We have already opened a second warehouse where we package and distribute our deliveries, and are building a third one now.

One of our newer partnerships is with the Piedmont Community College in southern Virginia. When food supply chains collapsed all over the country during COVID, they looked into starting a food hub, so they could buy food from local farmers and distribute it to local communities and especially to people in need of food. But when they did their research on local food hubs, they found that most of them are not commercially viable, and theirs certainly wouldn't be since their market was too small. So, rather than starting a nonprofit food hub that would require ongoing support through grants and donations, they asked us if we would run it for them. Now we provide local food from these farmers in southern Virginia to larger markets in metro areas, and we can add to the food offered to customers in their region by supplementing what their farmers produce with products from other farmers in our network.

By scaling our operation into a hub-and-spokes food ecosystem, we feel that we can build regional, regenerative, and equitable food ecosystems one region at a time. Of course, that's not easy, since we are running not one business but at least three: we build networks of farms that can provide high-quality, sustainably grown food; we build networks of customers who are looking for healthy, sustainably produced food; and we have our commercial partners, like the Food Is Medicine network, and the 800-plus schools where we deliver great-quality food.

So, what's next? If I had a magic wand, and assuming that I will be unable to change accounting practices so that they take full account of the benefits of restorative and equitable food systems, then the next-best thing would be to expand the Local Food Purchasing Assistance Cooperative Agreement (LFPA), which started during COVID. Under this program, produce purchased from local farmers is distributed to food-insecure clients. It has two goals: to support small, disadvantaged farmers and rangers; and to support food-insecure families who typically fall through the cracks of SNAP, WIC, and other food-assistance programs, like immigrants and homebound seniors who can't get to the nearest food pantry. LFPA is a step in the right direction, but it needs better checks and balances to ensure that the food is produced sustainably and that farmers who are genuinely disadvantaged are given priority, including black and Latino farmers. These farmers produce beautiful fruits, vegetables, eggs, and dairy and meat products, but can't access distribution systems that give them the kind of volume they can handle. The existing distribution systems want high volume and low cost. We can play an important role here by making sure that the right farmers and the right families benefit from the program by helping them work through the red tape and ensuring that the program's priorities are actually implemented. These are the kinds of models that can create win–win situations for small farmers and people in need of healthy food. But in the meantime we still need to work on changing general accounting practices so it is obvious to everyone what the actual win–win situations are.

Concluding thoughts

All the food system innovators interviewed for this book, and several others who could not be included, are committed to the social justice and environmental sustainability goals associated with a restorative food system. While they span a wide range of food production models and food system innovations, all emphasize the systemic issues that limit progress toward such a food system. Gotham Greens has been the most successful of our innovators in navigating the current food system, while Chispas Farm, Planting Justice, and 4P Foods are the most articulate in questioning the current measures of success.

Chapter 6 will take a more in-depth look at some of the systemic issues that have created the current food system—issues that must be addressed if we are ever to get the food system we want.

6

HOW DO WE GET THERE FROM HERE?

Pathways toward the food system we want

There is some good news. Food insecurity is solvable. Indeed, as the stories of urban food innovators, food-insecure individuals, and those working to address food insecurity illustrate, a number of smart, creative, and viable solutions are already out there. The problem is that, rather than smoothing the path toward the widespread adoption and implementation of these strategies, and rather than supporting the work that is already underway, the path remains full of boulders, potholes, and other barriers. Some of these obstacles can be bypassed or overcome. But the only long-term solution is to remove all of them permanently. This will require more than a few policies and smart implementation strategies. It will require a whole new way of thinking.

Getting the price right

Our price system is broken. This is nowhere more evident than with the price of food. Food that is highly processed, high in calories, and low in nutrients is cheap, even though its consumption should be discouraged. Food that is unprocessed, high in nutrients, and low in empty calories tends to be expensive, even though its consumption should be encouraged. This price distortion is bad enough in the short term, but it is especially problematic in the long run. Prices established through the free exchange of consumer preferences and producer interests in the marketplace are supposed to bring about a socially optimal situation. This is what economic theory tells us. It insists that markets are efficient mechanisms through which consumers can communicate what food they want and need, and producers can communicate what food they want to produce and sell; and, as these individual actors communicate their individual wants and needs, the best interests of all are served. In other words, everyone wins. Economists call this the "Pareto optimal state," named after

DOI: 10.4324/9781003322399-6

the Italian economist Vilfredo Pareto (1848–1923). Yet, a food system that results in over 30 percent of the population becoming obese, and diabetes in the region of 15 percent, as we have in neighborhoods across the six cities introduced in this book, is certainly not in the best interests of everyone. It creates high healthcare expenses, reduces people's ability to contribute to society, and causes premature death. These are clearly not socially desirable outcomes.

Economists blame this kind of distortion on a well-known phenomenon—negative externalities. These are the undesirable side-effects of economic activity. The goal of producing food (an economic activity) is to sell it to people and thereby provide them with the nutrients they need to lead productive lives. We assume that the price at which the food is sold accounts for the total cost of all the resources that went into its production, including labor, fuel to run the tractors, fertilizer, water, and so on. Yet, some costs are not captured in the price that consumers pay for their food: for example, when the production process causes pollution because the fertilizer leaches into the ground water, or when the end product contains so much sugar that it makes those who eat it ill rather than productive. These are the external costs of food, and they can be social or environmental. In other words, they can have negative consequences for people, the planet, or both (Gowdy and O'Hara, 1995; Daly and Cobb, 1994).

One of the first studies to acknowledge these economic distortions at the global level was the so-called "Brundtland Report" (officially titled the *Report of the World Commission on Environment and Development: Our Common Future*; United Nations, 1987). This called for a more sustainable approach to economic development that pursues a triple bottom line of profits, people, and planet. The implication is that economic activity must balance economic, social, and environmental goals, and account for the negative social and environmental impacts of all economic activity. Fifteen years earlier, a group of international scientists had prepared a report for the so-called Club of Rome, which had become concerned with the declining resources of our planet, especially non-renewables like fossil fuels (Meadows et al., 1972). They warned that the rate at which these resources were being used, and at which even renewable resources were being harvested, put our future in jeopardy. The crux of their argument was that extracting non-renewable resources and leaving nothing for subsequent generations made future economic success impossible. Moreover, while extracting ground water for irrigation and harvesting crops for food are, in principle, renewable processes, if the rate at which the ground water is pumped to the surface exceeds the rate at which it is replenished, and if the crops are harvested without putting nutrients back into the soil, then these renewable resources will eventually become non-renewable, too.

The Club of Rome managed to get a lot of countries' attention. To address the concerns raised and protect the planet's non-renewable resources, many nations introduced policies like the United States' Clean Water and Clean Air Acts. However, these policies were largely regulation based and failed to consider how prices might be adjusted to reduce negative externalities. This was hardly surprising, as accounting for the negative externalities of food, for example, is no small task. It requires us to think systemically, anticipate side-effects, and then try to minimize and counteract those side-effects. It also invariably means giving up some rewards today in order to retain the ability to generate rewards tomorrow—a proposition that is no easy sell.

That said, economists and policy-makers are at least aware of the need to correct negative externalities. By contrast, most of them seem to be wholly ignorant of the sink problem (see Chapter 4). One of the reasons for this ignorance is that economic losses and gains are registered almost instantly in private-sector companies' and government agencies' monthly cash-flow statements and quarterly reports. One of the most closely watched of these economic figures is GDP (Gross Domestic Product), which is a measure of the total production of final goods and services in a country, state, or region. By contrast, the timeframes of natural resources and sink capacities are measured in decades, centuries, or even millennia. For example, it took millions of years, enormous pressure, and very high temperatures to turn decaying plant material into coal, oil, and natural gas. And it takes decades of cultivation and care before a forest is productive or a field yields a bountiful harvest. When it comes to the timeframe in which sink capacities function, it's all about the long term, often exceeding the span of a single human life. As a result, we simply do not keep track of them. Economic reports provide regular updates on GDP, but we do not receive similar updates on remaining oil reserves, a region's forest cover, underground aquifers, the fish stocks in our oceans, or any of the other large and small resources nature provides for us.

Clearly, then, it is difficult to assess how quickly environmental resources and sinks are declining, or what the cost of their decline will be. However, for example, we do know that overusing carbon sinks exacerbates the problem of carbon-dioxide accumulation in the atmosphere. The resulting climate vulnerabilities are felt in the form of heatwaves, torrential rain, hurricanes, mudslides, wildfires, and other natural disasters. We also know that soils can be overused, and when one considers that a 30-centimeter layer of topsoil forms the outer skin of our planet, which is 12,742 kilometers in diameter, and that this paper-thin layer of soil constitutes all the arable land we have to grow our food, it is astonishing that we do not report regularly on its health and extent. Similarly, depleted soils below the thin topsoil layer will no longer absorb pollutants. Consequently, more and more contaminants will reach our ground-water reservoirs and leave us vulnerable to both water and food shortages. And the depletion of oxygen in our lakes, rivers, and oceans eventually leads to dying fish, plants, and other aquatic life. The list is long. Some researchers have advocated the introduction of natural resource accounts that would at least allow us to keep better track of the state of our natural resources (Harris and Fraser, 2002; Perrings and Vincent, 2003; Yang et al., 2021). Yet, sinks usually go unmentioned.

Economists have devised a variety of methods to measure the cost of the unintended side-effects of economic activity. For example, healthcare expenses and related costs may be used to estimate the full cost of obesity and diabetes (Tremmel et al., 2017; American Diabetes Association, 2018). Meanwhile, the cost of restoring a river or coastal area may be used to estimate the full cost of surface-water pollution (Mumbi and Watanabe, 2022; Easter and Zeitouni, 2018). In some cases, these estimates may be based on the perspectives of different stakeholders. For example, the value of an ecosystem and the cost associated with its demise may be based on the value assigned to that ecosystem by different individuals through a process called "contingent valuation" (Loomisa et al., 2018; Spash et al., 2009; Carson and Hanemann, 2006; Holmes et al., 2004). Regardless of the methodology, though, the focus is usually on the value of resources, and rarely on the value of sinks.

Ecosystems play a critical role in maintaining both resources and sink capacities. In a 2005 report, the Millennium Ecosystem Assessment defined "ecosystem services" as the many and varied benefits humans receive from a healthy natural environment. The report distinguishes between four types of ecosystem services:

- Regulating services, including filtering water, decomposing waste, detoxifying soils, regulating disease, and regulating our climate.
- Provisioning services, including the ability to grow food crops, timber, and other forest products, gather fish and other marine resources, collect minerals, and utilize genetic resources.
- Cultural services, including the spiritual and religious value drawn from nature, its recreational value, educational insights, and therapeutic aspects.
- Supporting services, including nutrient cycling, soil formation, habitat formation, and many other services necessary to maintain provisioning services (Millennium Ecosystem Assessment, 2005).

Based on these definitions, provisioning services are most closely aligned with the resourcing functions of the food system, regulating and supporting services are most closely aligned with sink capacities, and cultural services shape human perceptions of both resources and sinks.

A quarter-century ago, ecological economists calculated the total economic value of 17 ecosystem services at between $16 trillion and $54 trillion per year, with an estimated average of $33 trillion per year. At the time, the global GDP (i.e., the total value of all final goods and services added on earth) was $18 trillion (Costanza et al., 1997). More recent studies have demonstrated that the steady decline in ecosystem services has resulted in steadily rising costs (Costanza et al., 2014). The ecological economist William Rees (2020) writes:

A cascade of data shows that the human enterprise is in ecological overshoot, consuming nature's goods and services faster than ecosystems can regenerate and dumping (often toxic) wastes beyond nature's processing/recycling capacity. In short, we are currently "financing" economic growth by liquidating the biophysical systems upon which humanity ultimately depends.

Since our human bodies also act as sinks that absorb the pollutants that have accumulated in rivers, soils, the air, and our food, the burden of depleted sink capacities is not equally distributed. Those who live in less polluted areas, and those who have the capacity to shield themselves from the negative effects of pollution and waste, will suffer less. Meanwhile, others will suffer the burdens of overwork, isolation, and financial stress in addition to suffering the health effects of pollution. Some of these burdens are not absorbed by individuals alone, but by social networks such as family units and even whole communities. These disparities are well documented both nationally and internationally, not only with respect to our food system but more generally as environmental racism, classism, and sexism (Tessum et al., 2019; Hajat et al., 2015; Cushing et al., 2015; Dallen et al., 2020). But, just as ecosystems can collapse, communities can collapse, too. This may be reflected in a dramatic rise in post-traumatic stress, violence, and suicide when the collective burden becomes too heavy. Feminist scholars and ecological economists have long pointed out that vulnerable populations suffer disproportionately because they have so few opportunities to shift their burdens to somewhere else (O'Hara, 2014; Mellor, 2009; Spencer et al., 2018). Lower life expectancies in such areas may therefore reflect not only an inability to adopt healthier lifestyles but also a lack of the support that is needed to deal with the triple burden of illness, poverty, and isolation (Case and Deaton, 2020). The stories of food-insecure households in Brooklyn and Chicago speak especially eloquently to the connections between food, resource constraints, and time constraints. The neglect of ecosystems' sink services is therefore not only due to the difficulties in measuring them, or in thinking long term, but to long-held economic valuation biases. Standard economic theory holds that food sold in the marketplace is visible, has a price, and therefore has value. Meanwhile, food produced at home or in a community garden has no market price and therefore no value. Likewise, resources that are used to produce marketable food have value, whereas resources that are used to produce subsistence food have no value. And the sinks that sustain the resourcing and absorptive/buffering capacities of both marketable and subsistence food are not visible as either resources or final products, so they have no price and therefore no value. As a result, when they are undermined or even ultimately destroyed, no one will notice. This raises questions about the conceptual framework of standard economics, which would argue that the externality problem could be resolved simply by adjusting a product's price so that all costs are included. Yet, this may not be enough. Rather than merely internalizing the currently externalized costs of food, we may have to rethink how we assign value to the physical/environmental and social/cultural systems that support our food system in the first place. In other words, food pricing should not simply be based on the product's market value; nor should it even be based on a market price that has been adjusted to reflect the true cost of producing and consuming food. Rather, it should be based on transparent objectives like improving water quality, biodiversity, ecosystems' health, safe and meaningful work, diverse food cultures, and thriving social networks. In other words, food pricing must make invisible sink capacities visible and reflect our commitment to sustain and restore them. The story of 4P Foods in Chapter 5 speaks eloquently to the valuation biases of current accounting practices and their failure to register the benefits of a restorative and equitable food system.

One potential solution is a more circular economy framework where someone's waste product becomes someone else's resources. This principle is beautifully illustrated by the story of Bubbly Dynamics in Chicago. Some circular economy concepts expressly reference the circularity of nature's ecosystems as a basis for their circular design (European Commission, 2017; 2020). These circularity concepts seek not only to close existing resource and waste loops, but also to improve the health and scope of ecosystems in the process.

Some of the tools cities and metro areas can use to design their circular economies are material-flow and energy-flow analyses, including life-cycle analysis (Weisz and Steinberger, 2010; Pincetl, 2012; Kaufman, 2012). Such tools can help cities to better understand how materials cycle through their communities and where they can best be captured and reused, while also reducing the pressure on ecosystems. Cities can then steer away from potential critical thresholds of ecosystem collapse (Sasaki et al., 2015; Farley and Voinov, 2016). Not using but preserving resources may turn out to be of greater value if the demise of an ecosystem can be avoided. As Stahel (2013) points out, "concerns over resource security, ethics and safety as well as greenhouse-gas reductions are shifting our approach to seeing materials as assets to be preserved, rather than continually consumed" (see also Stahel, 2010).

Understanding the true value of ecosystem services will require at least a basic understanding of how they work. The resulting price system can then incorporate appropriate payments for ecosystem services (PES), and offer corresponding incentives to farmers and landowners in exchange for maintaining and strengthening them. Tacconi (2012) describes these payments as "a transparent system for the additional provision of environmental services through conditional payments to providers." Likewise, incentives can go to those who maintain and strengthen social networks. Prices can thus become a means to maintain and strengthen both environmental and social sink capacities.

Calling for a price system that reflects the realities of resources and sinks and moves us closer to a food system that sustains both is neither anti-market nor anti-economic. Instead, it recognizes that food prices must move us closer to what the Italian economist Mariana Mazzucato (2020) calls "market making," as opposed to our current system of "market taking."

Getting wages right

Food prices have to deal with a double whammy. Distortions in food pricing are not only created by the food system's failure to account for the complex side-effects of food production and consumption, but also by what economists call the "public goods" problem. This has profound implications for the inputs of food production, including wages. With public goods, the so-called "exclusion mechanism" of the market does not work. This is economics-speak for the fact that, when I want to buy a pound of tomatoes, I have to pay for them. Not doing so would be considered theft. The same is true of the fertilizer I need to grow the tomatoes. If I don't want to pay for it, I can't use it. However, this is not true of the sunlight and carbon dioxide that the tomato plants need to create carbohydrates and release oxygen. Ground water is typically another public good, as are the minerals in the soil, and a landscape of farmland or rolling hills. No one can be prevented from using these public goods, regardless of whether they are willing to pay for them. In other words, these resources are not covered by the market's exclusion mechanism, which stops anyone from using something unless they are willing to pay for it.

This can lead to two interlinked problems: free-riding and overuse. In a culture where value is closely tied to how much we have, the tendency is to use as much of a public good as possible without paying for it. If the consequence of this behavior is that the resource in question is overused, the free-rider will hope that someone else will pay to protect or restore it, as this will allow them to keep using it free of charge. In other words, public goods will tend to be overused while the use of costly private or market goods is kept to a minimum. Labor has been a market good since the abolition of serfdom and slavery. Farmers, farm workers, and food processors all have to be paid. Yet, the temptation is to minimize the use of this expensive market good by overusing a public good, such as an ecosystem, and/or utilizing a less costly alternative, such as machinery. Economists would describe this process as replacing labor with "capital" (an umbrella term for all human-made resources).

The assumption is that substituting capital for labor has no consequences other than lowering the cost of production by imposing constant downward pressure on wages. Needless to say, this is an erroneous assumption. If wages are reduced to a point where the workers can no longer afford to buy the items they produce, the consequences are profound. Farm workers who cannot afford to buy the tomatoes they harvest are a prime example. The price of tomatoes must fall so that those who receive low wages can still afford to buy them, and so the downward spiral continues: lower wages, lower, prices, lower wages. Planting Justice in Oakland and Chispas Farm in Albuquerque are both committed to disrupting this downward spiral (see Chapter 5). They recognize the importance of building a more egalitarian workplace and remunerating their team members fairly. Indeed, all of the food innovators who shared their stories for this study stated their commitment not only to improving food security but also to creating better workplaces.

Hunger Free America, which is based in New York City, argues that the United States' emergency food distribution system is fundamentally flawed because it relies on charity rather than the payment of living wages. The organization's executive director, Joel Berg, explains:

> The US emergency food system is a very small part of the answer to hunger. Taken together, all food distribution programs—including hunger programs in schools, summer meal programs, Health and Human Services senior programs, food assistance through the Federal Emergency Management Agency, and all the others—equal 17 times the food distributed through the US emergency food system. I've calculated that if we increase the emergency food safety net by 20 percent, that would be another $30 billion for emergency food. That's nothing to sneeze at. However, if we increase the wages of the lowest-paid Americans by two dollars an hour, that would equal $200 billion. Now, that would really make a difference. Unfortunately, when we've asked Congress to consider increasing the minimum wage, they have consistently rejected the idea.
>
> So, we suggested another solution, which is actually a market-based solution. You may be familiar with the Arboretum in Washington, DC. It is a beautiful, USDA-run facility that breeds, tests, and produces a great many varieties of plants. We've suggested that whenever the Arboretum develops a new pest-resistant shrub or tree for the horticulture industry, then the industry should pay a fee to the USDA. This would be similar to what the pharmaceutical industry pays the National Institute of Health when it develops a new drug. But we were told in no uncertain terms to forget it and that this suggestion would go nowhere. So, when we spend US taxpayers' dollars to develop new plants for the horticulture industry, we apparently have no interest in getting anything in return for the taxpayers' investment.
>
> Urban agriculture is a great place for education, community building, neighborhood safety and beautification, and a whole host of other benefits. But we have to be realistic that it doesn't make a dent in the need for quality food for low-income populations. We need to get healthier and more sustainable food, and better pay for those who work in the food system. But this will have to include better pay and better food for large and small food producers, and for those located in rural areas as well as those who operate in peri-urban and urban areas. The point is that we need to move to a compensation-based model for emergency food.
>
> Our current emergency food system is actually fairly new. It started in the 1980s when we shifted out of government-supported emergency food programs and into charity-based programs to address food insecurity. We all thought this was a temporary shift that occurred during the Reagan years when we deregulated everything and pretended to shrink government and demonized welfare moms in the process. Today, we have over 800 food pantries in New York City to serve the city's emergency food

needs. Most of these are very small and open only a few hours a month and they serve a limited number of people. In 1980, we had a few soup kitchens in New York and that was it. Nationwide, we used to have a few hundred emergency food programs. Today, we have an elaborate system of over 60,000 food pantries that rely mostly on volunteers, and most of them are very small. We should scrap the whole system and pay people decent wages. And while we're at it, we should scrap the whole agricultural subsidy system and use about a third of the subsidies to support small farmers to produce specialty crops, a third to reduce hunger, and a third for deficit reduction.

The American model of fighting hunger is broken, as is the relationship between Americans and their government sector. But, regrettably, the rest of the world seems to be following the broken US emergency food system model as we speak.

(Berg, 2023; see also Mozaffarian and Berg, 2021; Berg and Gibson, 2022)

This brings another value distortion into focus: namely, while better wages for those working in the food system are a necessity, not all work is created equal. Some workers produce food, others process and distribute it, still others prepare it, serve it, or clean up afterwards. But what of those who work to sustain the sink capacities of nature and our human communities? Of course, those who work in the labor market and contribute to creating market value must be paid. But what of those whose work contributes to the health and well-being of the planet's ecosystems, and of the old and young in our communities who cannot contribute to the market economy? How should we compensate the people who build thriving community gardens that produce fruits and vegetables that are consumed directly by low-income households rather than sold at the grocery store or the farmers' market? We generally accept that those whose work contributes to the produce that is sold in the marketplace have a right to earn a decent wage. Yet, we place no value on the contributions of those who maintain, restore, and care for our social/cultural and physical environment. Do those in high-paying jobs really make more valuable contributions to society than those who receive less money and those who earn no wages at all?

This raises serious questions about the conceptual framework that underlies standard assumptions about remunerating work. While work must be rewarded, care is equally indispensable to the economic process and must be remunerated, too. Feminist economists and other feminist scholars have long focused on the direct and indirect implications and valuation biases that prioritize paid work while neglecting the unremunerated contributions of care (Waring, 1989; Mies, 1986; Henderson, 1995). These scholars argue that all human activity—both economic and non-economic—draws upon a web of services provided in households, communities, social networks, and ecosystems.

Without these care-taking, regenerative, and reproductive services, there is no creativity, no innovation, and no muscle power. In short, all economic activity depends on a plethora of social, cultural, and environmental functions that sustain it. The burden of supplying these—typically uncompensated—sustaining services is not distributed evenly. It is disproportionately carried by nature, women, the very young, the old, the poor, and those without power. Those who provide the sustaining services may be prevented from utilizing their skills—or may lack the skills that are valued—in the marketplace. They receive little or no payment for their services, and have few opportunities to alleviate their burden. This was evident in some of the stories in Chapter 3, which described the difficulty of earning enough money to pay the bills and still having enough time for healthy and rewarding activities that benefit the individuals themselves and their communities.

The loss of unremunerated sustaining services translates into unmaintained gardens, declining social engagement, less time to participate in democratic institutions, and more stress. The Romanian-born economist Nicolai Georgescu-Roegen distinguished between productive resources that are stocks and those that are funds. A stock is a productive resource that may be used at any rate; a fund is a resource that can be used only at a certain rate. For example, seven tons of coal can be burned in one day, or one ton can be burned every day for seven days. By contrast, a worker can dig one ditch a day for seven days, but cannot dig seven ditches in a single day. A stock can produce flows at any rate, whereas a fund can produce services only at a certain rate. The latter rate is constrained by biological, ecological, and physical processes and the time they require. Georgescu-Roegen (1984: 24) explains:

> In every enterprise, in every household, a substantial amount of labor-time and material are steadily devoted to keeping the buildings, the machines, the durable goods, in a useful, workable state ... Undoubtedly, when a worker leaves a process, he is a tired individual. But when the same individual returns to work next day he is again a rested worker after being restored in an adjacent household.

The underlying biases that negate the value of care are also reflected in the wages we pay to those who provide care in the marketplace. Those who feed us and care for us are some of the lowest paid in our society. These are the farm workers, food service workers, childcare workers, and domestic workers who tend to our fields, look after our children and elderly, and maintain our homes and gardens. In the United States, 94 percent of domestic workers are women, 37 percent are African American, and 15 percent are Hispanic. Contrary to what we may think, however, care is not optional. It is a necessity and an essential part of being human. We humans have higher care needs for our young and old than possibly any other species. The care work that ensures that productive work can happen in the first place must therefore be recognized as the skilled and valuable work it is. According to the political scientist Joan Tronto (1993; 1998), there are at least four dimensions to care:

1. Caring About. This recognizes that care is a necessity and a fact of life. It is therefore erroneous to associate it with helplessness and inferiority.
2. Taking Care Of. Since care is indispensable, we must establish a flexible notion of it that does not adhere to cultural norms of what women are supposed to do or what black, brown, or Asian people are expected to do. Everyone must contribute to care.
3. Care-Giving. The actual work of care must be based on competence. We must recognize the value of care and view a lack of competence in care-giving as unacceptable. Skill and competence—not gender, race, or ethnicity—must define who provides care and who does not.
4. Care-Receiving. This recognizes that those in need of care may be vulnerable but they are also essential to defining what their care looks like and how it is provided. In other words, the care-receiver's response to care must form the basis for determining the type of care they need and its value.

All four of these dimensions reflect the fact that human life and its quality depend on a web of sustaining services and relationships. Yet, even if we understand that productive work and care work are complementary, care work is not accorded its proper value. The marketplace cannot resolve this problem. Instead, we need political commitments to valuing and remunerating the sustaining care services provided in households, communities, and ecosystems as well as the productive services provided in the marketplace. Policies and institutional frameworks must support rather than hinder more equitable and flexible notions of paid care work as well as arrangements where care is simply expected as an indispensable part of productive work. Moreover, the need for long-term care for the elderly will continue to grow as human life expectancy increases and ever more people experience the inevitable decline associated with the aging process or become chronically ill.

Rather than focusing on different age groups, ethnic groups, or other subsets of the population, a more generally applicable typology of care work is needed that recognizes at least three dimensions of care: rest, restoration, and recreation (O'Hara, 2014). First, the need for rest is almost ubiquitous. It is difficult to imagine any process that does not require at least some rest. Even a machine must be turned off occasionally for maintenance. Our need for rest reminds us of our biological and physiological limitations as well as our inescapable ties to the natural world. Yet many of us seem to find it difficult to accept this reality. Rest is often viewed negatively as we try to be active and productive around the clock. The expectations of this rest-less productivity are especially evident in the ubiquity of so-called "time-saving" electronic devices such as smartphones, tablets, and laptops. The overt and covert expectation is that we should work and remain accessible all the time. But non-human systems and materials are also subject to the expectations of limitless productivity. Fallow periods used to be an integral part of crop rotation to avoid the overuse of soils, yet the practice has become all but obsolete. There has been some kickback against the expectation of limitless work, as those who have resisted the pressure to return to the office post-COVID would testify. Yet, simply put, rest is not an option but a necessity. It reminds us that we need to feed our bodies and rest our minds in order to revive our capacity to work.

Second, restoration becomes necessary when signs of overuse, stress, and decline are evident. The caring work of restoration requires more than just rest. It requires renewing sink capacities to absorb, process, and buffer the stressors, emissions, and waste products that impact our ecosystems and human communities. The restoration of ecosystems such as coastal wetlands may be costly, but it is feasible. However, it demands a thorough understanding of how absorptive and restorative capacities work, and of the complex networks of processes that support and sustain them. The parallels between vulnerable ecosystems and human health are rather obvious. For example, activities associated with improving physical and emotional health can be viewed as restorative care activities. Yet, there is far more to human restoration than healthcare or caring for the sick. Relationships, social connections, and communal activities all help to restore and revitalize us. Restoration should therefore encompass maintaining and strengthening our connections with other people and the places where such restorative connections take place. However, rather than doing this, we tend to undermine our communities' capacity for restoration care. Whenever this happens, someone has to pay the price—most likely the victims of overuse, stress, and exhaustion themselves. This default position of "let the victim pay" seems to be entirely inconsistent with ethical standards of public responsibility, not to mention the legal principle of "polluter pays," which states that the costs of restoration should be borne by those who cause the damage.

Third, recreational care work encompasses more than merely restoring the status quo. It involves increasing our capacity, improving our creativity, and replenishing our ability to think new thoughts and be innovative. Therefore, making room for and supporting recreational care work is imperative, especially in the knowledge-based economies of the information age. So, what will it take to sustain the innovation capacity of the United States? The food innovators in our six cities provide some pointers. First, we can draw inspiration from their can-do energy. Second, we should celebrate their diversity and range of ideas. People of every gender, race, ethnicity, and socio-economic background are capable of out-of-the-box thinking, and we will need creative solutions from all of them if we are to create a sustainable food system on a planet of 8 million people.

The three dimensions of care work are most evident in the story of Chispas Farm (see Chapter 5), whose owner spoke so eloquently about heeding the warning signs that our own bodies send us. The owner's commitment to taking regular sabbaticals from work and delegating responsibility to the team members and volunteers who comprise the farm's sustaining network demonstrates their understanding that rest, restoration, and recreation are essential for future productivity. The natural consequence of this is a recalibration of our understanding of who gives and who receives, and whose contributions are valuable and whose are not. For example, those who receive in our current, charity-based food system may turn out to be the ones who make the most important contributions to defining the kind of food system we want in the future.

Getting subsidies and transfer payments right

Subsidies can mitigate the externality and public goods problems that have rendered our food system less than optimal for food producers, consumers, and society at large. They can even be used to protect sink capacities and achieve social goals like decent wages for farmers. They can do this by encouraging the production of some products while discouraging others, or by moving prices and production costs in the right direction. Subsidized crops, for example, can be offered at lower prices, therefore encouraging consumers to buy them. Subsidized production methods might, for example, reward farmers for using cover crops during the winter, which lowers the cost of avoiding surface and ground-water pollution.

US farm subsidies are exceedingly complex and consist of many layers of programs that use several of these strategies. The first few iterations of the Farm Bill in the 1930s provided subsidies to farmers who produced commodity crops like feed grains, wheat, rice, cotton, and wool. Commodity-crop subsidies have increased steadily since then, with the exception of a few years during the 1950s. In the 1940s, direct payments were added in large part because memories of the Dust Bowl were still fresh in everyone's mind, and it was widely viewed as imperative that farmers should get a decent wage for their labor. Fifty years later, the 1996 Farm Bill decoupled program payments from actual plantings and instead based them on historical production. Supplemental and ad hoc Disaster Assistance Payments, Fixed Direct Payments, Counter-Cyclical Payments, Peanut Quota Buyout Payments, and Milk Income Loss Payments were all added in 2002. Since then, programs like Cotton Transition Assistance Payments (CTAP), Average Crop Revenue Elections (ACRE), Price Loss Coverage (PLC), Dairy Margin Coverage, Tobacco Transition Payments, and the Biomass Crop Assistance Program (BCAP) have been introduced. This vast array of programs suggests that there is no clear definition of agricultural subsidies. While the first Farm Bill was divided into only two policy areas—Agricultural Adjustments and Agricultural Credits—by 2018 there were 12 policy titles across multiple agencies. Subsidies under these 12 titles related primarily to wheat, corn, soybeans, cotton, and rice. Some also went to dairy and animal feed. To make matters even more complicated, not only the programs but also the mechanisms through which farm payments are made have changed. Five primary types of subsidies are outlined in recent US Farm Bills:

- Direct payments that are paid annually based on a farm's history of crop production and regardless of whether they grow crops or not.
- Counter-cyclical payments that are triggered when market prices for certain crops fall below a predetermined threshold.
- Revenue assurance payments that ensure overall profitability for certain crops.
- Marketing loans that offer favorable terms to farmers, including loan deficiency payments (LDPs), where a loan can be forgone in return for an anticipated future payment for an eligible commodity crop.
- Disaster payments that recoup large losses due to a natural disaster; this also includes subsidized crop insurance to insulate farmers from risk.

Given the history of increasingly complex and layered subsidies, it is not surprising that precise figures about who receives what payments—and for what—are difficult to come by. Some watchdog groups have tried, but a lack of transparency makes their investigations challenging (Environmental Working Group, 2023; Stray Dog Institute, 2023; Gurian-Sherman, 2008). For example, when a recipient receives a loan through a bank or other financial institution, the USDA will release the name of the bank or financial institution, but not the recipient's name. This practice was introduced in 2019, during the Trump administration, presumably to veil the fact that the wealthiest (and predominantly white) farmers receive the bulk of the commodity subsidies. Further research established that almost 80 percent of the commodity subsidies allocated between 1996 and 2021 went to the top 10 percent of farmers, with almost 30 percent going to the top 1 percent. Meanwhile, just 9 percent of all subsidies were split between 80 percent of the nation's farmers (Schechinger and Faber, 2023; Agriculture Fairness Alliance, 2023). Despite these recent extremes, the practice of supporting the largest and wealthiest farms is not entirely new. In fact, farm subsidy programs are designed that way: payments are based primarily on acreage and premium tonnage of production, so the farms with the most acres and/or the most crops produced receive the largest payments. Meanwhile, those with small farms only qualify for small payments by virtue of the small size of their operations.

During the recent COVID pandemic, payments to US farms skyrocketed to close to $50 billion in an effort to stabilize the nation's food supply. Here, too, large commercial farms were the winners, receiving 97 percent of the subsidies provided by the Coronavirus Food Assistance Program (CFAP) (Schechinger and Faber, 2023; Agriculture Fairness Alliance, 2023). A few years earlier, the Market Facilitation Program (MFP), which the Trump administration introduced to mitigate the impact of the 2016 Sino-US tariff war, also subsidized large, wealthy farms, while those with the greatest need received the least direct support (Rosenberg and Stucki, 2019).

Of course, no one specifies that the bulk of agricultural subsidies should go to large, wealthy, and predominantly white farmers. Marketing companies have long honed the art of market segmentation based on demographic, psychographic, geographic, and behavioral data. Similar segmentation strategies have been employed by policy strategists intent on shifting the benefits of agricultural subsidies to their clients: namely, large farming enterprises that have amassed tremendous political and financial power. These commercial farming operations have access to capital, land, innovative technology, and political influence. In the process, the wealthiest farmers have become even richer due to policy segmentation that favors large, vertically integrated operations that control every step of the supply chain from field to fork (Agrolearner, 2023). Small farmers, in turn, lack the market power to influence regulations. As food safety standards, product specifications, and equipment standards are shaped by large commercial farms, small farms are finding it increasingly difficult, and increasingly costly, to meet both the regulations and the financial metrics that are tailored to large operations. Of course, this means that many of them find it impossible to stay in business, at which point one of the mega-farms will happily take possession of their land.

Since most farm subsidies focus on commodity crops, there is also little support for growers of "specialty crops" (USDA jargon for fruits and vegetables) or urban agriculture schemes. Unfortunately, little information is available about support for local production initiatives (Johnson et al., 2020; USA Facts, 2023), but it has been estimated that farmers received almost $45 billion in direct-payment subsidies in 2020, while $6 billion went to crop insurance premiums and only about $1.2 billion to fruit and vegetable production (Agriculture Fairness Alliance, 2023).

While subsidies are paid to agricultural enterprises in exchange for producing specific crops or adopting particular production methods, transfer payments are a one-way street, paid to a person or organization that is not expected to provide any product or service in return. This contrasts with a "simple payment," which in economic terms is a transfer of money in exchange for a particular product or service. The Supplemental Nutrition Assistance Program (SNAP) is the main vehicle through which transfer payments are made, but there are also domestic food assistance schemes, such as the Special Supplemental Nutrition Program for Women, Infants, and Children (WIC), and child nutrition schemes, such as the National School Lunch Program and the School Breakfast Program. Collectively, these and other assistance programs reached an all-time high of $182.5 billion in 2021, largely to counteract the surge in food insecurity US households experienced during the COVID pandemic (Martin, 2023). Two new, temporary programs—the Pandemic Electronic Benefits Transfer and the Farmers to Families Food Box Program—were introduced during the pandemic. Food banks and food pantries swiftly criticized the lack of checks and balances in both schemes. In addition, as we saw in Chapter 3, some small farmers were refused permission to deliver food to local food pantries, while some pantries complained that the food they did receive was substandard. More importantly, addressing the immediate food-security needs of local communities through transfer payments does little to address the underlying causes of food insecurity.

According to the Food Research and Action Center (2023), SNAP payments generate $1.79 in economic activity for every $1 invested. Ironically, though, this multiplier effect is created by allowing recipients to spend the transfer payments on items other than food. In other words, the transfer payments do not generate economic independence and self-sufficiency among the recipients; nor do they make any difference to how food is produced or how farm workers are paid. Therefore, SNAP would likely have a far greater impact if it were reconstituted as a work and empowerment program, rather than a transfer payments program. For example, recent data shows that 12 percent of New York City's residents fall below the federal poverty threshold, but 35 percent have incomes below a level that would make them self-sufficient (Reznickova, 2023). These gaps can be bridged only by supporting productive and self-sustaining work, rather than consumption. Such empowerment programs must include, or even prioritize, work that is considered care work rather than work that solely focuses on increased productivity. Another obvious problem with SNAP is the fact that the payments cannot be used to purchase prepared meals. This includes a ban on prepared foods that are sold at grocery stores. As some of the stories in Chapter 3 illustrate, food-insecure households often face intense demands on their time. Yet, while well-to-do families can free up time by heating up prepared meals or eating out, SNAP recipients do not have that luxury. The incubator kitchen projects referenced in Chapter 5 illustrate the economic capacity-building potential of prepared meals, so it seems silly to prevent SNAP households from participating in these community-based initiatives.

The SNAP and commodity crops examples illustrate that transfer payments and subsidies sometimes do not go in the right direction, and may even make things worse. Economists call this "intervention failure." US agricultural subsidies and transfer payments are riddled with intervention failures. Since subsidies support commodity crops, including animal feed, they run counter to both environmental and social objectives like reducing greenhouse gases and encouraging plant-based diets. For example, US rice, dairy, beef, and pork producers received an estimated $800 to $2,600 in federal benefits for every ton of methane (CH_4) emitted in 2020 (Agriculture Fairness Alliance, 2022). The Environmental Protection Agency (2022) estimates that methane emissions from the United States' agricultural sector stand at just over 10 million tons per year—roughly equivalent to the methane emissions generated by the country's energy sector. On the social front, dietary guidelines suggest that Americans should fill half of every plate with fruits and (preferably) vegetables (United States Department of Agriculture and United States Department of Health and Human Services, 2020). Yet, less than 3 percent of all farm subsidies support fruit and vegetable production and just 13 percent go to the cultivation of edible grains, while more than 30 percent support livestock and animal-feed production (Farm Action, 2022; O'Neill-Hayes and Kerska, 2021). Of course, farmers are likely to grow crops that they know will make them eligible for subsidies. Meanwhile, an estimated 80 to 90 percent of the US population falls short of consuming the recommended amounts of fruits and vegetables and instead consume too many processed foods, including refined grains and sugar. Yet, commodity-crop subsidies go to growers of wheat and corn—crops that are turned into white flour and corn syrup (O'Neill-Hayes and Kerska, 2021).

At a more basic level, agricultural subsidies run counter to economic theory itself. To ensure the best outcome for society, markets should be transparent and competitive, not murky and monopolistic. According to economic theory, markets are at their best, and achieve the best outcome for society as a whole, when they are decentralized, with a large number of players and widely distributed power. This is precisely why anti-trust laws were created. Yet, the food and agriculture sector is dominated by a small number of "superstar farms" that continue to grow at the expense of a fast-shrinking fringe of small and medium-sized operations. Similar market concentrations are occurring in other sectors of the economy, too. Amazon is a particularly interesting example in the retail sector. It uses artificial intelligence and social media not only to facilitate exchange in its marketplace, but to create both the marketplace itself and demand within it. The superstar retailer has created enormous market power through vertical and horizontal integration as it controls supply chains and functions across the production, distribution, and consumption of an array of products and services (Duhigg, 2019). Similarly, superstar farms have advanced the vertical and horizontal integration of the agricultural sector. Their vertical integration includes large food buyers and processors that leave small farmers with few options to sell their crops to anyone else.

In his book *The Great Reversal*, economist Thomas Philippon (2019) documents the decline of competition in US markets due to the unprecedented growth of a small number of superstar firms. As he explains, this phenomenon has been detrimental to US workers and consumers alike. A reluctance to enforce existing anti-trust regulations, coupled with a seemingly laissez-faire philosophy that suggests that all regulation is bad, has resulted in ever more sectors resembling the monopoly markets of early capitalism. Moreover, in agriculture, farm subsidies have exacerbated the process of the big getting bigger and the small disappearing.

Another intervention failure is the lack of coordination among federal programs. For example, SNAP allows recipients to buy seeds so they can grow their own food. In theory, this could enable them to be far less reliant on transfer payments, as just $1 of seeds and fertilizer generally yields about $25 of produce. Yet, SNAP is not connected to the specialty crop program or other USDA initiatives that provide technical and financial assistance to those who grow, preserve, process, and prepare food. Moreover, transfer payment programs are not linked to schemes that facilitate land acquisition and preservation, or those that assist the development of cooperatives. SNAP's strict work requirement also means that recipients are unable to enroll in training programs that would teach them how to grow their own food or even start value-added food-processing and -preparation businesses.

While current subsidies and transfer payments clearly do not facilitate a sustainable, resilient, and just food system, there are nonetheless a few signs of hope. For example, regenerative agriculture is starting to receive some attention. This term refers to an approach to food and farming systems that includes regenerating topsoil, protecting and increasing biodiversity, improving water quality, and restoring and enhancing ecosystems and the services they provide, mostly with a focus on maintaining productivity. While this productivity orientation means regenerative agriculture is not entirely the same as a restorative food system (which incorporates values beyond productivity), it is certainly a step in the right direction. Many regenerative practices are also the focus of sustainable agriculture that minimizes waste and closes loops wherever possible. Such practices are often integral to permaculture, agroecology, agroforestry, restorative ecology, and holistic management, all of which are usually associated with small-scale farming that is keenly aware of how its practices interact with the physical, ecological, and environmental context around it (see Chapter 5 for several impressive examples from Chispas Farms, Planting Justice, 4P Foods, Ponics, and others). Yet, larger enterprises are also starting to adopt regenerative techniques, such as non-till or reduced-till farming. It makes sense to support these initiatives through a reallocation of subsidies as long as specific program requirements are put in place that protect small growers and prevent large operations from receiving support for green-washing strategies that make no real progress toward a sustainable and just food system.

The USDA's Risk Management Agency (RMA) may be one of the first organizations to benefit from the reallocation of subsidies toward regenerative agriculture schemes. Created in 1996, it serves US agricultural producers through the provision of effective, market-based risk-management tools like crop insurance and strategies to reduce climate vulnerabilities. At present, the agency focuses primarily on conventional, rural agriculture. However, existing vehicles, such as the Whole Farm and Micro Farm Policy, could be used to provide small farmers, specialty crop producers, and urban growers with similar assistance. For example, the RMA recently announced revisions that will make it easier for specialty crop producers and others who sell through direct marketing channels to obtain insurance and file claims. It has also pledged to provide assistance to those who face the daunting task of navigating their way through filing requirements and eligibility definitions, and has announced an expansion of its Risk Management Education for Farmers Program. This is especially welcome news for historically under-served applicants. In 2021, the USDA invested $3.1 billion in its new Partnerships for Climate-Smart Commodities (United States Department of Agriculture, 2023d). Currently, these programs are primarily focused on conventional, rural agriculture, with the exception of a few sub-grant awards aimed at urban and peri-urban climate-smart mitigation schemes. However, they could be expanded to level the playing field for small peri-urban and urban producers as well.

Another step in the right direction would be to include soil-less production in USDA programs. Subsidies are currently limited to soil-based production, with soil-less and indoor production both ineligible to receive any assistance. This prohibition creates barriers for food innovators who wish to employ climate-smart and regenerative practices that conserve water and nutrients, reduce their reliance on pesticides and cold storage, and so on. It is time to recognize the benefits of these food production methods from both a risk-management and a sustainability perspective, and provide them with access to subsidies.

Support for regenerative agriculture must also extend to the next generation of farmers. Retaining top talent within the farming sector is difficult in rural America, and equally challenging for urban agriculture (Rangarajan and Riordan, 2019). One promising approach is a workforce development partnership between private industry, the Department of Labor, and the USDA modeled on the Department of Labor Apprenticeship USA Program, which was launched in 2013 and has seen a steady increase in participants since then (United States Department of Labor, 2023). More recently, an apprenticeship program specifically for agriculture was added in a bid to address the well-documented shortage of agricultural workers in the United States (Castillo and Simnitt, 2023). Up to now, the new apprenticeship program has focused on conventional and rural farming, but there are plans to expand it to urban and controlled-environment agriculture. In 2021, the USDA authorized grants for controlled-environment agriculture projects. The expectation is that these will be continuously expanded to test and implement new agricultural initiatives, including the new apprenticeship partnerships.

Moving toward a restorative food system requires both technical and human capacity-building as well as a new approach to subsidies and transfer payments. Following the model of the new Partnerships for Climate-Smart Commodities, transfer payments could be used to incentivize workforce development in the green and restorative economy and the care economy. Specifically, these payments could be used to provide living wages in the currently underpaid care sector and to establish a compensation scheme for people who currently receive no remuneration for their contributions, such as those who are working to enhance the resilience and quality of life of their local communities. Contributions that increase a community's capacity to maintain or improve the physical and mental health of the next generation, and those that lead to better learning outcomes, must be considered especially valuable since they facilitate improved economic, social, and environmental conditions in the future.

The restorative economy model introduced in Chapter 4 provides the framework for establishing this new subsidies and transfer payments system. It takes policy-makers' familiar objectives as its starting point, then adds neglected social and environmental objectives that undergird the long-term viability and success of any food system. It also recognizes the fact that such systems can be undermined by unfettered markets and even incentives to correct their failures. The food system we want and need must:

1. redefine efficiency as the efficient and prudent use of assets, including labor, capital, and natural resources;
2. reduce emissions and waste through improved processes and closed loops by design rather than as an afterthought;
3. strengthen sink capacities through improved ecosystem services and social support networks; and
4. redefine policy objectives as restorative by fulfilling principles 1, 2, and 3.

These four principles imply that estimates of the total cost of food production will need to consider not just familiar input factors like fertilizers, fuel, tractor hours, water, labor, and so on, but also emissions, such as nitrates that leach into the ground water, carbon dioxide that is emitted into the atmosphere, food waste, and, crucially, the impact of different production methods on sink capacities like water filtration, heat absorption, the reduced stress associated with better food access, and supportive social connections. Several of the stories introduced in Chapter 5 illustrate the multiple gains achieved by production methods that do more than improve the efficiency of labor and add the benefits of stronger social and environmental sink capacities. It would make sense to subsidize farmers who adopt these methods, rather than those who increase their yields by exploiting environmental and social assets. The current system of subsidies and transfer payments does the exact opposite. Supposedly "costly" decentralized, smaller-scale urban and peri-urban food production that creates meaningful, well-paid work, increases permeable surfaces in the urban landscape, sequesters carbon, preserves biodiversity, mitigates flooding, and alleviates the impact of heat islands is actually comparatively cheap—and highly valuable—when its total contributions are taken into account. Similarly, paying for work that improves the esthetics and safety of neighborhoods, reduces commuting times, and frees up time to engage with family members and neighbors may be considered a sound investment when the positive impact of such payments on environmental and social sinks is factored into the equation.

These examples illustrate the opportunities that the restorative food systems model can create and the political will that will be necessary to implement it.

Getting the metrics right

The sad state of existing food and agriculture policies raises questions about the metrics that are currently in use. The lobbyists of superstar farms have been very effective at defining these metrics. The result is a food system that is characterized by volume-based eligibility criteria and the notion that "bigger is better," both of which run counter to the four principles of a restorative food system.

Joan Tronto's research into care competencies provides some pointers toward an alternative, more equitable set of metrics by highlighting that those in need of assistance should be consulted when deciding how the performance of care is measured (Tronto, 1993). In other words, those in need of food, shelter, and support, rather than those who provide these things, should have the final say when the performance standards of a sustainable and just food system are defined. Several of those who discussed food insecurity in Chapter 3 spoke of the need to shift agency from care-givers to care-receivers and acknowledge the expertise of those who receive care. Such a shift is essential, as those who could make the most valuable contributions to changing the current, charity-based emergency food system are rarely at the table when policy objectives and performance metrics are defined (O'Hara, 1999; O'Hara et al., 2023).

This is one reason why diversity is so important. Those who are commonly excluded, and those whose competencies are routinely questioned, must be consulted when the performance metrics of a restorative food system are defined. There are sound practical, as well as moral, reasons to adopt this approach. For example, a recent study on urban agriculture found that cities that failed to include local residents and businesses in the decision-making process were more likely to waste time and resources on ineffective policies (Rangarajan and Riordan, 2019). Moreover, introducing a zoning policy in support of urban agriculture made little difference if other municipal services were misaligned and the policy implementation lacked the broad-based dialogue necessary to identify synergies and remove obstacles.

In 2021, the Biden–Harris administration signed Executive Order 13985, "On Advancing Racial Equity and Support for Underserved Communities through the Federal Government" (White House, 2021a). This compelled federal agencies to put their own houses in order and address discriminatory and exclusionary policies in their own ranks. Given the long history of excluding small, African American, and Hispanic farmers from subsidies, and of portraying low-income, African American, and Hispanic recipients of food assistance as welfare queens and social burdens, Section 1006 of the American Rescue Plan (ARP) directed the USDA to establish an Equity Commission and take action to ensure that under-served producers have the tools, programs, and support they need to succeed. The ARP states:

The COVID-19 pandemic and the corresponding economic crisis have undermined the health and economic wellbeing of American workers. Millions of Americans, many of whom are people of color, immigrants, and low-wage workers, continue to put their lives on the line every day to keep the country functioning through the pandemic. And more than 9.5 million workers have lost their jobs in the wake of COVID-19, with 4 million out of work for half a year or longer. Without additional government assistance, the economic and public health crises could drag on and our national vaccination program will be hobbled at a critical moment.

(White House, 2021b: 1)

Under the umbrella of the ARP, the federal government provided funding to the USDA Equity Commission to ensure that it was adequately staffed and well positioned to carry out its duties (United States Department of Agriculture National Institute of Food and Agriculture, 2021). The same funding mechanism provided the USDA with an additional $1 billion for equity initiatives in support of historically under-served farmers, ranchers, and forest landowners.

The USDA launched its Equity Commission in February 2022, having previously tasked it with analyzing how its "programs, policies, systems, structures, and practices contribute to exclusionary practices and systemic discrimination that exacerbate or perpetuate racial, economic, health and social disparities" (United States Department of Agriculture, 2022a). In addition, the commission was tasked with providing the US Secretary of Agriculture with recommendations for action. It comprised 15 members drawn from a broad range of stakeholders, including small businesses, farm workers' groups, higher-education institutions, members of organizations that advocate for under-served communities, minorities, women, individuals with disabilities, individuals with limited English proficiency, rural communities, and LGBTQI+ communities. Two of the expressed objectives were to improve access to resources and to restore trust in the USDA among constituencies that have long been excluded from its decision-making processes.

However, the section of the ARP that outlined the commission's equity and access work was almost immediately blocked by lawsuits launched by farmers in Wisconsin, Minnesota, South Dakota, Ohio, and Texas—states that, collectively, had received 24 percent of the subsidies provided under the previous Trump administration's MFP (Hayes, 2021). In response, Congress repealed ARP and instead appended several sections to the recent Inflation Reduction Act.

This example illustrates that the current food system will not be reformed by policy-making alone. Legislative and social support will be needed if we are to build a more sustainable and just, restorative food system.

The Equity Commission delivered its *Interim Report* in 2023 (United States Department of Agriculture Equity Commission, 2023). One of its initial objectives had been to document all policy recommendations related to equity that had been provided to the USDA since the publication of the Equal

Opportunity in Farm Programs Report in 1965. However, after six months of deliberations, the Equity Commission acknowledged that documenting every past recommendation to address historical inequities in USDA policies, practices, and processes was an impossible task, given the sheer number of recommendations that had been issued over the previous 55 years. Instead, the commission collated 748 recommendations from 11 historic reports into just 32 recommendations for consideration by the USDA and the Secretary of Agriculture (United States Department of Agriculture Equity Commission, 2023). The number of historic recommendations might lead one to think that the USDA has initiated numerous policy actions to address the plight of under-served groups since 1965. However, this is not the case. Despite the long list of recommendations, disparities actually increased over the years, and small producers (including urban producers) were consistently overlooked. Therefore, the *Interim Report* could be viewed as progress, even though there is still a long way to go. Two subcommittees helped to draft the report—one focused on policy goals and objectives, while the other looked into rural economic development—so only a few of the recommendations relate specifically to urban and peri-urban agriculture.

One of the *Interim Report*'s more important recommendations is to include beneficiaries in evaluations of the effectiveness of transfer payments. However, while SNAP is funded at the federal level, it is administered at the state level, so federal legislation would be needed to compel all states to include beneficiaries in their evaluations of food assistance programs. Historically, each state has had the freedom to design its own programs in the best interests of the state, but not necessarily the best interests of the beneficiaries. The Atlanta and Albuquerque stories in Chapter 3 are two great examples of customer-centered initiatives that could be expanded in the wake of such a shift in legislative authority (United States Department of Agriculture Equity Commission, 2023).

The Equity Commission also addressed long-term barriers to accessing land and capital. This has been a serious issue in the United States ever since the Homestead Act, which not only sanctioned the appropriation of land from indigenous people but also favored European settlers over those of African descent. The *Interim Report*'s conclusions confirm those of previous studies, which found that land-access programs routinely exclude a number of groups, including inexperienced farmers, women, people of color, and farm workers (United States Department of Agriculture Equity Commission, 2023). Moreover, these access barriers are often exacerbated in urban and peri-urban communities, where land values are high. Public and collective ownership models, such as land banks, community land trusts, and cooperatives, help to level the land-access playing field in urban and peri-urban areas. Chicago, for example, has created land banks that provide land, or at least land access, to urban growers. Land banks can also assist in the transition to landownership by making plots available for startup projects. Similarly, as we saw in Chapter 5, for-profit social enterprises like Bubbly Dynamics can provide small, food-sector businesses with access to land and facilities.

Two promising recent developments are the Farm Service Agency's announcement of $550 million in funding for the Increasing Land, Capital, and Market Access Program, which includes increasing access within under-served urban communities, and the launch of the Natural Resources Conservation Service's Cooperative Agreements for Racial Justice and Equity, which can be used for land acquisition. Both of these programs include funding for community-based land access, which should lead to greater equity (United States Department of Agriculture, 2022b). However, further funding and better coordination will be needed to convert vacant city lots, roofs, and abandoned factory buildings into viable food spaces, as the example of Bubbly Dynamics demonstrates (see Chapter 5). Many promising community enterprises have been undermined, and eventually forced to shut down, by tax policies that treat agricultural and investment space as standard commercial space. Another of the Equity Commission's recommendations is noteworthy here: namely, its suggestion that the current definition of "farm" needs to change. This is because the current definition creates barriers for very small and subsistence farmers whose operations are built on bartering, sharing, and other communal models. Since these models do not follow standard accounting practices, such enterprises routinely fail to meet eligibility criteria and are therefore excluded from a wide range of subsidies (United States Department of Agriculture Equity Commission, 2023).

As this section has demonstrated, the current subsidies and transfer payments system relies on metrics that exacerbate rather than reduce disparities. Table 6.1 suggests a new, more equitable set of metrics based on the four components of a restorative food system. However, those most affected by food insecurity, and the innovators who are attempting to address this problem, must be consulted to refine this list and create the food system we want.

TABLE 6.1 Suggested metrics of a sustainable and just food system

	Efficiency	Emissions/ waste	Sink capacities	Overall performance
Environmental impact	Reduce use of non-renewables Reduce use of renewables	Reduce emissions Reduce food waste	Paid care positions to improve environmental sinks Create ecosystem capacities	Meet at least one metric in each of the first three columns
Social impact	Remunerate work with living wages Increase skills through capacity-building	Improve food-related health outcomes Reduce nature deprivation Reduce stress	Paid care positions to improve social sinks Time for social interaction Time for democratic engagement	Meet at least one metric in each of the first three columns

Getting the right information

Almost all of the contributors to Chapters 3 and 5 highlight the importance of education, be it in the form of learning how to prepare food, understanding how to cook on a budget, teaching urban gardeners how to grow their own food, exploring new food-production techniques, or providing continuous learning. Early-childhood education on the benefits of fruits and vegetables is crucial, too (Kostecka et al., 2021), and is especially well articulated in the stories from Albuquerque (Chapter 3) and Atlanta (Chapter 5). Yet, learning opportunities are not equally distributed, either. This is because many people—especially those in under-served communities—simply do not have the time, energy, and financial resources that are needed to facilitate the learning process.

The resulting unequal educational playing field is nowhere more evident than in the USDA's grant-allocation system. As with subsidies and transfer payments, grants are generally delivered in the form of direct payments. Some of the USDA's grants are specifically reserved for land-grant universities. These were established as early as 1862, when one university per state was launched and funded through the sale of federal lands taken from native peoples. The expressed mission of the land-grant universities was to build the economic capacity of their home states by conducting research and educating students, chiefly in the agricultural and applied sciences. The third component of the land-grant university system, in addition to research and teaching, was to share research findings through a network of community outreach offices that became known as the Cooperative Extension Service. Since some southern states refused to hire African American faculty members and admit African American students, a second group of land-grant universities was formed in 1890; these institutions were known as "historically black colleges and universities" (HBCUs). Finally, in 1994, the government established a third group of land-grant colleges ostensibly dedicated to education and capacity-building in Native American communities. However, there was no allocation of public land to these institutions. Today, there are 112 land-grant institutions in total—58 1862s; 19 1890s; and 35 1994s—ranging in size from very small colleges to very large research universities (National Research Council, 2001; National Education Association, 2022).

The National Institute of Food and Agriculture (NIFA) administers two types of grant on behalf of the USDA: capacity grants and competitive grants. Capacity grants are recurring federal appropriations allocated on the basis of legislative formulas to US states, territories, and the District of Columbia. States are generally required to contribute matching funds in exchange for their capacity grant allocations. Recipient land-grant universities must conduct research and community outreach programs in fields defined by the NIFA, including the likes of food security, food safety, water resources management, and climate mitigation. Meanwhile, institutions may apply for competitive grants, which are awarded for specific projects. This dual system has resulted in a long history of unequal funding for the land-grant universities that continues to this day, despite some recent progress (Partrige, 2023; Lee and Keys, 2013; Humphries, 1991). Current funding formulas also disadvantage institutions that serve urban areas as both capacity grants and competitive grants frequently refer to rural programs in their eligibility criteria. The funding formula for 1862 research funds, for example, refers to 26 percent of the funding "to each state in amounts proportionate to the relative rural population of each state to the total rural population of all states"; and 26 percent "to each state in amounts proportionate to the relative farm population of each state to the total farm population of all states" (Congressional Research Service, 2022). Similarly, the funding formula for 1890 research grants requires 40 percent proportionality with respect to both rural and farming populations (Congressional Research Service, 2022). These funding formulas disadvantage not only urban populations but especially African American populations, who are known to comprise a smaller percentage of the population of rural America. In 2020, each of the 1862 institutions received an average of $11.6 million in research and cooperative extension funding, while the 1890 institutions received an average of $7.5 million; the 1994 colleges received only $137,000 per institution (Congressional Research Service, 2022; Partrige, 2023).

In addition to universities, grants typically go to research institutions and nonprofit organizations, although some are paid to businesses and individuals. There are also so-called "block grants," which are provided to states or land-grant universities for distribution to other organizations on the basis of strict eligibility criteria. One of these is the Specialty Crops Block Grant, which provides funds for organizations that promote increased consumption of fresh fruits and vegetables.

The grant-application process tends to be quite demanding. For example, urban food innovators have expressed frustration over what they view as an unnecessarily complicated application process. Similarly, food pantries and other nonprofit organizations have pointed out that the process is very time-consuming, which leaves them with less time to focus on their core mission. The first hurdle is simply identifying a potential grant. Since 2007, the USDA has issued over 2,500 grants and agreements totaling more than $210 billion (Grants.gov, 2023). Federal grants are typically announced on the Grants.gov website, which also accepts applications from grant-seekers. Yet, not all USDA grants are announced and managed in this way: some are issued directly to organizations that are deemed to have the necessary skills and knowledge to carry out a specific project. Of course, such grants tend to go to those who have already built up a funding relationship with the USDA, rather than those who are seeking grants for the first time. This two-tier system makes it impossible to determine either the total number of grants or the total level of funding.

Barriers to securing grant funding extend to other federal agencies as well. The Environmental Protection Agency (EPA), the Department of Housing and Urban Development (HUD), and the Department of Labor all have programs that support different aspects of urban agriculture. However, they lack coordination. For example, an urban farmer may receive a grant from the EPA for soil testing, or a community may receive a HUD Community Development Block Grant, yet neither of these grants can be used as leverage in applications for funds from the USDA to establish a local farmers' market. Therefore, it is hardly surprising that a study of 14 commercial urban farms conducted by the USDA's Agriculture Marketing Service and Cornell University found that several of them identified securing grant funding as their most persistent challenge (Rangarajan and Riordan, 2019).

In theory, the USDA values knowledge and bases all its policies on scientific research. For example, the 2018 Agricultural Improvement Act outlines standards for soil health, food safety, regenerative practices, and more (GovInfo, 2018). The USDA has also updated its guidance on geotextiles, raised beds, mulching, composting, urban cover crops, critical area planting, and biochar. Yet, these adjustments tend to lag considerably behind the availability of scientific data, and their implementation is generally slow. The same is true with regard to social-science insights about, for example, the importance of broad-based participation and local expertise (O'Hara et al., 2023). So, the question must be asked: are these delays due to a lack of information or a lack of political will?

Sensible policies can rapidly turn into political footballs if they are not properly funded. For example, the 2018 Farm Bill granted the USDA the authority it needed to begin working on urban and innovation agriculture. Yet, the funding mechanism to support such initiatives did not follow the Farm Bill's five-year funding cycle; instead, it was to be allocated on an annual basis. To ensure some continuity, the law provided the Secretary of Agriculture with a grant and an advisory committee to create the previously mentioned 17 Urban Agriculture Committees as well as funding for composting and food waste-reduction initiatives (GovInfo, 2018). Congress further stated that it intended to enable the Secretary of Agriculture to deliver financial and technical assistance for community gardens, nonprofit farms, education on food systems, nutrition, and the environmental impact of agricultural production, as well as startup funds for new farmers to assist with land acquisition, the purchase of equipment and supplies, and the development of farm cooperatives. Yet, it is unclear how these programs will be funded or how information on these opportunities will be communicated to a wide range of stakeholders, especially in historically under-served communities. This example illustrates that the Secretary of Agriculture and the USDA may have authority over the programs under their purview, but the US Congress has the authority to pass the laws and appropriate the funding that set the foundation for the programs. This invariably impacts when and how programs and policies can be implemented and communicated.

There are some positive signs, though, at least at the municipal and state levels. All of the cities introduced in Chapters 2 and 4 have engaged local stakeholders in their food system innovations and have made efforts to share information about new initiatives. New York City's Office of Food Policy, for example, consulted with a broad range of local stakeholders to develop a ten-year plan to address food insecurity and hunger, improve economic conditions for urban farmers, reduce food waste, increase access to healthy food, and create benchmarks to measure the city's progress toward achieving all of these urban food system goals. Meanwhile, Atlanta passed a zoning ordinance to encourage urban gardening, sustainable production, and economic development, while also minimizing environmental impact (Healthy Food Policy Project, 2023). California is another early adopter of policies to encourage participation in its urban agriculture initiatives: in 2014, the Bay Area established one of the first urban agriculture incentive zones to facilitate improved land access for urban producers in food-insecure neighborhoods (Zigas, 2014). Similar collaborations between the municipality and nonprofit organizations—such as the Urban Growers Collective and the Center for Community Land-Trust Innovation—have been implemented in Chicago.

Food and agriculture policies have multiple objectives, including ensuring an abundance of food, stabilizing food prices, securing living incomes and wages for farmers and farm workers, and slowing the rate at which farmers are leaving the land. These objectives must be universally known so that they can either be challenged, or the effectiveness of policies in achieving them can be monitored and tested. Increasing access to information is also key to augmenting or amending existing objectives to ensure that they still reflect the best interests of society at large. For example, ensuring an abundance of food may have to be augmented with a new objective to prioritize food that is high in nutrients and produced in ways that protect sink capacities. Similarly, the objective of stabilizing food prices may have to be amended to stabilizing the price of the right kinds of food (i.e., those that improve health outcomes) while making sugary foods and those that are high in saturated fats more expensive. Finally, the objective of mitigating the risks associated with climate change and an unsustainable reduction in the number of farms may have to be augmented with a new goal of ensuring that farms are sufficiently diverse to support a resilient food system and engage in practices that will lead to improvements in the health and vitality of the nation's ecosystems and communities.

A restorative food system will be able to realize all of these objectives. However, we have a way to go in making the distortions of current policies more transparent and in informing consumers about the real cost of food. Education and effective communication of the success stories already under way will be key to garnering wide-ranging support for moving toward a more sustainable and just restorative food system.

References

Agriculture Fairness Alliance. (2022). US farm spending in 2020 favored methane production. https://agriculturefairnessalliance.org/news/methane-subsidies-in-the-ag-sector/.

Agriculture Fairness Alliance. (2023). US farm spending in 2020. https://agriculturefairnessalliance.org/news/category/2020farmspending/.

Agrolearner. (2023). Top 5 richest farmers in the United States. https://agrolearner.com/richest-famers-in-america/.

American Diabetes Association. (2018). Economic costs of diabetes in the US in 2017. *Diabetes Care*, 41(5): 917–928. https://doi.org/10.2337/dci18-0007.

Berg, J. (2023). Interview with the author, 15 March.

Berg, J. and Gibson, A. (2022). Why the world should not follow the failed United States model of fighting domestic hunger. *International Journal of Environmental Resources and Public Health*, 19(814). https://doi.org/10.3390/ijerph19020814.

Carson, R. and Hanemann, W. (2006). Contingent valuation. In: Mäler, K.G. and Vincent, J. (eds.), *Handbook of Environmental Economics*, vol. 2. Amsterdam: Elsevier, pp. 821–936.

Case, A. and Deaton, A. (2020). *Deaths of Despair and the Future of Capitalism*. Princeton, NJ: Princeton University Press.

Castillo, M. and Simnitt, S. (2023). Farm labor. https://www.ers.usda.gov/topics/farm-economy/farm-labor/#:~:text=For%20example%2C%20according%20to%20NAWS,percent%20in%20the%202021%20ACS.

Costanza, R. *et al.* (1997). The value of the world's ecosystem services and natural capital. *Nature*, 387(6630): 253–260.

Costanza, R. *et al.* (2014). Changes in the global value of ecosystem services. *Global Environmental Change*, 26: 152–158. doi:10.1016/j.gloenvcha.2014.04.002.

Congressional Research Service. (2022). *The US Land-Grant University System: Overview and Role in Agricultural Research*. https://crsreports.congress.gov/product/pdf/R/R45897/7.

Cushing, L., Faust, J., August, L., Cendak, R., Wieland, W. and Alexeeff, G. (2015). Racial/ ethnic disparities in cumulative environmental health impacts in California: evidence from a statewide environmental justice screening tool (CalEnviroScreen 1.1). *American Journal of Public Health*, 105: 2341–2348. https://doi.org/10.2105/AJPH.2015.302643.

Dallen, K., Jung, L., Dhatt, R. and Phelan, A. (2020). Climate change and gender-based health disparities. *Lancet Planetary Health*, 4(2): E44–E45. https://doi.org/10.1016/S2542-5196(20)30001-2.

Daly, H. and Cobb, J. (1994). *For the Common Good: Redirecting the Economy toward Community, the Environment, and a Sustainable Future*. Boston, MA: Beacon Press.

Duhigg, C. (2019). The unstoppable machine. *New Yorker*, 21 October.

Easter, K.W. and Zeitouni, N. (eds.). (2018). *The Economics of Water Quality*. London: Routledge.

Environmental Protection Agency. (2022). Estimates of methane emissions by sector in the US. https://www.epa.gov/natural-gas-star-program/estimates-methane-emissions-segment-united-states.

Environmental Working Group. (2023). Farm subsidy primer. https://farm.ewg.org/subsidyprimer.php?_gl=1*185stvd*_gcl_au*MTQxMDM4NzE1NC4xNjgzOTE3MDc3*_ga*MTU1NjQ5NDAyNy4xNjgzOTE3MDc3*_ga_CS21GC49KT*MTY4NTMyOTE5NC4xNC4wLjE2ODUzMjkxOTQuMC4wLjA.&_ga=2.79424087.2103949398.1685329194-1556494027.1683917077.

European Commission. (2017). *The EU and Nature-Based Solutions.* https://ec.europa.eu/info/research-and-innovation/research-area/environment/nature-based-solutions_en.

European Commission. (2020). *A New Circular Economy Action Plan for a Cleaner and More Competitive Europe: COM/2020/98 Final.* Brussels: Directorate-General for Environment, European Commission.

Farley, J. and Voinov, A. (2016). Economics, socio-ecological resilience and ecosystem services. *Journal of Environmental Management*, 183: 389–398. doi:10.1016/j.jenvman.2016.07.065.

Farm Action. (2022). References: federal farm subsidies. https://farmaction.us/sub sidies-sources/.

Food Research and Action Center. (2023). The positive effect of SNAP benefits on participants and communities. https://frac.org/programs/supplemental-nutrition-a ssistance-program-snap/positive-effect-snap-benefits-participants-communities#:~: text=Economic%20Impacts&text=For%20example%2C%20SNAP%20is%20good, supports%20for%20low%2Dincome%20families.

Georgescu-Roegen, N. (1984). Feasible recipes versus viable technologies. *Atlantic Economic Journal*, 12: 21–31.

GovInfo. (2018). Public Law 115–334: Agriculture Improvement Act of 2018. https://www.govinfo.gov/app/details/PLAW-115publ334.

Gowdy, J. and O'Hara, S. (1995). *Economic Theory for Environmentalists.* Florida: St. Lucie Press.

Grants.gov. (2023). All Department of Agriculture funding instruments. https://www.grants.gov/web/grants/search-grants.html.

Gurian-Sherman, D. (2008). Direct and indirect subsidies to CAFOs: CAFOs uncovered. http://www.jstor.com/stable/resrep00054.8.

Hajat, A., Hsia, C. and O'Neill, M. (2015). Socioeconomic disparities and air pollution exposure: a global review. *Current Environmental Health Reports*, 2: 440–450. https://doi.org/10.1007/s40572-015-0069-5.

Harris, M. and Fraser, I. (2002). Natural resource accounting in theory and practice: a critical assessment. *Australian Journal of Agricultural and Resource Economics*, 46 (2): 139–192.

Hayes, J. (2021). USDA data: nearly all pandemic bailout funds went to white farmers. https://www.ewg.org/news-insights/news/usda-data-nearly-all-pandemic-bailout-funds-went-white-farmers.

Healthy Food Policy Project. (2023). *Healthy Food Policy Project Database.* https://healthyfoodpolicyproject.org/policy-database.

Henderson, H. (1995). *Paradigms in Progress.* San Francisco, CA: Berrett Koehler Publishing.

Hodgson, K., Campbell, M. and Bailkey, M. (2011). *Urban Agriculture: Growing Healthy, Sustainable Places.* Planning Advisory Service Report No. 563. Chicago: American Planning Association.

Holmes, T., Bergstrom, J., Huszar, E., Kask, S.B. and Orr, F., III. (2004). Contingent valuation, net marginal benefits, and the scale of riparian ecosystem restoration. *Ecological Economics*, 49: 19–30.

Humphries, F. (1991). 1890 land-grant institutions: their struggle for survival and equality. *Agricultural History*, 65(2): 3–11.

Johnson, R., Clifford-Billings, K., Benson, L., Aussenberg, R., Croft, G. and Monke, J. (2020). *Local and Urban Food Systems: Selected Farm Bill and Other Federal Programs.* Congressional Research Service Report No. 46538. https://crsreports.con gress.gov/product/pdf/R/R46538.

Kaufman, S. (2012). Quantifying sustainability: industrial ecology, materials flow and life cycle analysis. In: Zeman, F. (ed.), *Metropolitan Sustainability*. Sawston: Woodhead Publishing, pp. 40–54.

Kostecka, M., Kostecka-Jarecka, J., Kowal, M. and Jackowska, I. (2021). Dietary habits and choices of 4-to-6-year-olds: do children have a preference for sweet taste? *Children*, 8(9): 774. doi:10.3390/children8090774.

Lee, J.M., Jr. and Keys, S.W. (2013). Land-grant but unequal. https://www.aplu.org/wp-content/uploads/executive-summary-land-grant-but-unequal-state-one-to-one-match-funding-for-1890-land-grant-universities.pdf.

Loomis, J., Kent, P., Strange, L., Fausch, K. and Covich, A. (2000). Measuring the total economic value of restoring ecosystem services in an impaired river basin: results from a contingent valuation survey. *Ecological Economics*, 33(1): 103–117.

Martin, A. (2023). Spending on USDA's food and nutrition assistance programs reached a new high in 2021. https://www.ers.usda.gov/data-products/ag-and-food-statistics-charting-the-essentials/food-security-and-nutrition-assistance/?topicId=d7627f77-6cee-4ab9-bbb9-8c74d4778941.

Mazzucato, M. (2020). *The Value of Everything: Making and Taking in the Global Economy*. New York and Philadelphia, PA: Perseus Books.

Meadows, D., Meadows, D., Randers, J. and Behrens, W., III. (1972). *The Limits to Growth: A Report for the Club of Rome's Project on the Predicament of Mankind*. New York: Universe Books.

Mellor, M. (2009). Ecofeminist political economy and the politics of money. In: Salleh, A. (ed.), *Eco-Sufficiency and Global Justice: Women Write Political Ecology*. London: Pluto Press, pp. 251–267.

Mies, M. (1986). *Patriarchy and Accumulation on a World Scale*. London: Zed Books.

Millennium Ecosystem Assessment. (2005). *Ecosystems and Human Well-being*. http://www.millenniumassessment.org/documents/document.356.aspx.pdf.

Mozaffarian, D. and Berg, J. (2021). Failing public health is killing Americans, unequally. *The Hill*, 16 October.

Mumbi, A.W. and Watanabe, T. (2022). Cost estimations of water pollution for the adoption of suitable water treatment technology. *Sustainability*, 14(2): 649.

National Education Association. (2022). *Land Grant Institutions: An Overview*. https://www.nea.org/sites/default/files/2022-03/Land%20Grant%20Institutions%20-%20An%20Overview.pdf.

National Research Council. (2001). *Colleges of Agriculture at the Land Grant Universities: A Profile*. Washington, DC: National Academy Press.

Natural Resources Defense Council. (2023). Climate change, agriculture, and food. https://www.nrdc.org/issues/agriculture-food#overview.

National Sustainable Agriculture Coalition. (2023). House FY24 Appropriations Draft undermines farmers and food system. https://sustainableagriculture.net/blog/house-fy24-appropriations-draft-undermines-farmers-and-food-system/?emci=514cc16d-44f6-ed11-907c-00224832eb73&emdi=b01cff63-defb-ed11-907c-00224832eb73&ceid=1969
1398.

Oberholtzer, L., Dimitri, C. and Pressman, A. (2014). Urban agriculture in the United States: characteristics, challenges, and technical assistance needs. *Journal of Extension*, 52(6). https://www.researchgate.net/publication/287020120_Urban_agriculture_in_the_United_States_Characteristics_challenges_and_technical_assistance_needs.

O'Dell, R. and Penzenstadler, N. (2019). You elected them to write new laws: they're letting corporations do it instead. https://publicintegrity.org/politics/state-politics/

copy-paste-legislate/you-elected-them-to-write-new-laws-theyre-letting-corporations-do-it-instead/.

O'Hara, S. (1996). Discursive ethics in ecosystems valuation and environmental policy. *Ecological Economics*, 16(2): 95–107.

O'Hara, S. (1999). Economics, ecology and quality of life: who evaluates? *Feminist Economics*, 5(2): 83–89.

O'Hara, S. (2014). Everything needs care: toward a relevant contextual view of the economy. In: Bjørnholt, M. and McKay, A. (eds.), *Counting on Marilyn Waring: New Advances in Feminist Economics*. Ontario: Demeter Press, pp. 37–55.

O'Hara, S., Ahmadi, G., Hampton, M. and Dunson, K. (2023). Telling our story: a community based meso-level approach to sustainable urban development. *Sustainability*, 15(7): 5795.

O'Hara, S. and Stagl, S. (2001). Global food production and some local alternatives: a socio-ecological economic perspective. *Population and Environment*, 22(6): 533–554.

O'Hara, S. and Stuiver, M. (2022). Restorative economics: food hubs as catalysts of a new urban economy. In: Stuiver, M. (ed.), *Symbiotic Cities*. Wageningen: Wageningen University & Research Academic Press, pp. 187–204.

O'Hara, S. and Toussaint, E. (2020). Food access in crisis: food security and COVID-19. *Ecological Economics*, 180(2021): 106859.

O'Neill-Hayes, T. and Kerska, K. (2021). Agriculture subsidies and their influence on the composition of US food supply and consumption. https://www.americanactionforum.org/research/primer-agriculture-subsidies-and-their-influence-on-the-composition-of-u-s-food-supply-and-consumption/.

Partrige, S. (2023). The 2023 Farm Bill must address inequities in the land-grant university system. https://www.americanprogress.org/article/the-2023-farm-bill-must-address-inequities-in-the-land-grant-university-system/.

Perrings, C. and Vincent, J. (eds.). (2003). *Natural Resource Accounting and Economic Development: Theory and Practice*. 2nd edition. Cheltenham: Edward Elgar.

Philippon, T. (2019). *The Great Reversal: How America Gave up on Free Markets*. Cambridge, MA: Harvard University Press.

Pincetl, S. (2012). A living city: using urban metabolism analysis to view cities as life forms. In: Zeman, F. (ed.), *Metropolitan Sustainability*. Sawston: Woodhead Publishing, pp. 3–25.

Ramesh, G., Belardo, D., Gulati, M., Ostfeld, R. and Michos E. (2021). Agricultural policy and societal factors influence patients' ability to follow a healthy diet. *American Journal of Preventive Cardiology*, 8: 100285. https://www.sciencedirect.com/science/article/pii/S2666667721001409.

Rangarajan, A. and Riordan, M. (2019). *The Promise of Urban Agriculture: National Study of Commercial Farming in Urban Areas*. Washington, DC: United States Department of Agriculture Agricultural Marketing Service and Cornell University Small Farms Program.

Rees, W. (2020). Ecological economics for humanity's plague phase. *Ecological Economics*, 169. https://doi.org/10.1016/j.ecolecon.2019.106519.

Reznickova, A. (2023). A hunger cliff is looming: time to rethink nutrition assistance. https://blog.ucsusa.org/alice-reznickova/a-hunger-cliff-is-looming-time-to-rethink-nutrition-assistance/.

Rosenberg, N. and Stucki, B. (2019). USDA gave almost 100% of Trump's trade war bailout to white farmers. https://www.farmbilllaw.org/2019/07/24/usda-gave-almost-100-percent-of-trumps-trade-war-bailout-to-white-farmers/.

Sasaki, T., Furukawa, T., Iwasaki, Y., Seto, M. and Mori, A. (2015). Perspectives for ecosystem management based on ecosystem resilience and ecological thresholds against multiple and stochastic disturbances. *Ecological Indicators*, 57: 395–408.

Schechinger, A. and Faber, S. (2023). Updated EWG Farm Subsidy Database shows largest producers reap billions, despite climate crisis. https://www.ewg.org/research/upda ted-ewg-farm-subsidy-database-shows-largest-producers-reap-billions-despite-climate.

Spash, C., Urama, K., Burton, R., Kenyon, W., Shannon, P. and Hill, G. (2009). Motives behind willingness to pay for improving biodiversity in a water ecosystem: economics, ethics and social psychology. *Ecological Economics*, 68(4): 955–964.

Spencer, P., Perkins, P. and Erickson, J. (2018). Re-establishing justice as a pillar of ecological economics through feminist perspectives. *Ecological Economics*, 152: 191–198.

Stahel, W. (2010). *The Performance Economy*. Basingstoke: Palgrave Macmillan.

Stahel, W. (2013). Policy for material efficiency—sustainable taxation as a departure from the throwaway society. *Philosophical Transactions of the Royal Society A*. doi:10.1098/rsta.2011.0567.

Statista.com. (2023). Total lobbying expenses in the United States in 2022 by sector. https://www.statista.com/statistics/257368/total-lobbying-expenses-in-the-us-by-sector/#:~:text=In%202022%2C%20about%20165.86%20million,sector%20in% 20the%20United%20States.

Stray Dog Institute. (2023). Challenges and opportunities surrounding US agricultural subsidies. https://straydoginstitute.org/agricultural-subsidies/#:~:text=Currently%2C %20five%20commodity%20crops%20are,cost%20prices%20for%20animal%20feed.

Tacconi, L. (2012). Redefining payments for environmental services. *Ecological Economics*, 73(1): 29–36. doi:10.1016/j.ecolecon.2011.09.028.

Teachers College. (2022). Here's how NYC food policy is evolving. https://www.tc.colum bia.edu/articles/2022/october/heres-how-nyc-food-policy-is-evolving-thanks-to-tc-alum na-kate-mackenzie/.

Tessum, C., Ate, J., Goodkind, A. and Hill, J. (2019). Inequity in consumption of goods and services adds to racial–ethnic disparities in air pollution exposure. *Proceedings of the National Academy of Sciences*, 116(13): 6001–6006. https://doi.org/ 10.1073/pnas.181885911.

Tremmel, M., Gerdtham, U., Nilsson, P. and Saha, S. (2017). Economic burden of obesity: a systematic literature review. *International Journal of Environmental Research and Public Health*, 14(4): 435. doi:10.3390/ijerph14040435.

Tronto, J. (1993). *Moral Boundaries: A Political Argument for an Ethic of Care*. New York: Routledge.

Tronto, J. (1998). An ethic of care. *Generations: Journal of the American Society on Aging*, 22(3): 15–20. http://www.jstor.org/stable/44875693.

United Nations. (1987). *Report of the World Commission on Environment and Development: Our Common Future*. https://sustainabledevelopment.un.org/content/docum ents/5987our-common-future.pdf.

United States Department of Agriculture. (2021). USDA announces over $243 million in grants awarded to strengthen the specialty crop industry. https://www.usda.gov/media/p ress-releases/2021/10/28/usda-announces-over-243-million-grants-awarded-strengthen-sp ecialty.

United States Department of Agriculture. (2022a). Advancing equity at USDA. https:// www.usda.gov/equity-commission.

United States Department of Agriculture. (2022b). USDA announces up to $550 million in American Rescue Plan funding for projects benefiting underserved producers and minority serving institutions that create career development opportunities for next generation leaders. https://www.usda.gov/media/press-releases/2022/08/24/usda-announces-550-million-american-rescue-plan-funding-projects.

United States Department of Agriculture. (2023a). Biden–Harris administration announces historic funding to expand access to trees and green spaces in disadvantaged urban communities. https://www.usda.gov/media/press-releases/2023/04/12/biden-harris-administration-announces-historic-funding-expand.

United States Department of Agriculture. (2023b). USDA announces $72.9 million in grant funding available through the Specialty Crop Block Grant Program. https://www.ams.usda.gov/press-release/usda-announces-729-million-grant-funding-availabl e-through-specialty-crop-block#:~:text=%E2%80%9CSince%202006%20when%20t he%20program,in%20the%20U.S.%20and%20abroad.%E2%80%9D.

United States Department of Agriculture. (2023c). *USDA Equity Commission Reports.* https://www.usda.gov/equity-commission/reports.

United States Department of Agriculture. (2023d). USDA kicks-off effort to expand market opportunities for climate-smart commodities and learn from pilot projects. https://www.usda.gov/media/press-releases/2023/04/27/usda-kicks-effort-expand-marke t-opportunities-climate-smart#:~:text=USDA%20is%20investing%20more%20than,pr oducers%20as%20global%20leaders%20in.

United States Department of Agriculture and United States Department of Health and Human Services. (2020). *Dietary Guidelines for Americans, 2020–2025.* https://www.dietaryguidelines.gov/sites/default/files/2020-12/Dietary_Guidelines_for_Am ericans_2020-2025.pdf.

United States Department of Agriculture Economic Research Service. (2023). Federal government direct farm program payments, 1933–2023. https://data.ers.usda.gov/rep orts.aspx?ID=17833.

United States Department of Agriculture Equity Commission. (2023). *Interim Report.* https://www.usda.gov/sites/default/files/documents/usda-ec-interim-report-2023.pdf.

United States Department of Agriculture Food and Nutrition Service. (2023a). I'm new to farm to school. https://www.fns.usda.gov/f2s/im-new-farm-school.

United States Department of Agriculture Food and Nutrition Service. (2023b). Urban agriculture. https://www.nrcs.usda.gov/getting-assistance/other-topics/urban-agriculture.

United States Department of Agriculture National Agricultural Library. (2023). Agricultural subsidies. https://www.nal.usda.gov/economics-business-and-trade/agricultura l-subsidies.

United States Department of Agriculture National Institute of Food and Agriculture. (2021). American Rescue Plan Act, as amended by the Inflation Reduction Act. https://www.usda.gov/sites/default/files/documents/1006-nifa-fact-sheet.pdf.

United States Department of Labor. (2023). Agriculture Apprentice Program. https://www.apprenticeship.gov/apprenticeship-industries/agriculture.

United States Government. (2021). Intent to establish an Equity Commission and solicitation of nominations for membership on the Equity Commission Advisory Committee and Equity Commission Subcommittee on Agriculture. *Federal Register*, 24 September. https://www.federalregister.gov/documents/2021/09/27/2021-20840/intent-to-establish-an -equity-commission-and-solicitation-of-nominations-for-membership-on-the.

USA Facts. (2023). Agriculture: how, where, and what food is grown in the US?https://usafacts.org/topics/agriculture/.

Vitiello, D. (2022). "The highest and best use of land in the city": valuing urban agriculture in Philadelphia and Chicago. *Journal of Agriculture, Food Systems, and Community Development*, 11(3): 241–257. https://doi.org/10.5304/jafscd.2022.113.019.

Waring, M. (1989). *If Women Counted.* London: Macmillan.

Weisz, H. and Steinberger, J. (2010). Reducing energy and material flows in cities. *Current Opinion in Environmental Sustainability*, 2(3): 185–192.

White House. (2021a). Executive Order on Advancing Racial Equity and Support for Underserved Communities through the Federal Government. https://www.whitehouse. gov/briefing-room/presidential-actions/2021/01/20/executive-order-advancing-racial-eq uity-and-support-for-underserved-communities-through-the-federal-government/.

White House. (2021b). The American Rescue Plan. https://www.whitehouse.gov/wp -content/uploads/2021/03/American-Rescue-Plan-Fact-Sheet.pdf.

Yang, Y., Jia, Y., Ling, S. and Yao, C. (2021). Urban natural resource accounting based on the system of environmental economic accounting in northwest China: a case study of Xi'an. *Ecosystem Services*, 47. https://doi.org/10.1016/j.ecoser.2020.101233.

Zigas, E. (2014). San Francisco establishes California's first urban agriculture incentive zone. https://ucanr.edu/blogs/blogcore/postdetail.cfm?postnum=15017.

7

CONCLUSIONS

Food security is a mixed bag. There is some good news in the form of the steady increase in the supply of food around the world, and especially in the United States, which is not only the world's largest economy, but also a major food exporter. There is therefore no reason why an estimated 38 million people in the United States should be food insecure, either temporarily or long term. The US food and agricultural sector also receives substantial subsidies. However, these payments go almost entirely to commodity crops, not toward supporting the production of fruits and vegetables. In fact, the United States is a major importer of both of these. In the meantime, the bulk of the nation's commodity crops go to animal feed and energy generation.

When it comes to the distribution of the food supply, disparities persist at every level. Indeed, they are getting worse. To some extent, major shock events are to blame. The recent COVID pandemic created major supply chain disruptions as well as mobility restrictions; at the time of writing, the war in Ukraine was disrupting grain shipments to some of the world's poorest regions; and the droughts, floods, and temperature increases associated with climate change have affected crop yields even in some of the world's most productive regions, including the United States. All of these issues have placed enormous pressure on food systems at the global, regional, and local levels. However, despite these substantial challenges, food security is not a production problem. Rather, it is a distribution problem, which is why it's more apt to refer to "food justice."

An analysis of US policies shows that there is nothing unavoidable or "natural" about the nation's maldistribution of food or the mismatch between the kind of food we need and the kind we produce. Rather, the policies themselves have created massive intervention failures on both the supply and the demand side of the food system. Nevertheless, US food and agricultural policies remain firmly anchored in the myth that unencumbered markets create the most desirable outcomes for society, so the priority of policy-makers must be to protect markets. But what if those markets are not unencumbered but actually work to disrupt market ideals? What if an underlying belief in the American myth of the self-reliance of successful individuals is at the center of the forces that drive US food policy? And what if that belief in the power and ingenuity of individuals also offers some hopeful signs of a new, sustainable, and just food system? Such hopeful signs are evident in the stories of those who are dealing with food insecurity and the food innovators who are committed to addressing it. The vision of a sustainable and just restorative food system is therefore already emerging. However, we will realize its full potential only by taking a fresh look at policies that will support rather than undermine it.

What the data tells us

The data shows steady progress in food production since a series of agri-cultural breakthroughs in the 1960s. In principle, this means there is enough food for everyone, at least for now, and certainly in the United States. Glob-ally, food production reached 13 billion tons in 2020, and severe poverty—defined as those living on less than $2 per day—dropped below 10 percent of the world's population (i.e., less than 720 million people). In the United States, the country with the world's largest economy, the poverty level is set at $14,000 for a one-person household and $30,000 for a four-person household. Based on these standards, 11 percent of the US population (35 million people) were living in poverty in 2020. In the same year, US food production reached 360 million tons, in part due to the disbursement of a wide range of agricultural subsidies. Meanwhile, food transfer payments to low-income households shore up the demand side of the US food system. As a result, despite the persistent need for emergency food assistance, it may be said that there has been tremendous progress toward the dual goals of "ensuring an abundance of food" and "stabilizing food prices". Both have been at the heart of US policy-making since the long bread lines of the Great Depression and the crop failures of the Dust Bowl years.

Yet, this tells only half the story. Data from US cities indicate persistent disparities in preventable food-related health outcomes, such as diabetes and obesity. Both are also closely correlated with income, race, ethnicity, and other social determinants of health (Pollard and Booth, 2019; Price and Jeffery, 2023; Chapter 2, this volume). This is because food insecurity is not simply a matter of not getting enough food, but of getting cheap food that is highly processed and often contains high proportions of subsidized agricultural products, such as corn syrup. Sugary beverages are cheaper than fresh fruit juice, and high-sodium canned vegetables are cheaper than fresh greens. Therefore, it is hardly surprising that residents of low-income neighborhoods experience far higher rates of obesity, diabetes, and other negative health outcomes than residents of affluent neighborhoods. Moreover, as income is closely correlated with race and ethnicity, it is hardly surprising that neighborhoods where non-white populations are the majority tend to experience more negative health outcomes than predominantly white neighborhoods. However, this pattern is not entirely consistent, which suggests that cultural factors may also play a key role, and indeed provide some solutions to mitigating food-related illness. For example, some low-income ethnic neighborhoods in Oakland, CA, and Brooklyn, NY, have relatively low rates of obesity and diabetes, which may indicate that gradual adoption of the "American diet" over the generations eventually leads to worse health outcomes (Jeffery, 2020; Jeffery et al., 2020).

Moreover, the picture is no better than mixed on the purportedly successful supply side, too. The negative externalities of a food system that relies heavily on economies of scale, petrochemical inputs, pesticides, and irrigation are well documented. They are evident in the eutrophication of streams, contamination of ground water, soil erosion, bio-accumulation of chemicals throughout the food chain (including in human bodies), loss of biodiversity, and a host of other side-effects (Vermeulen et al., 2012; Loboguerrero et al., 2019; Udvardi et al., 2021; Read et al., 2022; Zurek et al., 2022). Furthermore, a large-scale, centralized food system in which the majority of the food is produced in remote rural areas but consumed in cities and metro areas creates another set of negative externalities associated with energy-intensive transportation systems, cold chains, storage facilities, and distribution centers. Such a system's long supply chains also impact the quality of the food and generate tremendous amounts of waste. Lower nutrient content and so-called "empty calories" exacerbate negative health outcomes even when food access problems are resolved; and up to 30 percent of all food produced in the United States is wasted due to losses incurred on the farm, in the supply chain, or after it has reached the consumer. These examples illustrate that negative externalities have significant consequences for the processing capacities—or sink capacities—of the natural environment, our own bodies, and our communities. The greater the externalities, the greater the burden carried by third parties, the greater the reduction in sink capacities, and the higher the cost to society (O'Hara, 1997; 2014; 2016).

Changing temperatures, precipitation patterns, and growing seasons—all linked to climate change—mean that the vulnerabilities of the current food system are only increasing. Consequently, business as usual will not do. Instead, constant innovation will be needed to counteract the increasing fragility of food systems both globally and locally. One such innovation should be a shift to smaller-scale, decentralized food systems that reduce the distance between food producer and consumer (Kumar, 2023; Maluf, 2021). Decentralized food systems are also better equipped to achieve specific sustainability goals and reduce the growing burden on ecosystems that provide vital sink capacities. However, they are sure to encounter resistance from existing large-scale, centralized food systems and their institutional representatives (Canfield et al., 2021). In addition, we must move food production from rural communities to urban and peri-urban locations, where the vast majority of food consumers live, and invest in new food production techniques, such as hydroponics and aquaponics, to reduce our reliance on arable land. While the energy needs of these innovative production methods are significant, their need for water, pesticides, and nutrients is typically far lower than that of conventional agriculture. Moreover, producing more of our food in cities and metropolitan areas can create meaningful work and introduce those who have rarely had access to fresh, unprocessed food to what fresh food can look and taste like.

Food subsidies and transfer payments routinely show large swings from year to year, depending on droughts, floods, wildfires, pest infestations, and, of course, viruses. These external shock events result in poor harvests, reduced food supply, higher prices, greater food insecurity, and, eventually, even hunger. They may also lead to higher energy prices, an erosion of household incomes, and high unemployment. Swings in much-needed payments can therefore occur both on the supply side of the food system (subsidies) and on the demand side (transfer payments). Of course, farmers are not entirely insulated from the impact of shock events, despite the subsidies they receive. When crop yields decline or the demand for food runs low, the result is lower revenues for farmers, liquidity problems, difficulties servicing loans, and foreclosures on land and equipment. Farmers may be buffered from the worst of these effects by crop insurance payments, price guarantees, and other mechanisms to keep them in business even in times of crisis. However, these mechanisms tend to be most beneficial to large farmers who produce enormous volumes of commodity crops, whereas small farmers who produce fruits and vegetables often receive nothing. Similarly, price guarantees that keep agricultural product prices low may be a necessity for those earning low wages, but they also benefit those in high-income brackets who could easily afford to pay the full cost.

Neither food distribution problems nor the growing vulnerabilities of the current food system will solve themselves. Both require targeted action in the form of policies. Hence, any proposal to discontinue all subsidies, transfer payments, and grants is nonsensical. Yet, all three of these mechanisms require significant adjustment. The first step must be to acknowledge that there is no such thing as a "free" market for food. Food markets are always full of interventions and intervention failures. Revisiting policy goals in a clear and transparent manner is therefore essential. Any policy that relies on markets to allocate resources, goods, and services must give some thought to sink capacities and the proper functioning of the market itself. First and foremost, this means that steps must be taken to stop the formation of monopolies, to protect market competitiveness, and ensure transparency by avoiding impenetrable procedures. These are important starting points for all new policy directions.

What the stories tell us

Chapters 3 and 5 offer a wide range of insights into food insecurity and food system innovations across six American cities. Each story speaks to one or more aspect of the valuation biases that are evident throughout the current US food system. Collectively, they highlight details and complexities that cannot be captured by data alone. These details are important in helping us identify potential pathways toward a more sustainable and just food system. In fact, several of the stories reveal that some of the groundwork for those pathways has already been laid, while others describe challenges that remain. They are both equally valuable.

One of the central questions this book has sought to answer is whether food system innovation will help us resolve the seemingly intractable problem of food insecurity in our urban communities. There is some reason for optimism, because all of the urban and peri-urban food innovators who have featured in these pages share a commitment to address food insecurity and other economic injustices in their communities. Every one of them wants to provide fresh food to those communities, create jobs, pay living wages, and create supportive work environments. At the same time, those who are dealing with food insecurity and those who are committed to addressing it are keenly aware of the benefits of fresh, unprocessed food. Every one of them hopes to eat more of it in the future, even though some struggle to find the time to prepare home-cooked meals, given the pressures of their life circumstances. Those with resources can free up time by paying others to deliver their groceries, look after their children, or do their household chores. These are luxuries that those without resources cannot afford.

The same stories also highlight the shortcomings of the current piecemeal approach to social support services. Illness and the need to care for family members feature prominently. If someone gets sick, if prices increase, or if a personal support network disappears due to relocation, the fragile balancing act of earning a living, paying the rent, and getting food on the table may collapse. Interestingly, none of the stories explicitly references a plant-based diet, although all mention the importance of eating fresh fruits and vegetables. Some also allude to generational differences and the need to share recipes and food preparation instructions, while others focus on understanding how to use greens and herbs and how to prepare fresh food on a budget. Several mention the importance of providing fresh produce to schools and preschools, and emphasize that young children must be taught to enjoy the unfamiliar flavors and textures of fresh vegetables. This need to focus on early childhood education is especially prominent in the story of Albuquerque's farm-to-preschool program, which also connects the dots between the consumption and production sides of the current food system and stresses the importance of ensuring that food quality remains high, regardless of where it is produced. This is a strong theme in the story of 4P Foods, too.

The Atlanta-based Ponics emphasizes the food production side of education by offering hydroponic systems that provide educational and even commercial opportunities for elementary and high schools. Most of the food innovators mention their interactions with food consumers, either directly as producers or indirectly through the businesses that come under their organizational umbrella. The importance of developing circular economies is another prominent theme, especially in the stories of Chicago's Bubbly Dynamics, the Bay Area's Planting Justice, and Chispas Farm in Albuquerque, which aims to replenish the soil and close resource production and waste loops whenever possible. While none of these stories explicitly refers to supporting and restoring sink capacities, several of them do express a commitment to caring for nature, their communities, and their own health and well-being, which suggests that they recognize the importance of maintaining and strengthening both social and environmental sink capacities. In turn, this goes some way to explaining why local markets that abide by the four principles of a restorative economy are already emerging:

1. They define efficiency in far more differentiated ways than merely increasing output.
2. They are committed to reducing emissions and waste.
3. They recognize the importance of protecting and strengthening the restorative capacities of both nature and people—from individual entities, to communities, to whole ecosystems.
4. And they understand that remaining productive is contingent on adhering to the first three principles.

Emerging local food systems are therefore anything but anti-market. Rather, they understand that markets can be effective allocation mechanisms if they are decentralized, as opposed to the dysfunctional, highly aggregated, centralized markets that have shaped the current food system. And decentralized markets are not only about scale; they are also about shifting agency from those in distant places to those who are affected by decisions about the quality and cost of food and its impact on local communities. For example, the Atlanta Food Bank demonstrates the importance of shifting agency from those in charge of food to those in need of food. When food-insecure consumers are given options, rather than simply handed a box of food, they tend to make healthier food choices. Meanwhile, Chispas Farm and Planting Justice speak to the power of connecting food producers with consumers and creating a culture of health and sustainability in the process, while 4P Foods speaks eloquently to the market opportunities that are created by linking urban, peri-urban, and rural producers with consumers in high-density markets. Not just the quantity but the quality of food is a key factor in defining the new restorative food system, and every one of these stories articulates a desire to make—and empower others to make—healthier and more sustainable food decisions.

The long-term viability of all of these local food systems rests on leveling the playing field. After all, the large-scale, centralized food system and its national, regional, and global markets did not happen by accident. They were created and managed by government policy. The markets that govern today's US food system are largely managed by the USDA, the US Congress, the US President, and whoever succeeds in exerting influence over these public-sector actors. Current food and agriculture policies have not created a level playing field for food system innovators, or indeed for those who understand that the need for care is not weakness but a fact of life. In fact, the innovators' achievements seem even more remarkable when one considers the minimal support they receive from government policies. Yet, policy intervention will be necessary if they are to get to the next level. This is sadly illustrated by the failure of several innovators who were celebrated as success stories only a few years earlier (Peters, 2023). The most recent example is AeroFarms, which produces leafy greens using a patented technology that needs even less water than hydroponics. Despite a much-publicized launch in 2017, and several years of successful operation, it filed for bankruptcy protection in June 2023 (Vertical Farm Daily, 2023).

This story and others like it illustrate one of the fundamental problems of the current food system. While innovators may be able to access capital to launch a new venture, they are rarely, if ever, eligible for ongoing subsidies. Moreover, in order to gain access to capital, there is typically a requirement to transfer power and authority from the innovators and the local community to national and global funders. Inevitably, this means that the new operation is managed according to externally imposed criteria, rather than local criteria. This is most clearly evident when urban controlled environment agriculture projects (CEAs) secure backing from venture capitalists. For example, estimates suggest that close to 600 companies invested more than $1 billion in the vertical farming sector between 2015 and 2019 (Biel, 2019). But venture capital funding always comes with strings attached, including the expectation that investors will receive a return on their investment. This typically takes the form of an equity share and commensurate decision-making power in the business. Alternatively, the US government's Small Business Administration (SBA) offers loans that are usually more flexible than venture capital funds, although applicants must still meet strict performance criteria. In addition, the SBA offers a limited number of grants through its Innovative Research (SBIR) and Technology Transfer (SBRD) programs. However, these are limited to research and development and technology transfer activities. Moreover, it is unclear how much of the $3.2 billion in annual funding has gone to food sector businesses (Small Business Administration, 2023). As mentioned earlier, government grants, including the proposed $4 billion in funding to strengthen the food system through the USDA's Build Back Better Program, are never equally accessible to all. It is therefore questionable whether existing funding mechanisms will ever provide the nation's food innovators with the ongoing support they need. For example, despite the success of its circular-economy business model, Bubbly Dynamics now faces a potentially insurmountable tax bill due to the lack of a supportive ecosystem of policies and rules.

It is doubtful that the food innovators themselves, or even the food and agriculture sector alone, will be able to realize the just, sustainable workplaces and living wages that virtually all of the contributors to this book hope to achieve. For this to happen, broader support and coordination across several economic sectors will be needed to level the playing field. For example, Hunger Free America argues that increasing the minimum wage will reduce the need for transfer payments to emergency food programs. Similarly, several commentators have advocated for a Universal Basic Income (UBI) that would provide all citizens with a guaranteed income without requiring them to meet eligibility criteria (Haagh, 2019; Hoynes and Rothstein, 2019; De Wispelaere and Stirton, 2004). Critics of this concept argue that it would be too expensive or simply unfeasible; that, at a time when the population is aging, UBI would reduce the workforce still further to unsustainable levels; or that it would be socially unjust for everyone to receive transfer payments regardless of their individual contributions or needs. Proponents counter that UBI would enable the government to abolish all of the disjointed and tremendously expensive programs that currently provide social support. Others argue that UBI would allow recipients to attain qualifications and therefore achieve long-term economic independence; that eliminating piecemeal social programs would make it possible to address the needs of vulnerable populations in a much more comprehensive manner; and that certain types of work (such as jobs that sustain and restore social and environmental sinks) could be prioritized, rather than simply insisting that all recipients of social support must be prepared to accept any kind of work.

Subsidies and transfer payments originated in the 1930s, when a confluence of economic and environmental shocks sent millions of Americans into poverty. Given the extent of unemployment, hardship, and hunger at the time, there was a gradual realization that everyone sometimes needs care, and that a reliance on individual responsibility is not always sufficient. This meant that those who required care were no longer stigmatized, at least for a time. A similar shift in mindset is needed today. Sinks provide the social and environmental services that absorb our emissions, waste products, stressors, and so much more besides, so we need to protect them, care for them, and, if possible, restore their capacities. Care is not some kind of deficit but a fact of life. A science-based food system would recognize not only the role of resources but also the role of sink capacities. Preserving both is therefore not an option but a necessity, and a fundamental reality of any healthy system, whether environmental, human, or economic.

Creating transparency

The power of education is evident in all of the stories in Chapters 3 and 5. They describe the sense of empowerment associated with learning to prepare meals and grow food; the joy of learning about fresh food and food cultures; and the satisfaction of sharing information about food connections and innovations.

At its best, education creates transparency and lets us see when the emperor is not wearing any clothes. It also enables us to reject previous misconceptions and acquire fresh insights. In other words, it does not simply answer questions but questions answers, including some that we have long held to be true. This is best achieved by listening to those who are actively involved, rather than simply poring over the data. In the case of food security, the general consensus is that credentialed experts will need to work alongside local activists and innovators to reform the current, unsustainable food system (O'Hara et al., 2023; Schroeter et al., 2016; Wesselink et al., 2011). Without engaging with local experts, and especially those who are most impacted by food insecurity, even the best-intentioned efforts will fail to accomplish their objectives and may even exacerbate existing problems. Therefore, this book has given some of those experts an opportunity to tell their own stories, with a view to broadening the conversation about food cultures, the barriers to adopting particular diets, the health benefits of certain foods, nutrient content, food waste, food and soil health, water use, and a host of other food-related issues. The United Nations' Food and Agriculture Organization (FAO) is already in the process of promoting further engagement between local and credentialed experts within what it calls "agroecology knowledge hubs" (Food and Agriculture Organization, 2022; Wezel et al., 2020; Sietz et al., 2022).

Another important theme that has emerged throughout the course of this book is the need to think systemically. This brings us back to the issue of food quality and the urgent need for a new food system that saves resources rather than squanders them, contributes to good health rather than illness, sustains rather than destroys biodiversity, and supports rather than undermines the vitality of ecosystems and communities. An FAO initiative highlights the integrative nature of food systems and the importance of focusing on the nexus between different fields and spheres such as food and water, food and health, and food and biodiversity in order to eliminate the unintended negative consequences of piecemeal policies. One such negative consequence is a labyrinthine funding system that discriminates against those who lack the time and resources to navigate an unnecessarily complicated grant-application process. The same is true with respect to food access. With more than 60,000 food pantries across the United States, all with different opening hours, eligibility criteria, and services, it takes a great deal of time, energy, and ingenuity to determine what kinds of food are available where, when, and for whom. Of course, in both cases, it is those in most need who tend to miss out.

Economic theory holds that transparency is a prerequisite for market efficiency. Information about the quality of a product, its direct and indirect impacts, and its price must be readily available to consumers so that they can make an informed decision about whether it represents value for money and meets other requirements. However, this kind of transparency is routinely lacking in food markets. Consumers often know nothing about the pesticides that have been sprayed on the apples in the grocery store, including their harmful side-effects. Indeed, the apple growers may go to great lengths to hide that information. Meanwhile, the growers need detailed information about resources (including their direct and indirect impacts), production technologies, and the purchasing power and desires of consumers when deciding whether to grow a particular species of apple and at what price to sell it if they do. Different levels of access to land, water, energy, seeds, irrigation techniques, and a host of other resources will result in different production costs for apple growers and different profit margins. Furthermore, the market for apples is only efficient when a very large number of consumers and producers interact with each other and clearly communicate their desire and ability to purchase apples and their desire and ability produce them, respectively. If there are only a few large apple growers, they will be able to collude and determine the price at which all apples are sold. Of course, this puts consumers at a serious disadvantage. To summarize, an efficient market comprises a large number of buyers and sellers, abundant, transparent information about resources, products, and consumer tastes, and low barriers to entering and exiting the marketplace. The current US food system meets none of these requirements.

Yet, even if government policy manages to level the playing field by creating a more transparent and competitive food marketplace, we still may not get the sustainable and just food system we want. As the father of market economics, Adam Smith, pointed out, this is because efficient markets are not simply mechanistic systems of exchange. They are instead living systems regulated by moral human behavior. In *The Theory of Moral Sentiments*, Smith writes: "Concern for our own happiness (self-interest) recommends to us the virtue of prudence (self-command), concern for that of other people, the virtues of justice and beneficence—of which the one restrains us from hurting, the other prompts (us) to promote that happiness" (Smith, 2006: 263). Furthermore, in his most famous book, *The Wealth of Nations*, he identifies the "social passions" that undergird a successful marketplace as "generosity, humanity, kindness, compassion, mutual friendship" (Smith, 1976: 38; see also Evensky, 2005). Today, we might suggest that similar generosity, humanity, kindness, compassion, and mutual friendship should are keenly aware of the benefits of be displayed toward our planet and its ecosystems.

In other words, successful markets do not just happen. They must be carefully managed lest they lose the social (and environmental) passions Smith envisioned, and therefore their efficiency. These passions must then guide the goals and objectives of our food and agriculture policies. As the stories in this book illustrate, they are clearly evident in the local food markets introduced in Chapters 3 and 5. Yet, they are either hidden in the morass of regional and national food policies or missing altogether. Federal and state governments should therefore support local food markets rather than undermine them with policies that discourage local innovation and the expression of local commitments to "generosity, humanity, kindness, compassion, and mutual friendship".

It will be no small task to create a sustainable and just food system that adheres to the four principles of a restorative food system and, more broadly, a restorative economy. Yet, it is worth persevering, not least because such a system would also be more resilient to the shock events that have become increasingly common over recent years. The next step should be a frank and transparent debate about the current (unspoken) objectives of a food system that prioritizes quantity over quality and operates on the assumption that bigger is always better. Even this may seem like a pipe dream, given the growing polarization of US society and other societies around the world. Yet, an honest discussion about food security and food systems would provide the perfect opportunity to identify the nexus points that connect us to nature and each other both locally and globally, as well as the local, national, and global governance structures we need to ensure a sustainable and just future.

References

Biel, J. (2019). How to get venture capital funding, from start to finish. https://www.netsuite.com/portal/resource/articles/business-strategy/how-to-get-vc-funding.shtml.

Canfield, M., Anderson, M. and McMichael, P. (2021). UN Food Systems Summit 2021: dismantling democracy and resetting corporate control of food systems. *Frontiers in Sustainable Food Systems*, 13 April.https://doi.org/10.3389/fsufs.2021.661552.

De Wispelaere, J. and Stirton, L. (2004). The many faces of universal basic income. *Political Quarterly*, 75(3): 266–274.

Evensky, J. (2005). Adam Smith's Theory of Moral Sentiments: on morals and why they matter to a liberal society of free people and free markets. *Journal of Economic Perspectives*, 19(3): 109–130.

Food and Agriculture Organization. (2022). Agroecology knowledge hub: ten elements of agroecology. https://www.fao.org/agroecology/overview/overview10elements/en/.

Haagh, L. (2019). *The Case for Universal Basic Income*. London: Polity Press.

Hoynes, H. and Rothstein, J. (2019). Universal basic income in the United States and advanced countries. *Annual Review of Economics*, 11: 929–958.

Jeffery, T. (2020). *Measuring the impact of acculturation on diet quality and metabolic syndrome among black and Hispanic minorities*. Graduate seminar, College of Agriculture, Urban Sustainability and Environmental Sciences, University of the District of Columbia, Washington, DC, 28 February.

Jeffery, T., Ardakani, A., Monroe-Lord, L. and Ordonez, M. (2020). Relationship between acculturation and diet quality among Hispanic adolescents. *Journal of Nutrition Education and Behavior*, 52(7): S69–S70. https://doi.org/10.1016/j.jneb.2020.04.160.

Kumar, R. (2023). Degrowth, diversity and decentralisation: building sustainable food systems for food and nutrition security. In: Fazli, A. and Kundu, A. (eds.), *Reimagining Prosperity*. Singapore: Palgrave Macmillan, pp. 171–187.

Loboguerrero, A., Campbell, B., Cooper, P., Hansen, J., Rosenstock, T. and Wollenberg, E. (2019). Food and earth systems: priorities for climate change adaptation and mitigation for agriculture and food systems. *Sustainability*, 11: 1372.

Maluf, R.S. (2021). Decentralized food systems and eating in localities: a multi-scale approach. *Revista de Economia e Sociologia Rural*, 59(4): e238782. https://doi.org/ 10.1590/1806-9479.2021.238782.

O'Hara, S. (1997). Toward a sustaining production theory. *Ecological Economics*, 20 (2): 141–154.

O'Hara, S. (2014). From sources to sinks: changing the rules of production theory. *World Future Review*, 6(4): 448–454.

O'Hara, S. (2016). Production in context: the concept of sustaining production. In: Farley, J. and Malghan, D. (eds.), *Beyond Uneconomic Growth*, Vol. 2: *A Festschrift in Honour of Herman Daly*. Burlington: University of Vermont, pp. 75–106.

O'Hara, S., Ahmadi, G., Hampton, M. and Dunson, K. (2023). Telling our story: a community based meso-level approach to sustainable urban development. *Sustainability*, 15(7): 5795. https://doi.org/10.3390/su15075795.

Peters, A. (2023). The vertical farming bubble is finally popping. *Fast Company*, 27 February. https://www.fastcompany.com/90824702/vertical-farming-failing-profita ble-appharvest-aerofarms-bowery.

Pollard, C. and Booth, S. (2019). Food insecurity and hunger in rich countries: it is time for action against inequality. *International Journal of Environmental Research and Public Health*, 16(10): 1804. https://doi.org/10.3390/ijerph16101804.

Price, M. and Jeffery, T. (2023). An analysis of socioeconomic determinants of the black–white disparity in food insecurity rates in the US. *Foods*, 12: 2228. doi:10.3390/foods12112228.

Read, Q., Hondula, K. and Muth, M. (2022). Biodiversity effects of food system sustainability actions from farm to fork. *Proceedings of the National Academy of Sciences*, 119: e2113884119.

Schroeter, R., Scheel, O., Renn, O. and Schweizer, P.-J. (2016). Testing the value of public participation in Germany: theory, operationalization and a case study on the evaluation of participation. *Energy Research and Social Science*, 13: 116–125.

Sietz, D., Klimek, S. and Dauber, J. (2022). Tailored pathways toward revived farmland biodiversity can inspire agroecological action and policy to transform agriculture. *Community Earth Environment*, 3: 211. https://doi.org/10.1038/s43247-022-00527-1.

Small Business Administration. (2023). Home page. https://www.sba.gov.

Smith, A. (2006) [1790]. *The Theory of Moral Sentiments*. Mineola, NY: Dover Publications, Inc.

Smith, A. (1976) [1784]. *An Inquiry into the Nature and Causes of the Wealth of Nations*. Edited by W.B. Todd. Oxford: Clarendon Press.

Udvardi, M., Below, F., Castellano, M., Eagle, A., Giller, K., Ladha, J., Liu, X., Maaz, T., Nova-Franco, B. and Raghuram, N. (2021). Research road map for responsible use of agricultural nitrogen. *Frontiers in Sustainable Food Systems*, 5: 660155.

Vermeulen, S., Campbell, B. and Ingram, J. (2012). Climate change and food systems. *Annual Review of Environment and Resources*, 37: 195–222.

Vertical Farm Daily. (2023). AeroFarms files for Chapter 11 bankruptcy protection. https://www.verticalfarmdaily.com/article/9536667/aerofarms-files-for-chapter-11-ba nkruptcy-protection/.

Walzer, N. and Hamm, G.F. (eds.). (2012). *Community Visioning Programs: Processes and Outcomes*. London: Routledge.

Wesselink, A., Paavola, J., Fritsch, O. and Renn, O. (2011). Rationales for public participation in environmental policy and governance: practitioners' perspectives. *Environment and Planning A: Economy and Space*, 43(11): 2688–2704. https://doi.org/10.1068/a44161.

Wezel, A., Herren, B.G., Kerr, R., Barrios, E., Rodrigues Goncalves, A. and Sinclair, F. (2020). Agroecological principles and elements and their implications for transitioning to sustainable food systems: a review. *Agronomy for Sustainable Development*, 40. https://doi.org/10.1007/s13593-020-00646-z.

Zurek, M., Hebinck, A. and Selomane, O. (2022). Climate change and the urgency to transform food systems. *Science*, 376: 1416–1421.

INDEX

Locators in **bold** refer to tables and those in *italics* to figures.

4P Foods 132–136, 176, 177

A&P 34
access to fresh food: Albuquerque, NM
45; Atlanta, GA **49**, 74; Chicago, IL
35, **53**; education about 176; food
deserts 33; impact on fruit and
vegetable consumption 37; New York
City **57**, 75–78; Oakland, CA **61**;
SNAP program 74; in urban areas 15,
37; Washington, DC 15, 35, 42, 70
aeroponics 97
Africa: demographic change 3; food
production and food security 3–13
African Americans: access to fresh food
37; American Rescue Plan (ARP)
157–158; Atlanta, GA 46; care work
146–147; Chicago, IL 50; getting the
right information 161–162;
Washington, DC 38–39
AgLanta 106
Agricultural Marketing Service (AMS)
88–89, 91, 93, 104–108, 110, 163; *see
also* United States Department of
Agriculture (USDA)
agricultural production: connection
between farm and food security 81–86;
food system innovators 116–136;
getting subsidies and transfer
payments right 149–156; global trends
1, **2**, 172, 173; global workforce

employed in 10; historical context 30;
negative externalities 8–9; new urban
food landscape 87–93; regional
progress 3–13; restorative urban
agriculture 100–102; top four countries
4–7; urban gardens/agriculture 93–102;
urban gardens/agriculture in six US
cities 102–111; *see also* United States
Department of Agriculture (USDA)
Albany, historical context 25
Albuquerque, NM: comparative statistics
61–62; connection between farm and
food security 81–86; food insecurity
landscape 42–45; the story of Chispas
Farm 116–119, 148–149, 176; urban
gardens/agriculture 104–105, **110**,
110–111
American Community Gardening
Association (ACGA) 93–94
American Rescue Plan (ARP) 157–158
aquaponics 97–98
Asia: demographic change 3; food
production and food security 3–13
Atlanta, GA: comparative statistics
61–62; food bank case study 71–75;
food insecurity landscape 45–49; food
system innovators 125–128, 177; urban
gardens/agriculture 105–106, **110**

Back of the Yards Algae Sciences
(BYAS) 129

Berg, Joel 144–145
Brazil, agricultural production 4, 6
Brooklyn *see* New York City
Brundtland Report 138–139
Bubbly Dynamics 128–132

carbon dioxide (CO2) 8, 101, 139
care work 146–149
the Caribbean: demographic change 3;
food production and food security
3–13
charities: emergency food distribution in
the US 144–145; food bank case study,
Atlanta 71–75; food pantry case study,
Washington, DC 67–71; the story of a
38-year-old mother of four 79–81; the
story of a 56-year-old immigrant in
Oakland 78–79; the story of a
64-year-old woman in Brooklyn 75–78;
see also Food Stamp Program (FSP);
Supplemental Nutrition Assistance
Program (SNAP); The Emergency
Food Assistance Program (TEFAP)
Chicago, IL: access to fresh food 35, **53**;
comparative statistics 61–62; food
insecurity landscape 50–53; food system
innovators 128–132; historical context
34–35; the story of a 38-year-old mother
of four 79–81; urban gardens/agriculture
106–108, **110**
children: education about food 161, 176;
Farm to Early Childhood Program
84–85, 176; farm-to-school movement
91; the story of a 38-year-old mother
of four 79–81; who is food insecure 12,
13, 69, 71, 72; Women, Infants, and
Children (WIC) nutrition program
29, 151
China, agricultural production 4
Chinese Americans 58
Chispas Farm 116–119, 148–149, 176
circular economy 97, 142, 177–179; the
story of bubbly dynamics 128–131
cities in the US, historical context 25; *see
also* Albuquerque, NM; Atlanta, GA;
Brooklyn, NY; Chicago, IL; green
cities; New York City; Oakland, CA;
Washington, DC
climate change 83, 124, 139, 164, 174
Club of Rome 138–139
community gardens 93–102, 108, **110**
community-supported agriculture (CSAs)
89–91, **110**, 132–136
controlled environment agriculture
(CEAs) 94, 178

cooking and food preparation 75, 176;
see also nutrition programs
cost of food 137–142
COVID-19 pandemic: Bubbly Dynamics
130–131; connection between farm and
food security 83–84; employment
situation 158–159; food bank, Atlanta
75; food pantry, Washington, DC
70–71; the story of a 56-year-old
immigrant in Oakland 78; the story of
Chispas Farm 118–119; subsidies
150–151; suburbanization/urbanization
35–36; suppler chain disruptions 172;
vulnerabilities of the food system
11–13, 14

DC Grocery Store Cooperative (DGS)
33–34
democratic engagement **160**; democratic
institutions 146; participatory
democracy 96
diversity, representation in metrics 157–158
Dust Bowl 26, 31–32

eco cities *see* green cities
ecological economics 140–142
economic context in the US: cost of food
137–142; Dust Bowl 26, 31–32;
ecological economics 140–142; getting
metrics right 157–160; getting
subsidies and transfer payments right
149–156; getting the right information
161–164; getting wages right 143–149;
grants and funding 161–163, 178;
historical data 26; market efficiency
181–182; restorative urban agriculture
100–102, 155–156, 177; as a result of
COVID-19 pandemic 158
ecosystem services 140–142, 148
education: in childhood 161, 176;
community gardens 94, 121; cooking
and food preparation 176; creating
transparency 180–182; CSA members
90; food hubs 92; getting the right
information 161–164; hydroponics 126,
128; National Farm to School
Network (NFSN) program 91; to
prisoners 121; in urban communities
98, 105, 124–125
The Emergency Food Assistance
Program (TEFAP) 37
emergency food distribution system
144–145
employment: care work 146–149; getting
wages right 143–149; global workforce

in agricultural production 10; as a result of COVID-19 pandemic 158
engineered soils 97
environmental issues: climate change 83, 124, 139, 164, 174; ecological economics 140–142; food waste 7, 99–100; metrics and equity **160**; negative externalities 8–9, 137–142, 149–156; sustainable cities 96–97, 98–99; water contamination 8, 9; *see also* green cities
ethnicities in the US 25; *see also* race
Europe: demographic change 3; food production and food security 3–13
eutrophication 8, 174
externalities: agricultural production 8–9; cost of food 137–142; getting subsidies and transfer payments right 149–156

families: Farm to Early Childhood Program 84–85, 176; farm-to-school movement 91; the story of a 38-year-old mother of four 79–81; who is food insecure 68–69, 70; Women, Infants, and Children (WIC) nutrition program 29, 151
Farm Bills 17, 26, 149–150
Farm Service Agency (FSA) Urban Agriculture Committees: launch of the committees 16, 18; metrics and equity 160
Farm to Early Childhood Program 84–85, 176
farm-to-school movement 91
Farm-to-Table initiative 88–89
farmers' markets 70, 89, 103–108, **110**, 118
farming *see* agricultural production
Federal Land Policy and Management Act 32
Feeding America 37, 104
fertilizers 8, 9
food access *see* access to fresh food
Food and Agriculture Organization (FAO) 2, 31, 180
food Apartheid 33, 35
food assistance programs *see* Food Stamp Program (FSP); The Emergency Food Assistance Program (TEFAP)
food bank case study, Atlanta 71–75
food deserts 33
food hubs 91–92, 122–123
food justice organization case study, New Mexico 81–86
food pantry case study, Washington, DC 67–71

food production *see* agricultural production
food-related illnesses: Atlanta, GA 49, 126–127; disparities in 9, 15, 62; Oakland, CA 59; Washington, DC 41
food security 25; definition 14, 30, 31; global trends 2; recent trends 12–13; regional progress 3–13; scope of 67; as solvable problem 137; as term 29–30; urban community 36; in the US 13, 14–19
Food Stamp Program (FSP) 27–31, 36
food system innovators 116; 4P Foods 132–136; Chicago-based projects 128–132; farming in Atlanta 125–128; future outcomes 176; Planting Justice 119–123; the story of Chispas Farm 116–119; the success story of Gotham Greens 123–125
food waste 7, 99–100
free-riding 143

gardens: in six US cities 102–111; urban gardens/agriculture 96–102
gentrification 35
Gini coefficient 4, 27
global population 1, 3, **3**
Gotham Greens 123–125
grant funding 161–163, 178
green cities: food production in the city 96–102; new urban food landscape 87–93; urban agriculture in six US cities 102–111; urban gardens/agriculture 93–96
Green Revolution 1, 7–8
green roofs 99, 101, 103, **110**
grocery store locations: access to fresh food 15; Albuquerque, NM **45**; Atlanta, GA **49**; Chicago, IL 35, **53**; food deserts 33; impact on fruit and vegetable consumption 37; New York City **57**; Oakland, CA **61**; SNAP program 74; Washington, DC 15, 35, 42, 70
gross domestic product (GDP) 10–14, **10–11**, 50, 54, 139–140
groundwater contamination 8, 9
Grows-A-Lot 106

high yield crop varieties (HYVs) 7–8
Hispanics: access to fresh food 37; Albuquerque, NM 43–45, **44**, 110; American Rescue Plan (ARP) 157–158; Atlanta, GA 47, **48**; care work 146–147; Chicago, IL 50, **52**;

New York City **56**; Oakland, CA 59, **60**, 111; urban gardens/agriculture 110–111; Washington, DC 39, **40**
historical context: agricultural production 30; Chicago 34–35; Dust Bowl 26, 31–32; early US cities 25; economic data 26; food assistance programs 27–31; urbanisation 32–33; Washington, DC 33–34, 35, 38
Homestead Act 6–7, 31–32, 159
hunger, as term 29–30, 31; *see also* food security
Hunger Free America 144–145
hydroponics 97, 98, 125–126, 177

immigrants: Chinese Americans 58; the story of a 56-year-old immigrant in Oakland 78–79; in US history 25, 31–32, 34, 35
incarceration 121
income inequality, global trends 4, *5*; *see also* economic context in the US; *see also* Gini coefficient
India, agricultural production 4, 5–6
inequalities: in America 13; COVID-19 pandemic 14–15
innovation *see* food system innovators
insurance for farmers 154–155
Interdepartmental Committee on Nutrition for National Defense (ICNND) 28–29

Jamestown, historical context 25
Johnson, President Lyndon B. 28
jobs 71; creating jobs 119–131; finding a job 74, 79–81, 105–108; job security 74; job training 80; need for job training 117–128, 154; providing job training 81–82, 92, 98, 100, 106–107

Kennedy, President John F. 27–28
Know Your Farmer, Know Your Food 87–88
Kroger 34–35

land values, urban gardens/agriculture 95–96
Latin America: demographic change 3; food production and food security 3–13
leak plugging 100
Local Agriculture Markets Program (LAMP) 88–89
local economy 100, 120
Local Food Purchasing Assistance Cooperative Agreement (LFPA) 135

malnutrition: nutrition programs 28–29; as term 29–30; *see also* food security
market making/taking 142
metrics, food and agriculture 157–160

National Farm to School Network (NFSN) 91
National Institute of Food and Agriculture (NIFA) 161–162
Natural Resource Accounting 139
Natural Resources Conservation Service (NRCS) 16–17, 26–27, 160; *see also* United States Department of Agriculture (USDA)
negative externalities: agricultural production 8–9; cost of food 137–142; getting subsidies and transfer payments right 149–156
New Deal (Roosevelt) 26
New York City: comparative statistics 61–62; food insecurity landscape 54–58; Hunger Free America 144–145; the story of a 64-year-old woman in Brooklyn 75–78; the success story of Gotham Greens 123–125; urban gardens/agriculture 95, 108–109, **110**
nitrate(s) 7, 8, 156
nitrous-oxide (N2O) 8
North America: demographic change 3; food production and food security 3–13
nutrition programs: cooking and food preparation 75, 176; effects of caloric deficit and deficiencies in specific nutrients 29; food bank, Atlanta 75; historical context 28–29

Oakland, CA: comparative statistics 61–62; food insecurity landscape 58–61; Planting Justice 109–110, 119–123; the story of a 56-year-old immigrant 78–79; urban gardens/agriculture 109–111, **110**
obesity: Albuquerque, NM 45, *45*; Atlanta, GA 49, *49*; Chicago, IL 53; New York City *53*, *57*, 58; Oakland, CA 59, *61*; as a result of food insecurity 14, 41, 173–174; Washington, DC *41*
Oceania: demographic change 3; food production and food security 3–13
Office of Urban Agriculture and Innovation Production (OUAIP) 94, 98
overuse 143

Pareto optimal state 137–138
pesticides 8, 9
Philippon, Thomas 153–154
Planting Justice 109–110, 119–123
policies for food distribution 172–173, 175, 181–182
Ponics 125–126, 177
population *see* world population
positive externalities 9
poverty: global trends 2, 12; length of time in 36–37; regional trends 3–4
price of food 137–142
prisoners, providing training and skills to 121
public goods 143, 149

race: Albuquerque, NM 43–45, **44**; American Rescue Plan (ARP) 157–158; Atlanta, GA 47, **48**; Chicago, IL 50–53; comparative statistics 61–62; demographic overview of the US 25; food security 17; New York City **56**; Oakland, CA 59, **60**, 111; representation in metrics 157–158; urban gardens/agriculture 109–111; Washington, DC 38–39, **40**
recreational care work 148
regenerative agriculture; regenerative farming 117–118, 154–155, 163; regenerative food system 135; regenerative production 133, 146
relocalizing 100; *see also* local economy
resilience: urban resilience 92, 97, 98, 102, 156
resilient food system(s) 16, 100, 154, 164, 182
restorative economics 155–156, 160, 177, 182
restoration of ecosystems 148
restorative food system 134–36, 142, 148, 154–156
restorative urban agriculture 100–102, 119, 155–156, 177
Risk Management Agency (RMA) 154–155
Rust Belt 95

St. Augustine (Florida), historical context 25
San Francisco 58, 109
Santa Fe 25
sinks 100, 139, 142, 145, **157**, 179; sink capacity(ties) 100–102, 139–140, 148–149, 156, **157**, 164, 174–175, 177
Small Business Administration (SBA) loans 15–16, 178

SNAP *see* Supplemental Nutrition Assistance Program
social determinants of food insecurity 17, 100, 111; social determinants of health and well-being 17, 62
Social and Solidarity Economy (SSE) 96
soil-less production 155
soils: engineered soils 97; erosion of 26; restorative urban agriculture 101
subsidies: agricultural production 7–8; getting subsidies and transfer payments right 149–156, 175
suburbanization, recent trends 35–36
Supplemental Nutrition Assistance Program (SNAP): food bank, Atlanta 74; New York City 58; subsidies and transfer payments 151–154; in urban communities 17, 36; Washington, DC *41*
sustainability: Brundtland Report 138–139; ecosystem services 140–142; urban gardens/agriculture 96–97, 98–99
Sustainable Development Goals (SDGs) 2, 19

TEFAP *see* The Emergency Food Assistance Program *under e*
transfer payments 149–156, 175
transparency in education 180–182
Tronto, Joan 147, 157

Ukraine-Russia war 12–13
UN Food and Agriculture Organization 2, 31, 180
unemployment 13; as determinant of food insecurity 36; and the Great Depression 26–27, 31; Albuquerque, NM **44**; Atlanta, GA **48**; Brooklyn, NY **56**; Chicago, IL **52**; Oakland, CA **60**, 175; Washington, DC **40**
United States: agricultural production 4, 6–7; demographic overview 25; food security 13; policies for food distribution 172–173, 175, 181–182
United States Department of Agriculture (USDA) 16–18, 26–27; grant-allocation system 161–163; metrics and equity 158–159; new urban food landscape 87–93; regional urban food production data 102, 110, **110**; Risk Management Agency (RMA) 154–155; soil conditions 98; subsidies 151–152; Urban Agriculture Committees 16, 18, 98, 107, 108; *see also* Agricultural

Marketing Service (AMS); Natural Resources Conservation Service (NRCS)
Universal Basic Income (UBI) 179
Urban Farming Act 96
Urban Growers Collective 107–108
urbanization: historical context 32–33; recent trends 35–36; *see also* green cities
USDA *see* United States Department of Agriculture (USDA)

wages 143–149
Washington, DC: access to fresh food 15, 35, 42, 70; comparative statistics 61–62; food hubs 92–93; food insecurity landscape 38–42; food pantry case study 67–71; historical context 33–34, 35; urban gardens/agriculture 95–96, 103–104, **110**
waste *see* food waste
water contamination 8, 9; *see also* eutrophication
water rights management 82–83
Women, Infants, and Children (WIC), nutrition program 29, 151; *see also* families
Works Progress Administration (WPA) 26–27
world population 1, **3**, 3

Printed in the United States
by Baker & Taylor Publisher Services